Understanding Trauma and

Understanding Trauma and Resilience

Louise Harms

 palgrave

First published 2015 by
PALGRAVE

Palgrave in the UK is an imprint of Macmillan Publishers Limited, registered in England, company number 785998, of 4 Crinan Street, London N1 9XW.

Palgrave Macmillan in the US is a division of St Martin's Press LLC, 175 Fifth Avenue, New York, NY 10010.

Palgrave is a global imprint of the above companies and is represented throughout the world.

Palgrave® and Macmillan® are registered trademarks in the United States, the United Kingdom, Europe and other countries.

ISBN 978–1–137–28928–5

This book is printed on paper suitable for recycling and made from fully managed and sustained forest sources. Logging, pulping and manufacturing processes are expected to conform to the environmental regulations of the country of origin.

A catalogue record for this book is available from the British Library.

A catalog record for this book is available from the Library of Congress.

Printed in China

Contents

List of Figures, Tables and Boxes   viii
Preface   ix
Acknowledgements   xi

Introduction   1
    The structure of this book   2

Chapter 1 **Theorising Trauma and Resilience**   4
    Introduction   4
    Defining trauma   4
    Defining recovery and resilience   8
    Theorising trauma and resilience responses:
      Introducing a multidimensional approach   13
    Implications for practice and research   22
    Practitioners' and researchers' critical reflections   24
    Conclusion   27

Chapter 2 **Psychodynamic Approaches: Reintegrating
the Self**   28
    Introduction   28
    Psychodynamic explanations of the developing self
      and resilience   29
    Psychodynamic explanations of trauma responses   30
    Implications for practice   39
    Critically reflecting on psychodynamic approaches 45
    Conclusion   45

Chapter 3 **Attachment Approaches: Regulating Self and
Relationships**   46
    Introduction   46
    Attachment explanations of resilience   46
    Attachment explanations of trauma responses   54
    Implications for practice   59
    Critically reflecting on attachment approaches   64
    Conclusion   65

Contents

Chapter 4   **Symptom Approaches: Reducing PTSD**   66
Introduction   66
Post-traumatic stress disorder as a trauma response   66
Resilience and recovery from post-traumatic stress   78
Implications for practice   78
Critically reflecting on symptom approaches   85
Conclusion   88

Chapter 5   **Person-Centred Approaches: Recreating Congruence**   89
Introduction   89
Person-centred approaches to resilience and recovery   89
Person-centred approaches to trauma   93
Implications for practice   99
Critically reflecting on person-centred approaches   103
Conclusion   105

Chapter 6   **Narrative Approaches: Re-authoring for Meaning and Coherence**   107
Introduction   107
Narrative understandings of resilience   108
Narrative understandings of trauma   110
Implications for practice   115
Critically reflecting on narrative approaches   121
Conclusion   122

Chapter 7   **Social-Ecological Approaches: Rebuilding and Sustaining Systems**   123
Introduction   123
Social-ecological understandings of resilience   123
Social-ecological understandings of trauma   133
Implications for practice   138
Critically reflecting on social-ecological approaches   141
Conclusion   142

Chapter 8   **Anti-oppressive Approaches: Recognising Rights and Redressing Oppression**   144
Introduction   144
Anti-oppressive approaches to resilience   144
Anti-oppressive approaches to trauma   149
Implications for practice   159
Critically reflecting on anti-oppressive approaches   163
Conclusion   164

Chapter 9   **Promoting Resilience and Recovery: An Integrative**
               Approach   165
               Introduction   165
               Drawing together understandings of trauma
                 and resilience   165
               Thinking dimensionally about trauma and resilience   168
               Thinking and working in multidimensional ways   174
               Conclusion   176

References   177
Index   203

Figures, Tables and Boxes

Figures

1.1 Variations in trauma and resilience conceptualisations   14
1.2 A multidimensional approach   23

Tables

5.1 The seven principles of post-traumatic growth   99
7.1 A comparison of individual-, family- and community-level
    resilience resources   132
9.1 A comparative analysis of practice implications according to
    theoretical approach   167
9.2 Reviewing the multidimensional aspects of the approaches   169

Boxes

1.1 The definition of trauma exposure in the *DSM V*   6
4.1 Intrusion criteria for post-traumatic stress disorder   69
4.2 Avoidance criterion for post-traumatic stress disorder   70
4.3 Hyperarousal criteria for post-traumatic stress disorder   70
4.4 Criterion D for post-traumatic stress disorder   71
4.5 Tasks involved in Psychological First Aid   80
5.1 The six necessary and sufficient conditions   91
5.2 The seven areas of adjustment to civilian life   94
7.1 Examples of Hobfoll's four resource 'caravans'   129

Preface

This book has come from my experiences as a social worker in different medical and academic settings over more than two decades. Initially, I worked in hospitals, where trauma was a core aspect of many people's experiences. In emergency departments, neurological and intensive care units of a paediatric hospital and then later in a rehabilitation hospital, I have seen people's lives turn upside down in a moment – due to a car accident, an injury, illness or violent incident. In these same environments, others were coping with the slow wear and tear of terminal illness or acquired disability experiences – each traumatic in their own ways as realities changed unpredictably and dramatically. Later, I worked for several years at a university counselling service, where sexual assault, substance use and misuse and self-harm, among many other experiences, were frequent causes of distress for students.

In my academic role over the last fifteen years, I have been engaged with social work teaching and research on the themes of trauma, resilience and recovery. In more recent years, my research has focused particularly on two key areas – on people's recovery from the Victorian bushfire disaster of 2009 and on patients and families dealing with major health crises. Throughout all these practice, teaching and research experiences – and personal ones – I have remained interested in the ability of people to cope with extraordinary traumas and losses.

This book introduces some of the key theoretical approaches that explain how we cope with traumatic life experiences. I was convinced of the diversity of this field while researching this book – with medicalised and psychiatrised views sitting alongside sociological and anthropological views, sometimes speaking to each other and at other times existing in seemingly parallel universes. The evidence for these approaches differs too – some approaches, such as cognitive approaches to trauma interventions, gain more evidence for their efficacy at a rapid rate. Others, such as psychodynamic and narrative approaches, may lack the same body of evidence, yet they continue to resonate with survivors, practitioners and researchers alike.

One of the major motivations for this book has been to build a resource that brings together these many perspectives on trauma, resilience and recovery. In writing this book, I have contended with feeling overwhelmed on a regular basis – knowing that for each idea I have sought to put on the page, decades of research, debate and literature sit behind it. My intention here is to introduce you to the research and key debates from a breadth rather than a depth perspective. I hope this broad overview encourages you to become curious about specific areas and to follow those leads to satisfy your search for depth and detail.

Acknowledgements

A book always emerges from a wealth of discussions and reading. This book is no different on that score. I have reflected on many discussions that I have had and continue to have with people – those I have worked with through their most difficult times in my role as a social worker, those in my own personal circles whose lives have been affected by trauma and loss, research colleagues in various teams with whom I share and dispute opinions and approaches and the students in lectures, tutorials or doctoral supervision. All remind me of the core questions and issues we have been grappling with and will continue to do so. Thank you to all who have been such critical influences in this way.

Many others supported this book in additional ways. Marie Connolly made it possible for me to take two critical windows of time to write. Lauren Kosta gave meticulous and dedicated care and attention to key literature searches. Catherine Gray and India Annette-Woodgate of Palgrave have helped bring this work together. Three anonymous reviewers provided feedback that was critical for focusing this book for a range of readers. Last but not the least, I thank my parents, Glenys and Peter, who have been constant sources of encouragement and support, and Jane Sullivan, who is my source of balance, wisdom and good humour.

The authors and publisher would like to thank the following individuals and organizations for permission to reproduce copyright material:

The American Psychiatric Association for their permission to reproduce Box 1.1, 'The definition of trauma exposure in the *DSM V*'; Box 4.1, 'Intrusion criteria for post-traumatic stress disorder'; Box 4.2, 'Avoidance criterion for post-traumatic stress disorder'; Box 4.3, 'Hyperarousal criteria for post-traumatic stress disorder'; and Box 4.4, 'Criterion D for post-traumatic stress disorder' from the *Diagnostic and Statistical Manual of Mental Disorders,* fifth edition (2013).

The National Child Traumatic Stress Network and National Centre for PTSD for their permission to reproduce Box 4.5, 'Tasks involved in psychological first aid', from *Appendix A: Overview of Psychological First Aid* (2016).

Oxford University Press for their permission to reproduce Figure 1.2, 'A multidimensional approach', from L. Harms *Understanding Human Development: A Multidimensional Approach*, second edition (2010).

SAGE Publications for their permission to reproduce and adapt Table 5.1, 'The seven principles of post-traumatic growth', from R. Tedeschi and C. Calhoun *Trauma and Transformation: Growing in the Aftermath of Suffering* (1995).

Introduction

As health and counselling professionals, we are frequently working with people who are survivors of trauma. Our involvement may be in the immediate aftermath of their trauma experiences and/or in the longer term. This involvement may be actively sought out by them or mandated by service systems. One of our challenges in working effectively is that experiences of trauma can be understood in so many ways. To work as trauma-informed practitioners and researchers requires that we are aware of these many standpoints relating to trauma, recovery and resilience.

This book introduces you to seven key theoretical approaches and ideas, to provide you with a broad overview of the ways in which they conceptualise trauma, recovery and resilience experiences. These seven approaches – psychodynamic, attachment, symptom (particularly post-traumatic stress disorder, PTSD), person-centred, narrative, social-ecological and anti-oppressive – understand the impacts of traumatic stress responses on lifelong psychosocial functioning in particular ways. They stem from very different traditions of medical, psychological and sociological discourses, although all primarily within Western ones. Thus, each of these approaches carries core assumptions about pre- and post-trauma states of being – what it is to be human and what well-being or optimal functioning looks like. They differ in their emphasis on psychological, physical, spiritual, relational, social, structural and cultural dimensions of human experience. In turn, concepts of adaptation and recovery are founded on certain assumptions. The depth and breadth of these disciplinary and theoretical approaches are vast, each backed by an extensive literature and evidence base.

These approaches provide a way of focusing our attention as practitioners and researchers. They move us from a theoretical explanation as to why difficulties have occurred, to a particular practice approach in terms of broad principles and finally through to practice strategies or specific skills (Connolly & Harms, 2012, p. 15). Ultimately, they encourage us to think about how to respond and optimally support and work with survivors: how to work with people in the context of therapeutic encounters through to collective and social responses of advocacy and social change. They also determine research priorities and prevention strategies with survivors. That is why it is so important to critically reflect on the beliefs and evidence that underpin our trauma practice and research.

The intention of this book is to broadly overview a variety of approaches, dominant and emerging, to look at their current and core assumptions and to consider the implications for practice and research. You may be working in school, child protection service, counselling service or health contexts – all of these approaches can be applied in these different settings.

Some approaches have a very long history. For example, psychodynamic approaches have endured over more than a century, albeit incorporating multiple adaptations over the decades. Others, such as neurobiological ones, are relatively new, in part because of the rapid shifts in medical technology and the ability to assess traumatic impacts in new ways. Every decade or so, a significant paradigm shift seems to occur in response to a range of factors in the wider contexts in which we live – sometimes socio-cultural or political, other times scientific.

The structure of this book

We begin, in Chapter 1, by exploring some of the prevailing definitions of trauma, resilience and recovery. A multidimensional approach is presented as a broad map that we will use throughout this book. This approach offers a way of holding together the inner and/or outer world dimensions of a person and their circumstances. It enables us to look at each of the seven theoretical approaches and understand the particular focus of interest. In turn, this helps us understand some of the core strengths and limitations of each theoretical approach.

Chapter 2 looks at psychodynamic ideas and how they focus on the disruption to the self, both conscious and unconscious. In Chapter 3, we look at attachment theory, a theory of regulation, which now integrates both psychodynamic and neurobiological approaches. In Chapter 4, we explore the ways in which 'symptom' approaches, primarily through post-traumatic stress disorder understandings, have dominated trauma theories. We focus on how neurobiological approaches have expanded understandings of trauma impacts in relation to symptoms of the body and the mind. Chapter 5 introduces person-centred approaches, which grew in response to the perceived limitations of psychodynamic approaches. They focus on restoring congruence and trust in self-structures. In Chapter 6, we look at the emergence of narrative approaches. With a focus on narrating and re-authoring experience, these approaches focus on both individual and collective witnessing of trauma and resilience. Chapter 7 looks at social-ecological approaches, examining trauma's impact on people and their environments, looking at what makes social systems resilient in particular. This focus reverberates through Chapter 8 also, where we explore anti-oppressive approaches, which locate the source and the recovery from trauma much more broadly in socio-cultural and political domains. Key themes of interest relate to traumatic experiences of powerlessness and oppression and the subsequent recovery experiences of empowerment and liberation.

Throughout Chapters 2–8 we look at the practice implications of each approach. While they are oriented towards therapeutic interventions, the practice implications provide a focus on research priorities as well. A case scenario is also included. These scenarios are amalgams, drawn from multiple situations into one, to stimulate your thinking about the trauma and resilience issues inherent in them. While these scenarios are presented across the chapters, you are encouraged to reconsider them through each of the theoretical lenses, to see what different approaches highlight.

In Chapter 9, we draw together the themes of the book into an integrative practice and research approach, revisiting the multidimensional lens set out in Chapter 1.

1
Theorising Trauma and Resilience

Introduction

We begin this discussion with a look at some of the issues in theorising trauma and resilience. In professional and lay contexts, 'trauma' and 'resilience' have become widely and popularly used words. For many survivors of different life events, these words capture the heart of their experiences, and for others, they miss the essence altogether. Many practitioners embrace these words as important areas of their professional specialisation, and others reject these categorisations. Researchers grapple with the diversity of ways in which these words are used and the challenge of operationalising these concepts rigorously and comparatively in the context of research. We look at these concepts, along with a multidimensional approach and self-care issues, as the foundations for this book.

Defining trauma

One glance at the research and practice literature shows that the word 'trauma' refers to many different events, from single incidents to chronic and complex post-traumatic stress experiences. In addition to referring to a particular triggering event, it can refer to the impact and aftermath experience, beginning to confuse notions of trauma as exposure and trauma as response.

Traumatic exposure

In relation to the exposure focus, the debate around what can and should be defined as 'traumatic' has continued over many years (Burstow, 2003; Weathers & Keane, 2007; Friedman et al., 2011a). While this debate may seem overly focused on semantics, the definition of trauma ultimately leads to what in turn becomes legally, socially, culturally and politically recognised. Recognition of events as traumatic or not determines whether wider systems of social support, for example, are put into place or whether people are expected to resume everyday life relatively unaffected.

In practice and research and in the wider community, commonly recognised traumatic events include natural and human-made disasters, war, forced migration and displacement, forced separations of children from their parents, abuse and neglect, torture, accidents and injuries, health crises and private assaults to emotional, physical, social and spiritual well-being. However, this list is by no means exhaustive; even beginning to list such events in this way raises the likelihood of omission or exclusion. Critically listing some events as inherently traumatic and others as less so will not help identify their impact on people. A term that has emerged in more recent years is 'potentially traumatic events' (PTEs; see Keyes et al., 2013, for example), avoiding the assumption that an event is, per se, traumatic.

Other distinctions lie in classifying trauma exposures as single incidents (such as a car accident or an assault) or multiple, long-term conditions of extreme adversity (such as wars, homelessness or droughts) where death and threat may be continually encountered. Other traumas are intergenerational in nature. It is often challenging to untangle the beginnings and endings of such interconnected events and their impacts on successive generations of families. This is particularly the case in child protection work. What may be a critical distinction is the perceived source or cause – whether the trauma is perpetrated by other people (intentionally or unintentionally) or seen as 'natural' events.

Typically, traumatic events are recognised as external events in people's lives. Yet, some experiences are less widely recognised, if at all, as traumatic events and afforded little attention from others. Some events can be defined as 'disenfranchised trauma' experiences, adapting Doka's (1989) 'disenfranchised grief' term. They are not recognised as being traumatic, yet they can create extreme distress and fear for people – for example, an episode of psychosis. An emerging body of literature has also highlighted the ways in which some human service responses can be traumatic in and of themselves, both in the immediate and longer term. While services (such as child protection) are about promoting well-being ideally, the surveillance and supervision by counsellors and protective services can create a suffocating environment in which it is impossible for families to function (Carolan et al., 2010). Other studies have highlighted that legal and service systems can be more problematic in the longer term for people than the traumatic event itself (Holman & Silver, 1996).

Less widely recognised, too, is the pre-existing vulnerability in many communities that can escalate into traumatic events over time. For example, Bankoff and colleagues (2004) have provided an insightful account into the importance of mapping vulnerability as it relates to where disasters occur and why – that is, taking into account the social and economic hierarchies in which people live prior to a disaster occurrence and the exposures to traumas that result. This challenges us to think about the extent to which vulnerability and trauma can be separated and the importance of working preventively with vulnerability so as to avoid the traumas occurring in the first place. In just skimming briefly over these issues of event type, frequency, intensity, cause and recognition, we can start to see that understanding the nature of 'trauma' is a nuanced, complex and contextual task.

In many ways, these debates have been reflected in the American Psychiatric Association's *Diagnostic and Statistical Manual of Psychiatric Disorders* (*DSM*; APA, 1980, 2000, 2013), evolving definition of trauma for the purposes of a diagnosis of post-traumatic stress disorder (PTSD), since its first inclusion in the 1980 version (Weathers & Keane, 2007). The purpose of the definition in this case is to determine whether someone has been exposed to trauma and therefore can be assessed as having a diagnosis of PTSD. A diagnosis of PTSD is significant not only in terms of access to appropriate mental health support in many contexts but also often in terms of access to appropriate legal recognition and compensation.

The new definition of trauma exposure in the *DSM V* (APA, 2013) reflects significant shifts yet again in the effort to define trauma exposure, as shown in Box 1.1.

Box 1.1   The definition of trauma exposure in the *DSM V*

The person was exposed to one or more of the following event(s): death or threatened death, actual or threatened serious injury, or actual or threatened sexual violation, in one or more of the following ways:

- Experiencing the event(s) himself/herself
- Witnessing, in person, the event(s) as they occurred to others
- Learning that the event(s) occurred to a close relative or close friend; in such cases, the actual or threatened death must have been violent or accidental
- Experiencing repeated or extreme exposure to aversive details of the event(s) (e.g., first responders collecting body parts; police officers repeatedly exposed to details of child abuse); this does not apply to exposure through electronic media, television, movies or pictures, unless this exposure is work related

Source: The American Psychiatric Association (2013).

This new definition is much narrower compared to previous editions. In the new definition, the primary emphasis in the events described is on embodied threat (death, injury and/or sexual violation) – to a person or to others they are closely connected with or where someone directly witnesses the actual or threatened physical harm. The extent to which this focus on physical threat will accurately convey the breadth of traumatic events is yet to be tested. Emotional abuse is known to lead to similar psychosocial outcomes as physical abuse, yet it may no longer qualify as a traumatic exposure, given the difficulties in linking emotional abuse with actual or threatened physical harm. Similarly, the separation of children from families may not qualify – previously, acknowledgement of the PTSD caused by the experience of forced government removal of Aboriginal children in Canada and Australia (Petchkovsky & San Roque, 2002; Bombay et al., 2009) or others into foster care (Salazar et al., 2013) has been an important step in establishing healing and reconciliation resources.

Traumatic impacts

As you can see, trauma is understood as a trigger or exposure event in diverse ways. The same is true in terms of how trauma is thought of as an impact or a response. Commonly, traumatic events are recognised as such because they have disrupted, overwhelmed and destroyed a person's or community's sense of well-being and safety and capacity to cope as before.

Each of the theoretical approaches we look at understands these traumatic disruptions differently. Rights-based approaches emphasise that traumatic events violate a fundamental sense of social justice, control and agency, for example. Psychodynamic approaches seek to explain the impact of past, often childhood traumas on adult functioning and development. There is consideration of the emotions of trauma – shame, guilt and anger, for example – and both the unconscious and conscious expressions of anxiety. The impact of trauma is seen as not only lasting but also highly influential on later adult experience. Psychiatric approaches focus on the presence of disorders such as PTSD or depression – that is, the symptoms of trauma.

Grief also has an important place in trauma understandings. Many traumatic events evoke both trauma and grief reactions. The losses inherent in many traumatic events – of life, world views and beliefs, a sense of safety, places, roles and routines – can lead to profound experiences of sadness and yearning and processes of mourning and remembrance. Despite this, trauma and grief research and theories have tended to remain separate, with relatively few people considering the overlap in traumatic bereavement (Raphael & Meldrum, 1994; Stroebe et al., 2001). As a result, as Parkes (2008, p. 464) notes: 'Bereavement services have developed separately from the field of traumatic stress.' Throughout this book, we will touch on the points of connection between trauma and grief, although maintaining a dominant focus on trauma understandings.

Many people also report positive trauma impacts in the form of post-traumatic growth, recovery and resilience (Tedeschi & Calhoun, 1995; Harms, 2001). These broader understandings of traumatic impacts are also critical, and we now look at some of these ideas.

Defining recovery and resilience

While the previous discussion considered the ways in which traumatic experiences leave people with negative outcomes, a vast evidence base exists for people adapting and surviving well, that is, evidence for a salutogenic approach to the impact of trauma. Others experience oscillation between functioning well in some parts of their life at some times, and not so well in other parts and/or other times. Therefore, concepts such as recovery, resilience and post-traumatic growth are helpful in understanding the full reality of people's experiences.

Recovery

Recovery, like trauma, is also defined in many different ways. From a practice and research perspective, it is an important concept to consider – what is regarded as the 'outcome' point for therapeutic work with people? What words best reflect these states? What are we there to 'do' or to encourage? How does a person come to see themselves and their coping capacity in the longer term? The evidence base for trauma recovery is mixed, in large part due to these varying definitions of what it is.

One approach is to understand recovery as the absence of PTSD or post-traumatic stress symptoms. This conceptualisation has dominated a lot of studies – the absence of psychopathology is seen as the presence of recovery. In this sense, research highlights that for most people, recovery is possible, given the prevalence rates for PTSD. For example, Johnson, Thompson and Downs (2009, p. 331) highlight prevalence studies that show the following:

> Among persons who have experienced a traumatic event in their lifetime, the prevalence of current PTSD is 9% to 12% for women and about 6% for men.

Thus, based on these types of prevalence figures, 88–91% of women and 94% of men recover. This conceptualisation of recovery, however, does not extend to the full possibilities of trauma aftermath experiences, nor does it reflect the World Health Organisation's (WHO) definition of health: 'A state of complete physical, mental and social well-being, and not merely the absence of disease' (WHO, 2003).

A second approach, therefore, is to see recovery as a return to functioning, typically along a trajectory of experiences. One of the early conceptualisations of this model came from O'Leary and Ickovics (1995), who outlined trajectories from survival, to recovery, to thriving. Whereas survival is seen in the manner 'the individual affected by a stressor continues to function, albeit in an impaired fashion', recovery is seen as 'a return to baseline' functioning (O'Leary, 1998, p. 425). In this model, the possibility of thriving is defined as 'the ability to go beyond the original level of psychosocial functioning, to grow vigorously, to flourish' (O'Leary, 1998, p. 425). Others adapted this model to define the possible experiences as succumbing, survival with impairment, resilience (recovery) and thriving (Carver, 1998, p. 246). Bonanno and colleagues' (Bonanno et al., 2011; Bonanno & Mancini, 2012) more recent work has continued to chart this idea of trajectories people may follow as they adapt post-trauma. Bonanno (2004, p. 20) defined recovery as

> a trajectory in which normal functioning temporarily gives way to threshold or sub-threshold psychopathology (e.g., symptoms of depression or Posttraumatic Stress Disorder (PTSD)), usually for a period of at least several months, and then gradually returns to pre-event levels. Full recovery may be relatively rapid, or may take as long as one or two years.

This conceptualisation of recovery highlights the resumption of 'normal functioning', or a return to everyday living where participation is possible. The idea is one of learning to 'live with', in the sense that experiences become part of who we are, part of our unique story, to the point where it enables us to engage with the demands and possibilities of living and even living well. Throughout the chapters of this book, we look at the conditions, both internal and external, that promote this experience of recovery.

A third approach is a stage approach to recovery based on the achievement of specific tasks, as outlined by Judith Herman (1992). These specific tasks, however, are seen in the context of the following two statements:

> Resolution of the trauma is never final; recovery is never complete. The impact of a traumatic event continues to reverberate throughout the survivor's lifecycle. (Herman, 1992, p. 211)

Understood in that way, Herman (1992, p. 155) proposes the following:

> Recovery unfolds in three stages. The central task of the first stage is the establishment of safety. The central task of the second stage is remembrance and mourning. The central task of the third stage is reconnection with ordinary life.

This understanding of recovery highlights a strongly embedded social model of trauma recovery. Relational, social and cultural reconnection is the final process and marker of recovery. As Herman (1992, p. 212) reminds us: 'Though resolution is never complete, it is often sufficient for the survivor to turn her attention from the tasks of recovery to the tasks of ordinary life.' However, it still raises questions as to what 'ordinary life' means. For a person living in highly conflicted parts of the world, 'ordinary life' over many years may be lived in the context of civil war. A focus on ordinary life may bring us into thinking about our basic human needs and rights and what promotes a fulfilling or good life.

Throughout the chapters ahead, you will see that the different approaches emphasise different conceptualisations of recovery – as an outcome, as a process, as a baseline we return to or as an improved state of living after trauma.

Resilience

Bonanno and Mancini (2012, p. 77) note that 'the ability to maintain normative or baseline levels of functioning is not rare but often the most common response to potential trauma'. Despite the acknowledgement of how common the response of resilience is in the aftermath of trauma, research has tended to focus less on this aspect and more on the psychopathological outcomes. Broadly speaking, resilience focuses our thinking on people's capacity and the resources to 'bounce back', or as Froma Walsh (2002, p. 35) suggests:

> A more apt metaphor for resilience might be 'bouncing forward' to face an uncertain future. This involves constructing a new sense of normality as we recalibrate our lives to face unanticipated challenges ahead.

The study of resilience is 'a search for knowledge about the processes that could account for positive adaptation and development in the context of adversity and disadvantage' (Crawford et al., 2006, p. 355). However, there is widespread debate about what resilience is and how it can be understood and measured.

Agaibi and Wilson (2005, p. 198) propose that resilience is 'the ability to adapt and cope successfully despite threatening or challenging situations... Resilience is sustained competence in response to demands that tax coping resources'. By these definitions of both process and outcome (dependent upon both personal and contextual qualities), while resilient people may 'experience transient perturbations in normal functioning (e.g., several weeks of sporadic preoccupation or restless sleep)', they 'generally exhibit a stable trajectory of healthy functioning across time, as well as the capacity for generative experiences and positive emotions' (Bonanno, 2004, p. 21). In this sense, resilience differs from recovery in that there is a much shorter period of initial negative impact and more evidence of positive outcomes in the face of trauma.

For resilience to be present, theorists argue that there is a need of two critical conditions: firstly, there is 'exposure to significant threat or severe adversity', and secondly, there is '[t]he achievement of positive adaptation despite major assaults on the developmental process' (Luthar et al., 2000, p. 543). That is, people cannot be deemed to be resilient until 'tested' through adverse circumstances. People may have many protective factors or assets in their lives, but it is the exercising of positive adaptation in the face of adversity that is indicative of resilience.

The literature highlights that there are 'multiple and unexpected pathways to resilience', including 'hardiness, self-enhancement, repressive coping and positive emotion and laughter' (Bonanno, 2004, pp. 25–26). Such factors were identified in the early studies of resilience by Werner and Smith (1992). They showed that there were defining dimensions of resilience in their longitudinal study of children growing up in circumstances of high poverty, high parental mental illness and conflict, and low education. The resilient children were identified as those having temperamental characteristics that elicited positive attention, alertness and autonomy as toddlers, a positive self-concept and internal locus of control, nurturant characteristics and four or fewer siblings; also, they rarely had a prolonged separation in infancy. Importantly, they had a close bond with at least one caregiver; they had emotional support outside their own families. They had positive constitutional factors and were highly achievement-oriented.

What makes positive adaptation possible is an important consideration. Payne (2011, p. 11) proposes that resilience can be usefully associated with a sense of security:

> Security is people's belief that they will be safe from harm and exploitation in their social environment and remain free to make choices that develop their self.

The qualities that sustain security, including physical, legal, economic and psychological, are the qualities that ensure resilience. This focus on broader social, structural and community security and resources is important. A risk is that resilience is seen only as an inner world quality, a trait, rather than something highly contextual. Conceptualised in this way, as much focus needs to be placed on relational, social, structural and cultural dimensions of a person's circumstances, as inner world ones. This is reflected in Ungar's (2009, p. 32) conceptualisation of the capacities of resilience:

1. The capacity of individuals to navigate their way to resources that sustain wellbeing

2. The capacity of individual's physical and social systems to provide these resources

3. The capacity of individuals, their families and communities to negotiate culturally meaningful ways for resources to be shared

As Ungar's definition highlights, resilience is more than an individual's experience of positive adaptation. Community and family resilience can also be understood in terms of processes and outcomes, or as 'a set of capacities' (Norris et al., 2008, p. 135). We explore these ideas further in Chapter 7.

Resistance

Some theorists have also revisited the concept of resistance. From the early work of Werner and Smith (1992), when they first termed the resilient children as 'stress resistant', through to today, the idea has endured that people can withstand the impacts of traumatic life events. In part, this is because the idea of resistance can be interpreted in so many different ways. Resistance can convey the idea of being well protected or withstanding the impact of trauma in the first place; or the idea of political resistance and protest, the refusal to succumb; or the idea of defence mechanisms, picking up on our unconscious buffers to anxiety, which we explore in looking at psychodynamic concepts. All of these definitional aspects of resistance are considered in the chapters ahead.

Transilience

Another term that is currently emerging in resilience thinking is 'transilience'. Borrowed from geology, this term refers to a changing state or identity, typically of geographical forms, whereby there is 'a leaping from one thing to another' in terms of 'an abrupt transition' (Brown, 1993, p. 3369). For example, it refers to the transition of some minerals or rocks into new forms (Brown, 1993, p. 3369). This term may well be applicable in some circumstances to experiences of traumatised individuals, families and communities when the changed state is such a new condition or identity, so beyond the original state of being, that 'bouncing back' to a former state is no longer possible.

Post-traumatic growth

In the 1990s, researchers Tedeschi and Calhoun (1995) proposed the term 'post-traumatic growth' (PTG), referring to the unexpected growth that many people report in the aftermath of traumatic life events. Terms such as 'perceived benefits' (McMillen, 1999) and 'thriving' (Blankenship, 1998) have been used also to refer to these positive post-trauma experiences, which often coexist with the negative (Frazier et al., 2009).

In their studies of PTG, Tedeschi and Calhoun identified five domains of PTG frequently reported by survivors: an appreciation of life, an enhanced self-concept, enhanced relationships with others, a sense of new possibilities and spiritual change. Various studies have shown that many people report these positive impacts of trauma (Weiss & Berger, 2010; Joseph, 2011), such as life-threatening health conditions (Weiss, 2002) and road trauma (Harms, 2001). In the chapters ahead, we will look at these areas in more detail. These concepts help us to understand what living well with trauma looks like – how these areas may become a key focus of therapeutic and research work. As Bonanno and Mancini's (2012, p. 77) words highlighted earlier in this section, returning to functioning is the 'most common response to potential trauma', and therefore the processes that activate this return to living, and potentially living and functioning well, need to be understood better.

Theorising trauma and resilience responses: Introducing a multidimensional approach

To date, we have looked at some of the definitional debates that reflect the different theoretical and political approaches to understanding trauma and resilience. Figure 1.1 below highlights these points of difference and enables a way of thinking about the points of difference in the theories we consider from Chapter 2 onwards. We now consider a multidimensional approach to theorising trauma and resilience.

Drawn broadly and liberally from ecological approaches such as Bronfenbrenner's approach (1979), a multidimensional approach causes us to think about human experience as deeply connected within our particular contexts (Harvey, 1996; Greene & Greene, 2009; Green & McDermott, 2010). A multidimensional approach considers the interactions of our inner worlds – our physical or biological self, our psychological selves and, for many people, our spiritual selves – and the reciprocal influence with our outer world contexts: relational, social, structural and cultural (Harms,

Figure 1.1   Variations in trauma and resilience conceptualisations

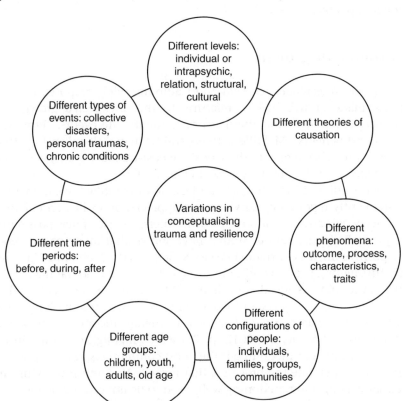

2010). These outer worlds reflect our political, economic, religious, gendered and social contexts. These inner and outer world experiences are lived out within particular time periods and places. The intersection of risk and protective factors comes to light with this approach – it provides a way of thinking about the experiences and identities of individuals, families and communities as comprising constantly interacting and mutually influential inner and outer world dimensions.

Listening to trauma and resilience through this approach provides a way of attending to the complexities of people's experiences, as well as the various risk and protective factors that are part of their experiences. It encourages us to see trauma not just as an inner world experience of psychological 'symptoms' or as an outer world experience caused solely by the social environment. A multidimensional approach encourages thinking about the extent to which different dimensions can be considered risk and/or protective factors.

The theoretical approaches we look at vary in the degree to which they are focused on inner world (intra-psychic) experiences and/or focused more on outer world experiences – for example, the degree to which traumas lead to social suffering and negative impacts at a community level and the degree to which a particular society provides resources and acknowledgement of what has occurred. Some approaches have come to provide more of a bridging focus between our inner and outer worlds – such as recent approaches to attachment theory. Before we look at these specific approaches, a multi-dimensional approach is briefly overviewed, noting that each of these dimensions could be the subject of a book in its own right.

Inner world dimensions of trauma and resilience

Inner world dimensions can be thought of as those that relate to our own unique, individual experiences. Our inner world can be thought of in the following way:

> no one else can ever experience what goes on in another person's thoughts and emotions, or know what it is like to live in someone else's body or to experience their sense of spirituality. (Harms, 2010, p. 5)

In considering a person's inner world dimensions, a focus is on their interacting psychological, physical or biological and spiritual experiences of trauma and recovery. Most of the theoretical approaches that we look at focus on the impact of trauma on individuals and at an inner world level.

Psychological dimensions

> how we think and how we feel emotionally influences every aspect of our daily experience . . . . Our capacities for thought and memory, for emotion and for anticipating the future reflect some of our most uniquely human qualities. (Harms, 2010, p. 7)

Within Western practice and research contexts, the dominant understanding of trauma has been on people's psychological dimensions – in particular, traumatic stress symptoms and PTSD. The interest has been on how individual psychological functioning is disrupted and restored during and following traumatic events. In Chapter 4, we look at the research and practice responses to PTSD – the trauma-related psychiatric disorder that has had three symptoms: intrusion, avoidance and hyperarousal; recently, a fourth symptom cluster has been added, relating to negative alterations in cognition and mood.

Traumatic impacts can include a variety of other cognitive and emotional responses. Survivors describe shock, disbelief and immense sadness – not as 'symptoms' but as profound human experiences and emotions. They describe the hurt, anger, rage, frustration, shame and despair that under-pin so many human experiences of trauma and suffering (Frost & Hoggett, 2008; Clarke et al., 2006). The loss of a sense of meaning and coherence is frequently reported. These intense emotional experiences are explored in the chapters ahead, along with the positive emotions ascribed to sur-viving trauma experiences – the often-renewed hope, optimism, solidarity, commitment, cause and value (Little, 1999).

Memory plays an important role in trauma aftermath experiences. From psychoanalytic through to neurobiological approaches, theories have been offered to understand the nature of traumatic memories. These understand-ings have changed quite significantly over time from a view that traumatic memory had to be remembered and reintegrated for cathartic release (see Chapter 2) through to the understandings that traumatic memory is encoded and processed in different ways from everyday memories in a non-stress state (see Chapter 4).

Biological dimensions

The body has long been a central part of trauma conceptualisations – from the early studies of hysteria manifested in bodily symptoms through to the focus on the neurobiology of traumatic stress responses. The body is considered in three ways, at least, as we shall see throughout our discussions.

The first way of thinking about the body's involvement in trauma is as the site of the traumatic event. That is, a person's body experiences the physical impacts of an event and/or a threat to life itself. Often, the body is phys-ically hurt and acquires an injury as a result of the traumatic event – for example, through a road trauma incident, a natural disaster or an assault. Babette Rothschild's (2000) work on how the body remembers these trauma experiences highlighted a key turning point in recent times back towards understanding the mind/body connection of trauma, which will be explored in Chapter 4.

Not only is the body implicated in direct experiences of trauma but in recovery experiences as well, which is the second way of thinking about the body and trauma. Increases in violence and assault and in drug and alcohol use (Flory et al., 2009), along with changes in overall health, have been noted in many studies as expected responses (Kendall-Tackett, 2009). Indeed, the *DSM V* definition of PTSD has included these dimensions as part of the behavioural responses to trauma (APA, 2013). So, the body is a site affected by the trauma aftermath processes a person engages in.

The third way in which the body is implicated is in relation to gender and chronological age. Research highlights that women and men experience traumatic events differently and arguably experience different traumatic responses. Chronological age and developmental stage can profoundly influence trauma exposures and impacts.

Physical age is important in many ways. In the first instance, it can be determinative of the types of traumatic events that people experience, given, for example, the physical vulnerability and dependence of infants and with some older adults. Developmental stage will also influence the extent to which a person can cognitively process and narrate their experience – for children who experience trauma when they are preverbal, this has a very different impact than on children who can verbalise and therefore externalise their experience through language, for example. It can be determinative of the voice that a person can give to their experience if age leads to other vulnerabilities – as in the case of elder abuse. It can also influence the accessibility and availability of support services – young people who experience sexual assault within the family may have very few resources to which they feel they can turn.

Some of the approaches tend to focus on a particular stage of the life course more than others. For example, neurobiological approaches focus primarily on the developing brain and attachment theory on the infant–carer relationship. Similarly, early psychoanalytic theories focused on childhood experiences, particularly of psychosexual trauma and their enduring impact on the adult person. These reflect approaches to human development that regard development as incremental, building upon earlier foundations and experiences. Other approaches tend to be focused more on adults, on narrative processing and on re-authoring, for example, which will be explored in Chapter 6.

Spiritual dimensions

Spirituality has been recognised as playing an important part in trauma recovery (McIntosh et al., 2011). The term 'spirituality' is used in a very broad and inclusive sense at this point in the discussion. Some people associate their spirituality with a strong religious faith and tradition, expressed through shared and public religious practices. Others see their spirituality as a connection with transcendence and a belief in a positive spirit beyond themselves. For some, spirituality is about meaning and coherence in the world around them and, therefore, related to a more existential phenomenon. For others, spirituality and religion play no role in their daily experience at all.

Throughout our exploration of the theoretical approaches, we look at the extent to which spirituality is emphasised as a possible risk or protective factor. Most of the literature exploring the role of spirituality in recovery identifies positive outcomes – that is, spirituality is a protective factor, providing meaning and ritual after trauma and often social support. Within narrative approaches, in particular, this has enabled indigenous spirituality to be recognised and drawn on as a major cultural and healing strength (Wingard & Lester, 2001; Atkinson, 2003).

However, spirituality and religion can play a key role in causing trauma. Many conflicts around the world are seen to be occurring because of religious differences of opinion, and many people experience significant oppression and trauma as a result of religious persecution. Within Ireland, Australia and the United States, major enquiries have been undertaken in relation to decades of physical, sexual and emotional abuse occurring within religious institutions. Similarly, abuse has been reported within cults where extreme spiritual and religious beliefs have given rise to the perpetuation of harm on people. Thus, spiritual and religious experiences for people are not always positive and supportive experiences but, rather, profoundly traumatic.

Outer world dimensions of trauma and resilience

A multidimensional approach emphasises that as individuals we live in particular contexts and that we cannot be understood without understanding the particulars of these contexts. These 'outer' world dimensions profoundly influence our daily experiences, as in turn we shape them. The outer world dimensions can be conceptualised as including our relational, social, structural and cultural ones and our time and place contexts.

Relational and social dimensions

The relational dimensions of trauma and resilience are critical in two ways at least. Firstly, our relationships with other people can be the source of trauma. That is, trauma can be inflicted by those with whom we are in close relationship as is the case with domestic violence or child abuse within the family. Some chapters focus more on this latter experience of complex trauma, which 'is defined as experiences of multiple traumatic events within the caregiver system, in place of the safety and stability that is normally provided therein' (Jaycox et al., 2009, p. 339).

Secondly, traumatic events often disrupt relationships and attachments. Sudden experiences of forced displacement through war or natural disasters, for example, can mean that people are never reunited with neighbours or even family members.

Thirdly, relationships are a critical source of support in the aftermath of trauma, and people can find themselves building new relationships and/or appreciating the depth and strength of existing ones. The protective and positive role of relationships for human well-being is long established. Throughout the approaches that we examine, the human connectedness, acknowledgement and recognition and relational warmth play key roles in promoting recovery and resilience. Secure attachments and the availability of role models are emphasised consistently in the literature as key resilience supports.

Linking our relational connections together is our wider social context – the web of connections within which we live. These connections again can be the source of trauma and/or resilience. Our social networks can provide both perceived and received social support. Our social connectedness can occur face-to-face or in online interactions. Many see the Internet and social media as providing critical, de-identified practical advice and emotional support in the aftermath of traumatic events.

By focusing on the relational and social dimensions, we can begin to see how people are connected and interwoven with the particular social historical political and economic contexts. As Hilhorst and Bankoff (2004, p. 5) note: 'Vulnerability then is not a property of social groups or individuals, but is embedded in complex social relations and processes.'

Structural dimensions

Our structural context plays an important part too in determining our trauma exposures and trauma recovery resources. Key systems in our everyday contexts, such as our legal, health, education, political, religious and environmental ones, influence our degree of access to resources and the level of freedom or oppression we experience on a daily basis. Everyday life in England, Afghanistan and China differs dramatically because of the ways in which these dimensions are exercised.

Known protective factors are community resources and facilities, high-quality human services, including social and health services, and adequate safety nets around housing, financial and employment needs. These protective factors can prevent some traumas from happening in the first place, such as strong policies around family support or disaster prevention, and/or provide essential support in an aftermath period.

The responsiveness of our broad social structures plays a critical role in trauma recovery. An established body of research now confirms that '[w]hat happens after a trauma has been shown consistently to have the biggest impact on whether a person develops PTSD' (Allen, 2012, p. 256). Some theoretical approaches have long recognised this interaction – for example, Betrayal Trauma Theory (Freyd et al., 2007) integrates a social, structural and cultural approach by looking at not only the ways in which an event or experience is terror inducing, but also the extent to which there is social betrayal or social acknowledgement and support following traumatic incidents. Feminist approaches generally have long identified the importance of this dimension in the prevention of violence against women. However, many approaches, such as psychodynamic and symptom ones, in focusing so intensively on inner world experiences have paid less attention to these areas of influence.

Cultural dimensions

Culture is a complex, elusive and multidimensional concept in and of itself. For the purposes of this discussion, culture is seen as referring to the 'taken for granted' ways of living – the values, beliefs and norms that exist among groups of people at global, national, local and/or familial levels. Bronfenbrenner (1979) described culture as the 'blueprint' for our behaviours, beliefs and rituals within the communities in which we live. Within cultures, world views evolve that can differ profoundly from other cultural groups, whether these cultural groups are based on ethnicity, sexuality, geography, religion, politics and many other defining aspects of our human experience and whether we are talking about dominant or minority cultures. World views about health, illness, trauma (Breslau, 2004) and resilience can differ profoundly, as is the case, for example, between Indigenous and non-Indigenous world views (Ypinazar et al., 2007), with implications for post-trauma interventions.

Therefore, our cultural contexts shape whether a trauma is acknowledged as such in the first instance and then influence the aftermath experiences profoundly. Many cultural practices and rituals are formally and informally enacted following traumas and disasters – for example, supporting people as they grieve and come to terms with the horrors of what they have been affected by. Within societies, the processes of both acknowledging and remembering and even forgetting (Rieff, 2011) are important adaptive processes.

Our cultural contexts can give rise to the particular traumas we face or inflict on others, both knowingly and unknowingly. Cultural identity as it relates to ethnic identity can be the source of traumatic events occurring. The Holocaust, along with the Rwandan and Bosnia-Herzegovina wars, involved mass genocide justified by a belief in 'ethnic cleansing'. The persecution of Indigenous Australians by governments, with the intent of eradicating the Aboriginal race (Haebich, 2000), brought trauma for generations in the form of forced family separations (Atkinson, 2003). Such beliefs in cultural superiority have been profoundly destructive on vast scales throughout human history.

As many authors note, as well as cultural beliefs creating traumas, significant cultural shifts can often come about as a result of traumas. The recognition that many veterans returned from the Vietnam War in the 1960s and committed suicide (Lester, 2005) because of their subsequent social marginalisation back home, given the unpopularity of the war, has profoundly shaped the public responses to soldiers going to war in similarly complex and controversial wars today. Following the massacre of 35 people in Tasmania by Martin Bryant in 1996, Australian gun laws were changed, with the restriction on firearm access changing dramatically the number of gun-related deaths and injuries. The belief in the right to own and use a gun was transformed in Australia, yet continues to be upheld in the United States with tragic consequences. These are just two examples of the ways in which public attitudes and subsequently public policy (structural context) can profoundly shift at key points in time, creating lasting cultural practices and beliefs.

Each of the theoretical approaches we explore in the chapters ahead understands trauma through its own cultural lenses. The explicit and implicit beliefs about human behaviour, human rights and dignity and the impact of trauma and resilience will emerge in the discussions. Throughout this book, we look critically at these different social constructions of trauma and resilience, knowing that we are each embedded in our own cultural context and therefore social constructions.

Time and place dimensions

Traumas occur in specific places at specific times. Many of them mark specific places and times in enduring ways.

As we look at the theoretical approaches, we will see that some pay attention to these dimensions and some do not. As noted earlier, for example, chronological age is a core aspect of a number of the theories we consider. Some theories speak to childhood as well as adulthood trauma experiences. A focus on time enables thinking about other aspects of time – the intergenerational nature of many traumas and how this affects people who are currently living under the influence of generations of trauma experiences. It enables thinking about the sense of future time that a person, family or community may engage with. Recurrent time, as in anniversaries, for example, is often a difficult time for people, when we are reminded of the events of the past.

The place-based nature of trauma is also important, yet it is rarely acknowledged in many of the theories, given their psychosocial emphasis. Pre-existing vulnerabilities in geographic locations or emergent risks characterise profoundly the types of traumas people encounter and the resources that are available in the aftermath – for example, in child protection practice. Whether survivors have a place to return to is another important consideration, with some traumas annihilating familiar places altogether, eradicating any traces of what was previously there. 'Place' now extends beyond physical spaces also into our virtual worlds. In this digital age, trauma often reverberates beyond geographical locations to others around the world, transforming sensory and immediate traumas of individuals into collective informational traumas.

For survivors, revisiting the places of trauma can be an important aspect of recovery, such as those who have returned to war zones, concentration camps or accident sites. Memorials provide an important place for people to revisit, providing people with a focus for their grief and trauma and their resilience. Narrative approaches, in particular, highlight the importance of time and place in these ways.

Some argue that a place itself becomes traumatised when atrocities have been carried out there (see, for example, Tumarkin, 2005). Others have certainly highlighted the impact that a loss of place has on us: 'Let us not underestimate the effect which the loss of dead and dying places has on our own self-identity, mental well-being and sense of belonging' (Read, 1996, p. xii). Very few theories that we look at, however, adequately incorporate this lived sense of place in our lives.

Implications for practice and research

The issues that we have considered so far provide some insight into why people respond so differently to specific trauma experiences. Figure 1.2 highlights how the various dimensions that have been described so far can be mapped, showing their interconnectedness. Many people make good recoveries in the aftermath of their traumatic experiences, recovering from any immediate mental health impacts and living well despite these experiences. Therefore, careful assessment is needed before any therapeutic interventions are provided, including in the immediate aftermath of traumatic incidents when practitioners may be keen to implement crisis interventions. In the chapters ahead, we consider the evidence that supports these various interventions and look broadly at the implications for therapeutic practice.

In recent years, clinical guidelines have been established for therapeutic work with trauma survivors. In the United Kingdom, the National Collaborating Centre for Mental Health (2005) has published the document, *Post-Traumatic Stress Disorder: The Management of PTSD in Adults and Children in Primary and Secondary Care*. The Australian Centre for Posttraumatic Mental Health (2007) has published the *Australian Guidelines for the Treatment of Adults with Acute Stress Disorder and Posttraumatic Stress Disorder*. In the United States, Foa, Keane, Friedman and Cohen's (2009) *Effective Treatments for PTSD: Practice Guidelines from the International Society for Traumatic Stress Studies* is also influential in the specific examination of the evidence for and approaches to the treatment of PTSD. We look at these documents as we continue with our theoretical discussion in the chapters ahead. From the

Figure 1.2   A multidimensional approach

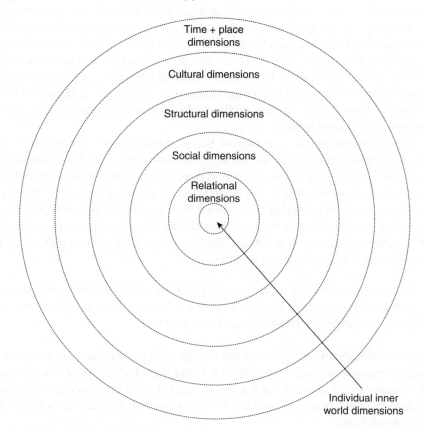

Source: Adapted from Harms (2010).

outset, though, it is critical to note that 'certain treatment approaches are more amenable than others for scientific study' (Foa et al., 2009, p. 13). This creates a bias in the evidence base that exists for various treatments and interventions. As Foa et al. (2009, pp. 13–14) state:

> Short-term and structured treatments, such as CBT and medication, are more suitable for controlled trials than longer, less structured treatments. As a result, there is more knowledge about the efficacy of the former than of the latter.

In addition to this evidence bias, for all the intervention approaches that we explore, some research to keep in mind is drawn from application of the 'common factors approach' (Lambert, 2005). Lambert and Ogles' (2004) meta-analysis of the literature relating to successful interventions found that around 40% of positive change relates to extra-therapeutic factors (i.e., factors outside of the therapeutic relationship), 30% relates to the therapeutic relationship (i.e., the working alliance and sense of rapport and support), 15% relates to hope and expectancy of the client and only 15% relates to the therapeutic technique used. This last figure is important to hold in mind, as often theoretical approaches and new trauma techniques are presented as the solution, when in fact the actual therapeutic technique used may be less influential than the therapeutic relationship itself and the sense of empathy, support and understanding.

This emphasis on the primacy of the working alliance is consistent in many ways with the five principles of mass trauma interventions, interventions on a much larger scale than individual therapeutic work. A panel of international trauma experts has agreed that an evidence base exists for five factors in successful interventions (Hobfoll et al., 2007). The evidence suggests that positive outcomes occur when practitioners have promoted a sense of (1) safety, (2) calm, (3) self and collective efficacy, (4) connectedness and (5) hope. Importantly, the panel notes:

> The heterogeneity of traumatic events and their aftermath defies any specific guidelines, and there is a need for flexibility of interventions and adaptations to specific circumstances. (Hobfoll et al., 2007, p. 284)

This encourages an evidence-informed approach rather than an evidence-based approach, whereby practitioners bring both the available knowledge of trauma and resilience responses to bear and their practice wisdom. Knowledge and practice wisdom are consolidated through processes of critical reflection.

Practitioners' and researchers' critical reflections

> The expectation that we can be immersed in suffering and loss daily and not be touched by it is as unrealistic as expecting to be able to walk through water without getting wet. (Remen, 1996, p. 52)

As practitioners and researchers engaged in trauma work, we are engaged with many people whose experiences have been and may continue to be horrific, distressing, sad and intolerable. We may come to be engaged in trauma work because of our own personal life experiences. Whether as insiders or outsiders to direct trauma, we are inevitably affected by the work we are engaged in. To use Remen's metaphor as quoted above, we cannot avoid getting wet unless we do something protective in this work.

Given this, critical reflection is a vital process for us to engage in for at least two reasons. Firstly, we need to be aware of how we are conceptualising trauma and resilience, as these ideas in turn justify our therapeutic and sociopolitical interventions (Payne, 2011). Critical reflection is about maintaining a focus on the role of power (Fook, 2002) and how we as practitioners and researchers use this power in our work with trauma survivors – including responsible and positive use of power to enable empowerment or negative uses of power to disempower trauma survivors further, either consciously or unconsciously. Trauma and power are inextricably linked – politically, personally and relationally (Afuape, 2011).

As we will see throughout the chapters ahead, we bring our own experiences and ways of thinking to trauma work and research. Reflecting on what has brought us to engage in this work with traumatised people is a key part of working transparently and productively in this area. No person's trauma experience is the same, and reflecting upon our own experiences and reactions is an essential component of knowing where we are coming from and what has influenced our thinking about trauma and recovery. Critical reflection requires that we also reflect on the ways in which we may be perpetuating or causing difficulties for clients (Fook, 2002).

The second imperative for engaging in critical reflection is in relation to self-care. Our capacity to stay engaged with the work, in whatever context, is influenced by our own well-being and motivation. Therefore, throughout the book, we look at the degree to which each of the approaches emphasises the role of the practitioner, both as an agent of influence and change and as someone profoundly influenced by the trauma work in which they are engaging.

Critical reflection and supervisory processes assist in identifying the potential negative impacts of trauma work. Concepts relevant to the practitioner and researcher in trauma work are burnout, compassion, fatigue and vicarious traumatization. Burnout refers to 'a syndrome of emotional exhaustion, depersonalisation, and reduced personal accomplishment that can occur among individuals who work with people in some capacity' (Maslach, 1982, p. 4). Emotional exhaustion, depersonalization and a reduced sense of personal accomplishment can all be experienced as a result of, typically, longer-term exposure to trauma work. Some of the risk factors that have been proposed for burnout include inexperience, high expectations, a heavy workload, a lack of support, a lack of autonomy or participation in decision making, frequent direct client contact and complex or severe client problems, a lack of reciprocity in relationships and a constant sense of giving in an environment where there may be little organisational support and often role blurring. Strategies to prevent burnout (Vachon, 1998) include maintaining a sense of competence, control and pleasure in work, maintaining and revising a personal philosophy of death and illness, focusing on lifestyle management and stress-relieving activities, distinguishing between personal and professional variables and reviewing your motivation for working in the area.

Compassion fatigue is a complex concept in that it can be seen to be an extension of burnout by some and as secondary traumatic stress (Figley, 1995) by others, 'the cost of caring' (Figley, 2002). It refers to the physical and emotional exhaustion, related to the cognitive schema, and can lead to a cynicism and detachment and a dread of working with clients.

Vicarious traumatisation is a different concept, although often confused with compassion fatigue and burnout. It 'refers to a transformation in the therapist's (or other trauma worker's) inner experience resulting from empathetic engagement with the client's trauma material' (Pearlman & Saakvitne, 1995, p. 40). Your cognitive schema is altered by the work that you do – there is a degree of disruption to your view of yourself and the world and a loss of faith in the essential goodness or trustworthiness of people. It is not as related to an experience of exhaustion as much as to a trauma response, whereby your world view is altered. It is defined as 'a normal reaction to the stressful and sometimes traumatizing work with victims' (McCann & Pearlman, 1990, p. 145), involving intrusive images, nightmares and negative attitudes such as cynicism and suspicion. However, as some have noted:

> [T]he evidence to support the existence of VT is meagre and inconsistent. Future research needs to be directed at distinguishing VT from other sources of distress arising in the workplace. (Sabin-Farrell & Turpin, 2003, p. 449)

What may be missing from some of these understandings of the impact of the work is the extent to which many practitioners and, to a lesser extent, researchers are directly involved in traumatic events – directly witnessing and relating to people through their trauma experiences. Teachers, for example, are interacting daily with children who are living with ongoing traumatic circumstances and seeing the daily impact on these children. Hospital staff and paramedics are often intervening in the midst of traumas as they unfold and are therefore active participants in the traumatic events themselves. Workers in refugee camps are witnessing the traumas of displaced people and their ongoing struggles. Thus, both informational trauma and sensory trauma are being experienced regularly. This is not vicarious in the sense of being removed from the trauma itself. It is trauma work as a chosen area of professional practice, with high exposure to traumatic events on a daily basis.

Thus, within services in many countries, a strong emphasis is emerging in relation to trauma-informed care. This acknowledges an awareness and centrality of the influence of trauma in people's lives, both the survivors and the service providers. By definition:

> Trauma-informed care is a strengths-based framework that is grounded in an understanding of and responsiveness to the impact of trauma that emphasises physical, psychological and emotional safety for both providers and survivors and that creates opportunities for survivors to rebuild a sense of control and empowerment. (Hopper et al., 2010, p. 82)

Many practitioners may want to see trauma-informed responses taken one step further than the dyad of providers and survivors – so that we act at structural and cultural levels for social change as well as within the privacy of therapeutic work. This ensures practice is both trauma-informed and critically reflexive.

Conclusion

In this first chapter, the focus has been on setting up some of the commonalities and differences in conceptualising trauma and resilience in a general sense for practice and research, before we look at the specific approaches in the chapters ahead. As you can see, trauma practice and research can be conceptualised in so many different ways as a result. A multidimensional approach has been presented as a way of considering where the key areas of focus are within a particular theoretical approach – whether inner worlds, with an emphasis on biopsychospiritual experiences, are privileged in thinking about trauma responses and recovery or outer worlds, with an emphasis on relational, social, structural and cultural experiences and influences. This enables us to keep thinking critically as practitioners and researchers about the elements of experiences that we in turn come to privilege or neglect. To conclude the chapter, we examined concepts of critical reflection and self-care. These processes enable us to focus on what we are doing in our practice and research, as well as what the implications of this practice and research may be for trauma survivors and ourselves.

2
Psychodynamic Approaches: Reintegrating the Self

Introduction

In this chapter, we begin our focus on specific theoretical approaches for understanding the impact of trauma experiences, starting with psychodynamic approaches. In a general sense, psychodynamic theories have provided ways of understanding the development and adaptive capacities of our inner life. These theories provide explanations of our instincts and motivations, our internal psychological organisation and our sense of self (both conscious and unconscious) and, in turn, how these influence our expectations within relationships and our overall capacity to engage with life. More specifically, psychodynamic ideas contribute extensively to understanding the types of disruption to self that occurs through experiences of trauma and the reorganisation processes that promote recovery and resilience. They also contribute to understanding broader sociocultural aspects of trauma.

Psychodynamic theories have developed over more than a century, and so it is beyond the scope of this chapter to explore these developments in great depth. The concepts that are in use today come from many different schools of thought, each with important histories behind them and points of divergence between them. Given this, we look at some core concepts of trauma and resilience in a broadly introductory way. We look at how these concepts have been profoundly influential in acknowledging and addressing the inner world distress and disruption that occurs during and after traumatic experiences and therefore at the implications for practice.

28

Psychodynamic explanations of the developing self and resilience

In order to understand the impact of trauma, it is important to consider how psychodynamic theories focus on non-traumatic processes of psychological experience. Psychodynamic theories are typically developmental theories, in that they seek to understand the experiences and influence of infancy and early childhood as foundational, setting down patterns of relating that are learnt through our relationships with primary caregivers. In these early experiences, to varying degrees we encounter predictability and routine, having our needs met and unmet, trusting ourselves and others and forming an internal set of assumptions about the world around us based on our experience of ourselves and those around us. We experience our helplessness, rage, pleasure, gratification, shame, guilt and a range of emotions – and we come to understand and manage these experiences of self. Non-traumatic psychological development and change across our lifespan therefore involves processes relating to our conscious and unconscious feelings and thoughts, our instincts or motivations, and how we incorporate past and present experiences.

Each of us varies in our capacity for, and states of, focused psychological presence and attending, our day dreaming and fantasising and our sleeping. We vary in our feeling states, our mindfulness of them and our understandings of their causes. This variation is both within our own experience and in comparison to others. These aspects of our conscious and unconscious experience are influenced by many factors, including, as some theorists propose, our collective unconscious experience (Jung, 1977, p. 160). The dynamic nature of our inner psychological life comes about through these constantly interacting processes.

Psychodynamic theories propose that from infancy we are motivated by different instincts. For example, Freud proposed that we are governed by two basic instincts from early in life – 'Eros and the destructive instinct' (Freud, 1969, p. 5), later elaborated upon as the pleasure principle and the death instinct (Freud, 1969; 1984). He proposed that these two instincts are in tension with each other, as they relate to our motivation to seek a sense of preservation and unity, and our simultaneous motivation to 'undo connections'. In this sense, we are striving to manage 'attraction and repulsion', simultaneously (Freud, 1969, p. 6).

While earlier psychodynamic thinking focused on drives or instincts, more recent emphasis is on a person's affective experience, or 'subjective emotional experience', according to Stolorow (2008, p. 114). Attention is focused on how affect 'from birth onward is regulated, or misregulated, within ongoing relational systems' (Stolorow, 2008, p. 114). When we experience the anxiety of such dysregulation, we use various defence mechanisms, typically unconscious strategies such as repression, splitting, denial and dissociation, to tolerate this painful or frightening effect, to protect ourselves from becoming overwhelmed – that is, from experiencing intense emotions or thoughts that are outside our sense of safety and security (Freud, 1968).

Psychodynamic theories typically emphasise the cumulative and integrative nature of these early experiences of self and defence, such that we bring these assumptions into our adult experience of self and others, again both consciously and unconsciously. Brothers (2009, p. 53) proposes that

> a sense of integration and regulation, a capacity to feel, know and remember, a capacity to be an autonomous individual, a capacity to use language to express inner and outer experience, and a capacity to play mentally with alternate realities are all part of building a continuing and coherent sense of being. This is central to our sense of self, our identity and our daily functioning.

Such integrated functioning enables the coping with stressors of everyday living and balancing in an integrated way the tasks of functioning well. This sets a benchmark for what resilience and recovery might look like in the longer term – the reorganisation and reintegration of inner life after major disruption and a capacity to relate with others. Trauma experiences are seen as disrupting or shattering these experiences of self (Ulman & Brothers, 1988).

Psychodynamic explanations of trauma responses

Through the late 1800s, psychoanalysis emerged as a therapeutic practice for people presenting for treatment of various psychological, physical and behavioural difficulties (Ellenberger, 1970). The manifestation of these difficulties as hysteria was a major area of focus (Showalter, 1997). The 'talking cure' (Breuer & Freud, 1936), as psychoanalysis came to be known, assisted people in making connections between past traumatic events and current physical and psychological symptoms of hysteria, which in turn were then often alleviated or abated. A connection was made with the symptoms of hysteria, past traumatic experiences and the unconscious. With earlier trauma experiences being recognised as a core reason for people's distress, the focus began to move onto understanding trauma differently.

A new understanding of the integration of experience from infancy onwards began to emerge, as the recognition of the impact of overwhelming experience came to be better understood. As an early trauma theorist, Freud proposed the following definition:

> We describe as 'traumatic' any excitations from outside which are powerful enough to break through the protective shield. It seems to me that the concept of trauma necessarily implies a connection of this kind with a breach in an otherwise efficacious barrier against stimuli. Such an event as an external trauma is bound to provoke a disturbance on a large scale in the functioning of the organism's energy and to set in motion every possible defensive measure. At the same time, the pleasure principle is for the moment put out of action. (Freud, 1984[1928], pp. 56–57)

Within this definition, some core aspects of psychodynamic understandings of trauma can be seen. Firstly, trauma is related to 'excitations from the outside', that is, external event/s, 'which overwhelms normal ego functioning' (Wilson, 1995, p. 14). Secondly, the impact of trauma is a disruption to everyday functioning, given disruptions to a person's sense of equilibrium. As individuals (or 'organisms' according to Freud), the usual barrier we have built around our self to manage our everyday anxieties is broken down during traumatic experiences. Thirdly, the anxiety stimulated by trauma activates a person's defence mechanisms. That is, in order to cope with this overwhelming traumatic stress, we unconsciously draw on processes of information and emotion management that will enable us to continue functioning, albeit often in a less optimal way. Fourthly, a person loses a sense of pleasure and engagement with life and with others. A loss of a sense of future focus occurs.

This definition provides a psycho-economic view of trauma, which remains relevant to many of today's definitions of trauma. That is, trauma overwhelms a person's ability or energy to maintain a focus on and engagement with daily life, given how overwhelming and dangerous particular experiences have been to their emotional and psychological functioning. As Lieberman, Ippen and Marans note (2009, p. 371), 'The helpless response to overwhelming danger is the key feature that distinguishes the traumatic experience from anxiety.'

What lies at the heart of this overwhelming danger is important to consider. The core trauma is in many ways the threat of annihilation, of non-existence – a threat to self. As Brothers (2009, p. 53) notes:

> we may readily acknowledge that we inhabit a world in which nothing is certain, not even our psychological survival, trauma appears to expose us to this truth in a way that we experience as unbearable.

This is similarly expressed by Van der Kolk (1994, p. ix): 'Trauma confronts people with the futility of putting up resistance, the impossibility of being able to affect the outcome of events'. This exposure to a new truth often involves a shattering of pre-existing meaning structures. Thus:

> Trauma is a brute fact that cannot be integrated into a context of meaning at the time it is experienced because it tears the fabric of the psyche. This creates special conditions for its remembrance and retroactive integration in present experience. (Bohleber, 2007, p. 335)

This futility and loss of meaning is compounded further if trauma occurs within the context of relationships, particularly ones in which a child is dependent upon for care and nurturance or where other relational violations occur. Thus, another part of the threat occurs intersubjectively – as Stolorow states:

> Painful or frightening affect becomes enduringly traumatic when the attunement that the child needs to assist in its tolerance, and integration is profoundly absent. (Stolorow, 2008, p. 114)

Writers such as Laub and Auerhahn (1993, p. 287) have emphasised this relational failure as inherently traumatic in their analysis of Holocaust trauma experiences during the Second World War: 'the essential experience of trauma was an unravelling of the relationship between self and nurturing other, the very fabric of everyday life'. From survivors of the Holocaust, one of the major traumas identified in therapeutic work was not only the atrocity of the brutality and violence towards people and the extreme anxiety provoked by witnessing and experiencing these difficulties, but also the added dimension whereby there was a refusal to witness and/or validate the suffering of those who were experiencing these traumas (Reiter, 2000). Accounts of concentration camp life include reference to instances when prison guards laughed at prisoners when prisoners were faced with the most traumatic and horrific of experiences. This failure of human empathy or mirroring of distress on the part of the prison guards compounded prisoners' already-extreme circumstances.

Core psychodynamic understandings of trauma's threat are therefore that trauma confronts us with the threat of annihilation, a sense of utter powerlessness, overwhelming emotion and a shattering of assumptions about self and others. With this confrontation, psychodynamic approaches propose a number of conscious and unconscious processes that occur, primarily, in relation to memory and the activation of defence mechanisms.

Memory

Trauma is a complex phenomenon involving both a shattering experience and efforts at restoration. (Brothers, 2009, p. 52)

In the aftermath of traumatic experiences, memory plays a critical, if not *the* central role in shaping our coping capacities. When traumatic experiences end, memory is the legacy. Memories are the psychological scars of trauma, the mechanism by which traumatic experiences are relived. Like all scars, these psychological ones can be a constant reminder of prior damage and suffering as well as a constant reminder of survival and recovery.

Before we look at these issues further, some consideration of everyday memory is needed to understand this type of memory functioning and then the disturbance traumatic events cause to information processing and subsequent traumatic memory formation. According to Mendez and Fras (2011), for example, we have a need for complete and integrated memories, so we have a tendency for the completion and 'filling in' of memories when memories are incomplete and lack integration. Memory construction not only relies on real-life experiences, but we bring into these constructions our imagination, wish fulfilment and magical thinking. We build a sense of familiarity into our memories, and so we embed this in our reworking of memories. We create memories based on self-relevance – that is, we include autobiographical information and information that is related to our survival. Our memories are shaped emotionally by events, pictures and words around us, so that personal and public sources of information become important influences. Studies show repeatedly that we are suggestible – that is, likely to be influenced by those around us and in the longer term in relation to the details of memories to varying degrees. Memory formation is profoundly influenced by our developmental age, which influences our verbal capacities in particular (Howe et al., 2008). All of these dimensions of memory are impacted upon through experiences of trauma, as the following discussion highlights.

Freud and his contemporaries, Charcot and Breuer, brought to attention the link between past traumatic memories and current difficulties in everyday life. Breuer and Freud (1936[1895], p. 17), in their studies of people experiencing hysteria, noted that 'hysterics suffer from reminiscences'. The link was beginning to be made between current distress, symptoms of hysteria and memories of past traumatic events. Freud was one of the earliest theorists to note the fixation that seems to then occur with traumatic memories of experiences:

The traumatic neuroses give a clear indication that a fixation to the traumatic accident lives at their root ... It is as though these patients had not yet finished in the traumatic situation, as though they were still faced by it as an immediate task which has not been dealt with. (Freud, 1966[1917], pp. 274–275)

Psychodynamic interest has focused on the experiences relived in night-mares:

These patients regularly repeat the traumatic situation in their dreams; where hysteriform attacks occur that admit of an analysis, we find that the attack corresponds to a complete transplanting of the patient into the traumatic situation. (Freud, 1966[1917], pp. 274–275)

Indeed, some see these recurrences as the core trauma experience:

Perhaps the hallmark of reaction to traumatic experience is the traumatic dream or nightmare ... In a typical dream, almost regardless of setting, the individual tends to be helpless in the face of attack. (De Fazio, 1978, p. 36)

This recurrence is seen as enabling over time the unconscious processing and integration of material too traumatic to process in waking life.

This idea of trauma's hold on people in the present was initially conceived of as a repetition compulsion, a repeating and reliving of the trauma, yet an inability to simultaneously gain a sense of control over it:

as the compulsion to repeat is a repetitive, self-defeating, and rigid way of being in the world that causes the individual distress, this process needs to be understood as a maladaptive attempt at mastery. It is an established and unchangeable coping style based on the past. (Levy, 2000, pp. 48–49)

Many different hypotheses are given as to why repetition, through intrusive thoughts, flashbacks, nightmares and actual behaviours, occurs as part of a trauma response. The behavioural repetition of traumas has been a controversial and contested area of focus – the concern has arisen particularly in relation to survivors of childhood sexual assault who are particularly likely to experience adult re-victimisation. In order to understand this phenomenon, some propose that repeating behaviours is a way of staying with the new familiar (Zepf & Zepf, 2008). Judith Herman proposed that it reflects 'repeated futile efforts to gain containment around occasions of extreme chaos or terror' (Gleiser, 2003, p. 31). Others propose that this idea of repetition provides the conceptual link with or pathway to PTSD, something we shall look further at in Chapter 4.

This early work, however, led Freud and others into the contested territory of memory and trauma that continues today. Both in Freud's day and more recently in the 1980s, different theoretical and therapeutic understandings of traumatic memory have been the focus of bitter disagreement among practitioners and researchers alike. Indeed, the emergence in the 1980s of what is now termed 'false memory syndrome' led to what is referred to as the 'memory wars' (McNally, 2003, 2005). Throughout history, debate has centred on the nature and veracity of traumatic memories (Mendez & Fras, 2011). These debates have not only therapeutic implications but also social, political and legal ones.

The first debate relates to an emphasis of psychodynamic theorists and therapists in relation to the connection between prior and current traumatic experiences and how these are influenced by the phantasies we bring to these experiences and in their aftermath. This is exemplified in this view of therapeutic work:

> the goal of reconstruction is to comprehend this pattern and its superimposed revisions in order to be able to trace the development in reverse back to the original event and its associated unconscious phantasy. (Bohleber, 2007, p. 333)

Psychodynamic theories of trauma persisted with a link between childhood traumatic experiences, often sexual in nature, and later traumatic reactions, evoked by adult experiences of trauma. For veterans during the First World War, for example, these concepts were found at the heart of their psychotherapy.

Freud's famous retraction of his theory of trauma exemplifies the debate about the connection between real experiences of trauma in childhood and subsequently triggered adult trauma reactions. He initially argued that all adult difficulties had their origins in early traumatic experiences, which were reactivated by adulthood experiences. Hearing the many accounts of childhood sexual trauma from the adult patients he was treating and experiencing the enormous pressure from colleagues within the Psychoanalytic Society, he came to the conclusion that the prevalence of such high rates of sexual assault could not be true – rather, these patients were imagining the sexually abusive experiences of their childhoods (Gay, 1988). He came instead to see these as part of an instinct-driven Oedipal theory, whereby these women were recounting childhood fantasies not realities. Freud had entered into the political territory of trauma work.

In the 1980s–1990s, clients in therapy in the United States and the United Kingdom, in particular, reported recovering childhood memories of sexual abuse and satanic ritual abuse (Ost et al., 2013). Some therapists claimed that clients had completely repressed memories of these experiences earlier in their lives, but had been able to recall them as a result of therapy, leading to several enquiries (Poole et al., 1995). In some cases, families were torn apart by false allegations of abuse and the subsequent legal and emotional consequences. Many of the claims were later retracted, found to be 'recollections that [were] factually incorrect but strongly believed' (Mendez & Fras, 2011, p. 492). These claims raised questions, though, about traumatic memory that remain today – what is the nature of remembering and forgetting of traumatic life experiences and is it possible to completely 'forget' a traumatic experience of the past, particularly in childhood?

A third debate, however, links to the extent to which 'real' traumas should be acknowledged and these realities addressed. With an emphasis on a phantasised past, the truths of these often horrific historical events can be lost:

> Historical truth is replaced by narrative truth. The framework of narrative reality becomes all encompassing and the connection with the real world goes unmentioned. The fundamental problem with these narratological and constructivist conceptions of psychoanalysis consists in their exclusion or obscuration of any connection with the reality behind the narration. (Bohleber, 2007, p. 333)

As we will see later in Chapter 8, this lack of attention to the truths of people's traumas and the engagement in the political and social redress of them is a criticism of psychodynamic approaches. However, these views are not necessarily theoretically incompatible, and authors such as Boulanger (2012) have argued strongly that psychodynamic therapists are morally obliged to not only individually and therapeutically witness people's stories but also engage in political acts of witnessing, such as actively participating in court processes.

Memories are not only influenced and re-experienced, therefore, by the individual who holds them. In many ways, the broader family and social context influences them also, through the sharing or silencing of these narratives – the extent to which they are social memories as well as individual ones. Sharing traumatic memories can often occur only with generational distance and/or the realities of the impending loss of history through the death of those who experienced the trauma – for Holocaust survivors, the perceived social imperative for others to remember has encouraged many survivors to recount the atrocities that were inflicted upon them. This social imperative has been the motivation to recount some of their experience, often after decades of silence (Reiter, 2000).

Thus, psychodynamic approaches highlight the challenges in therapeutic work in relation to the 'truth status' of memories (Bohleber, 2007) as well as 'the role of the historic past in the therapeutic presence' (Blum, 2003). As this brief discussion highlights, there are 'many levels of remembering and preserving the horror of atrocity' (Laub & Auerhahn, 1993, p. 299).

Defence mechanisms

Psychodynamic approaches propose that when we are faced with overwhelming traumatic circumstances, we are unable to process them cognitively and emotionally. Therefore, we employ defence mechanisms to protect ourselves from being completely overwhelmed and non-functioning. This enables a traumatic experience to be dealt with somehow at the time of its occurrence and subsequently in the aftermath period, however dysfunctional in the longer term the defence mechanism may be. As Price (2007, p. 344) states:

> These defences generally act to block conscious awareness of distressing material, rather than allowing the individual to consciously acknowledge it.

The result of this activation of defence mechanisms is as follows:

> Distressing material is consequently denied from full conscious awareness as it is (unconsciously) feared that it may overwhelm the ego and result in personality disintegration. (Price, 2007, p. 344)

At the time of the traumatic experiences and in their aftermath, these processes may well be adaptive, protecting someone from experiencing the intensity of their circumstances. What the defence mechanisms allow for is a partialising of the experience. Acknowledgement of this process has been one of the major reasons why debriefing strategies in the immediacy of trauma have been strongly questioned (Rose et al., 2002) on the basis that these defence mechanisms fulfil an important self-protective process, and should not be tampered with. Two commonly identified defence mechanisms are dissociation and repression, each considered briefly in this discussion.

Dissociation

There are many definitions of traumatic dissociation. One broad definition from Gleiser (2003, p. 37) is as follows:

> Clinical dissociation is understood to be a primitive response to traumatic over-stimulation of the ego and psychic pain (Brenner, 2001), in which aspects of the traumatic event, such as affect, memory, or meaning, are internally split off from awareness, or from each other, thereby shielding the individual from their immediate effects.

Other key writers, Van der Kolk and Fisler (1995, p. 10), define dissociation as 'a compartmentalization of experience: elements of the experience are not integrated into a unitary whole, but are stored in memory as isolated fragments consisting of sensory perceptions or affective states'. In defining dissociation, they highlight the multiplicity of ways in which dissociation is applied – to 'the sensory and emotional fragmentation of experience', 'depersonalization and derealization at the moment of the trauma', 'ongoing depersonalization and "spacing out" in everyday life' and 'containing the traumatic memories within distinct egostates' (Van der Kolk & Fisler, 1995, p. 10). Some argue that this tendency to dissociation is the key predictor of complex PTSD in adulthood (Lyons-Ruth et al., 2006).

Moving away from that which cannot be tolerated is described as 'splitting off, (Bragin, 2010), and therefore the therapeutic task is to tolerate rather than split off from the intolerable material. Bragin gives the example of working with war veterans. Not only do they face the war traumas, but they must also face their own anger and aggression and that of others. On returning home, the therapeutic task requires a shared tolerance of these emotions and drives; that is, the therapeutic relationship needs to

> create the atmosphere in which thinking about the violence of war could be tolerated. But for that to happen, both parties would have to be able to keep the violence in mind. Each party, starting with the clinician, would have to be able to take in and acknowledge, as opposed to splitting off, their own anger and aggression. (Bragin, 2010, p. 324)

These understandings of dissociation as a result of trauma within primary caregiver relationships have led to very different understandings of borderline personality disorder (APA, 2000). Borderline personality disorder has been predominantly diagnosed in women, mainly in women who have experienced sexual trauma in childhood, with prevalence estimates in the order of 85%. While it was previously thought to be a disorder that was non-responsive to treatment, recognition of the violation of the attachment relationship that was inherent in the trauma has led to new understandings of the origins of the disorder and therefore the appropriate treatment. At its most extreme, trauma is seen as the underlying cause of dissociative identity disorder, formerly known as multiple personality disorder. The core work of complex trauma interventions is to reinstate or introduce a state of internal, emotional regulation.

Repression

The other most commonly noted trauma defence mechanism is repression:

> As a result of the degree of threat experienced to the ego and the subsequent anxiety, the victim typically used repression as an ego defense to remove unpleasant memories and emotions of the traumatic event from awareness. (Wilson, 1995, p. 11)

There are other ways in which traumatic memories can be repressed. One is in relation to the verbal capacity that we may have at the time of the traumatic experience. Depending upon our developmental stage, we may have no verbal memory of a traumatic event we have witnessed. This has been noted in psychotherapeutic work with children who have witnessed parental homicide (Kaplan et al., 2001). It was noticed from their drawings and their lack of articulation of what had occurred that young children did not have the words to match their visual memory, given that they were preverbal at the time of the experiences. Changing working style, to focus on giving words to children's experience, enabled them to form a verbal narrative that accompanied their visual memory. Thus, being preverbal at the time of trauma experiences may be a way of living with an overarching repression of what had occurred.

Repression can happen also for children and adults in terms of a social repression. As Laub and Auerhahn (1993, p. 288) note:

> Much of knowing is dependent upon language – not only our knowing trauma through hearing the victim's language, but the ability of victims to grasp and recall their experiences through the process of formulating them in language. Because of the radical breakdown between trauma and culture, victims often cannot find categories of thought or words for their experience.

Many of the processes operating at individual levels, such as denial and repression, as part of the helplessness of trauma have been mirrored in social and cultural levels. These social processes of forgetting or repressing often compound survivors' distress as they have no external validation of their experiences and are often silenced or negated as a response.

Implications for practice

As the chapter has highlighted, there are many different psychodynamic theories and concepts, and, therefore, there are many different practice approaches and models. It is well noted that, for psychodynamic approaches to PTSD, the overlap with cognitive behavioural approaches and interpersonal approaches makes it 'difficult to circumscribe the boundaries of what constitutes psychodynamic treatment' (Lieberman et al., 2009, p. 383).

Psychodynamic approaches are typically used in the longer-term aftermath of trauma rather than as immediate interventions. This is in part because of the conditions that need to be in place for someone to engage in more insight-oriented therapeutic work.

While there is great diversity in the depth and focus of psychodynamic trauma therapies, perhaps the most appropriate summary of the focus of psychodynamic work is contained in the following few lines:

> All of us who work psychodynamically have committed to explore the tension between past and present; identifying the roots of the past as they are multiply manifest in the present, establishing psychic and historical continuity, a more fully lived subjectivity, and more engaged intersubjectivity. (Boulanger, 2012, p. 319)

Much of the therapeutic work involves building a trusting working alliance and, within that context, bringing into awareness and language the trauma that has been experienced, and building a subsequent integration of these experiences into conscious and manageable awareness. Insight into conscious and unconscious influences is encouraged, and connections with past traumas and coping patterns may be made. The aim is to prevent the disruption of trauma through conscious management of its impact in the present.

Building a trusting working alliance

Psychodynamic approaches have given a high level of consideration to the role of the therapeutic relationship, generally, and specifically in relation to trauma work. The first step in therapeutic work is establishing a working alliance so that insight-oriented work can proceed. This may sound straightforward; however, with lack of trust in oneself and in others being one of the major disruptions of trauma, the re-establishment of trust in a therapeutic context can be an enormous challenge.

Trust occurs when a person can reveal themselves fully to their therapist, without fear of rejection, blame, disgust or hostility, for example. This is particularly important in trauma work, where people's experiences of trauma may actually be characterised by these emotions. The therapist as witness to often horrific experiences that someone has endured or been engaged in is an important role (Laub & Auerhahn, 1993).

Initial approaches to the therapeutic relationship within psychoanalysis encouraged distance and objectivity between the analyst and the 'patient'. The analyst was removed from the client's sight so that the client could talk in ways that allowed for free association to occur – that is, conversation unmediated by both the verbal and non-verbal responses of the therapist that influence the direction of the conversation. It was thought that this enabled the client to provide the material that was relevant to them and also facilitated the projection of earlier relational expectations and patterns – primarily those with parents earlier in life, to highlight the ways in which these were influential on current functioning and expectations. This method was likened to a 'blank screen' and continues in some psychoanalytic contexts today. Trauma therapy work occurs in typically highly boundaried relational settings – the predictability of availability, safety and understanding being important components of the therapeutic space. Providing a supportive, understanding presence is critical to building or rebuilding trust, often reparation for a parental relationship that was not so. Within such a space,

> it is the analytic encounter that allows traumatic repetition to take on the quality of a communication, an address to another, rather than remain meaningless reproduction. (Reis, 2009, pp. 1359–1360)

A strong working alliance enables mutual engagement in this task, breaking the hold of traumatic memory and experience.

Working with transference and countertransference issues

Psychodynamic approaches pay particular attention to the therapeutic relationship, as the main factor in facilitating insight and understanding. Two key relational processes are transference and countertransference. As a complex reaction,

> transference is a compromise formation, an unconscious fantasy, including components of real experience, self-and object-representations, defense, superego factors, and associated affects. (Blum, 2003, p. 499)

Within the context of trauma work, the trauma transference is an intensified reaction, as the projection onto the therapist also relates to the trauma injury in terms of relational expectations and/or anxieties about safety. The aim of this work around the transference is to understand the patterns of past and present thoughts and feelings and how they are enacted in close relationships. Ideally, this leads to an improved reflective capacity and reliance on mature defences (Schottenbauer et al., 2008).

In a traditional sense, 'countertransference traditionally has referred to the activation of the therapist's unresolved or unconscious conflicts or concerns ... the work of psychotherapy may reactivate therapists' early experiences and memories' (McCann & Pearlman, 1990, p. 134). The therapist's own insights and self-understanding are similarly a critical part of the work, through your own therapy or analysis and ongoing supervision. Attention to the countertransference is a key part of trauma therapists' understanding and insight (Wilson & Lindy, 1994). As a practitioner, the ability to tolerate the realities of human atrocities that have been experienced by people and inflicted by others is an essential quality to have.

In the context of work with trauma, however, the concept of trauma countertransference is particularly important. While working with Holocaust survivors who had endured profound horrific traumas in the concentration camps during the Second World War, Laub noted a particular countertransference that was a trauma countertransference, unlike a countertransference with non-traumatic material. With a trauma countertransference, or event countertransference (Hafkenscheid, 2005), the reaction is to the traumatic material, and the confrontation with how horrific the experiences were in the concentration camps. The violence, cruelty and exposure constantly to threat of death that survivors had endured confronted therapists with new realities that were previously unheard of. In order to cope with this unprecedented material, therapists found that they were reacting in different ways to the client and to their narratives. Whereas previously the countertransference was seen largely as in response to the client's material and what that client evoked in the therapist by way of the therapist's own past and present, a trauma countertransference involved reaction to not only the client but also their traumatic material. This awareness of the countertransference associated with the traumatic material itself, not just the client's world and experiences, has been embedded in supervision practices in many settings.

This thinking is reflected in the awareness of vicarious traumatisation, described in Chapter 1, whereby the therapist's world view and belief system is disrupted by the material they are encountering in their daily work (Pearlman & Saakvitne, 1995). The reactions can be similar to the trauma reactions evoked in the client – dissociating from the information, becoming hypervigilant to the possibility of the trauma happening in their own life and/or developing a trauma response of intrusive or avoidant symptoms.

Some more psychoanalytically oriented approaches focus extensively on these aspects of the work, whereas, at other times, these developments are noted by the practitioner but not necessarily explicitly addressed.

Bringing to conscious awareness the trauma that has been experienced

Psychodynamic sessions are typically unstructured sessions, unlike other treatments that are structured by guidelines. The aim is to provide a space where a person can talk about whatever is on their mind. This arose from the early recognition that the practice of 'free association', as it was termed, led to a person talking about their core concerns and anxieties and simultaneously encountering the defences that prevented their cure. This 'talking cure' was noted in interactions with Breuer and a particular client, who told him to stop asking questions and listen to her instead. This free association brings to conscious awareness the traumatic experiences of past and present.

It enables a person to form a more coherent narrative and meaning structure for containing experiences that have exceeded pre-existing narratives of the self. This enables a restoration or establishment of a sense of self in an enduring way, which enables a person to experience the world as more predictable and organised than was rendered by the traumatic experiences.

Psychodynamic trauma therapy is oriented towards enabling fragments of feelings or thoughts to be brought into conscious awareness and enabling a new conscious regulation of these thoughts and feelings to emerge. This is based on an understanding that traumatic memory is stored unconsciously and is able to be retrieved, at least in part, and remembered over time when a tolerance can be built up to accommodating the awareness and emotionality of the trauma. In bringing together memory and emotion, a cathartic release is thought to occur. That is, the energy being expended on repressing the traumatic material, on keeping emotion and thought separate, no longer needs to be expended on this defensive behaviour. Bringing these often traumatic memories into full conscious awareness, understanding their origins in past realities and fantasies and being able to tolerate them emotionally became and remains the focus of therapeutic work.

From early psychodynamic treatments that were conducted with the military during the First World War (see Kardiner, 1941, for example), another focus of practice emerged in relation to flooding techniques. Soldiers hospitalised for psychiatric disorders following front-line action were flooded with their sensory trauma experiences rather than sheltered from them. The direct relived exposure to the source of the trauma was thought to result in a cathartic release from shellshock. Today, prolonged exposure therapies are proving effective for people with PTSD (Foa, Gillihan & Bryant, 2013); this will be explored in Chapter 4.

Integrating experiences into conscious awareness

Insight into conscious and unconscious influences is encouraged, and connections with past traumas and coping patterns may be made. With a new and increasing awareness of traumatic experiences that disrupt functioning, longer-term therapy focuses on understanding the defence mechanisms that have been used to manage the trauma and bring them into a more conscious coping repertoire. This enables active engagement around the management of trigger experiences – that is, deliberate avoidance or exposure to trauma triggers rather than unknowingly being confronted by trauma triggers.

It also means tolerating our unconscious lives, our many motivations and desires. It enables exploration of previously intolerable feelings, thoughts and realities, contained now in the context of a positive therapeutic alliance and a newly forming trauma narrative. This is all with the aim of preventing the disruption of trauma through conscious management of its impact in the present.

As mentioned earlier, some more intersubjectively oriented approaches have emphasised the moral obligation that practitioners have to witness the traumas people have experienced, not just privately but also publicly:

> The moral witness who can validate the experience privately and testify to it publicly, if required to do so, is essential in enabling the survivor to lay claim to experiences that are so dehumanizing that they cannot be borne in mind without the help of another. (Boulanger, 2012, p. 320)

This political engagement with people's suffering is addressed further in Chapter 8.

Reintegrating the self and relationships

The overarching intention of psychodynamic interventions is for a person to develop a capacity to relate well to themselves and to others – this is resilience in a psychodynamic sense. With psychodynamic approaches highlighting that trauma foreshortens a sense of hope and a future focus, resilience is about restoring a sense of pleasure and engagement with life and with others.

A case scenario

How would you go about working with Jasmina using a psychodynamic approach?

Jasmina presents to the Counselling Service as a very chaotic 38-year-old woman. She is always late for her counselling sessions, if she arrives at all, and is often angry with the reception staff when she turns up. After several sessions, she talks about the sexual abuse that her grandfather had inflicted upon her from the age of 7 to 15. Her mother and father, both of who are now deceased, were health professionals, and she remains distraught that neither of them knew what was going on. She has frequent nightmares about her abuse, which often lead to days of confusion afterwards, when she feels lost in time and place. She describes herself as useless and worthless, and yet she rages against this self-perception. She has recently returned to university study, excelling as a mature-age veterinary science student. She is passionate about this career pathway.

Critically reflecting on psychodynamic approaches

A vast literature exists critiquing psychodynamic approaches, generally (Masson, 2012), and in relation to trauma, specifically. Part of the critique lies in concerns that psychodynamic approaches generally were in their early days 'patriarchal, ethnocentric and claiming a universality that does not allow for the uniqueness of women's voices' (Magnavita, 2002, p. 466). Psychoanalysis was founded on primarily male practitioners and female 'patients' and on trying to understand and alleviate the disruption of childhood experiences of trauma in adult life (Carr, 2011). The failure to address these childhood experiences of trauma explicitly and instead focus on women as 'patients' and pathologise their reactions is also part of the critique of earlier practices. The extent to which gender and ethnicity are now seen as addressed adequately in current practices and thinking is still the subject of debate. As we see in Chapter 4, these criticisms are not only made of psychodynamic approaches.

Another part of the critique focuses on the difficulties in establishing an evidence base for the efficacy of psychodynamic interventions so that theories remain relatively untested. However, this situation arises because of the very strengths of the approach – it is a relationally oriented approach driven by human connectedness, insight and understanding, rather than a symptom–relief approach, which tends to be driven by a manual or guidelines (Lieberman et al., 2009, p. 383). It is difficult to 'control', therefore, the various factors that are seen to be part of gold standard interventions. Research in this area is complex (Cohen, 2011). Roth and Fonagy (2005) provide an excellent discussion in their book, *What works for whom?* Thus, clinical case studies have tended to provide the evidence for the approach and of course, subjective reports of satisfaction. These are both the strengths and weaknesses of the approaches that fall within this theoretical domain.

Conclusion

Psychodynamic approaches have contributed enormously to the identification of core trauma and resilience issues over decades. They highlight the impact of traumatic memories and the vital role of defence mechanisms, along with the importance of containing, ventilating and narrating experience, at individual and social levels. Resilience is understood as our capacity to manage our inner worlds, particularly our anxieties, and to engage in relationships with others and our worlds. These elements will recur in so many of the approaches in the chapters ahead.

3

Attachment Approaches: Regulating Self and Relationships

Introduction

In this chapter, we focus on attachment theory approaches to trauma and resilience. Attachment theory is an approach to understanding the internal regulation and social relatedness from infancy into adulthood. In this sense, it provides a way of bridging inner and outer world experiences across time.

Attachment theory contributes to practice understandings in two distinctive ways. In the first place, it provides an explanation of adaptedness and resilience through the important protective role of secure attachment and the development of appropriate internal working models. For this reason, we look at the core tenets of attachment theory initially as a way of understanding resilience. In the second place, it provides a way of understanding the often devastating impacts when trauma occurs within the attachment relationship itself, that is, complex trauma arising as a result of caregiver trauma. The chapter therefore examines these negative impacts and draws out the implications for practice with individuals and more broadly with families.

Attachment explanations of resilience

When the British psychiatrist John Bowlby originally proposed his attachment theory in the 1950s, he argued that it provided a critical link between our biological, psychological and social worlds – our inner and outer worlds. As noted six decades later:

> Attachment theory is one of the few conceptual frameworks in psychology that integrates evolutionary biology, primate ethology, psychodynamic conceptions of personality, lifespan cognitive and social developmental psychology, and the study of adolescents' and adults' relationships. (Shaver & Mikulincer, 2010, p. 342)

Bowlby's approach was a significant departure from earlier psychodynamic thinking and, as a result, was vehemently opposed by many of the psychodynamic theorists and practitioners of the time (Fonagy, 2001). Since then, attachment theory has emerged as a dominant theory for understanding the ways in which we, from infancy, come to organise our inner emotional and cognitive worlds and ultimately our sense of self in relation to others.

Bowlby was psychoanalytically trained himself, and attachment theory has psychoanalytic origins (Fonagy, 2001). He developed his theory from observing the impact on children of prolonged separations from their parents, focusing on the real-world distress these children were exhibiting. He observed children in hospitals, who were frequently separated from parents for long periods of time due to illnesses and injuries. The prevailing belief of the time was that it was better for children to have no contact with their parents at all throughout a hospitalisation. He noted the distress and responses that children exhibited throughout these prolonged separations – protest and shock, disorganisation and then typically reorganisation on reunion (Bowlby, 1969). For many children, these institutional experiences were traumatic. Not only were they experiencing the distress of separation from their parents, but they were often experiencing painful, unexplained medical and physical procedures. Mary Salter Ainsworth (1993), the Robertsons (1971) and Mary Main and Judith Solomon (Main & Solomon, 1990) extended the evidence for and application of Bowlby's theory for work with traumatised children and their families.

This research brought a focus on the protective caregiving systems around us, particularly throughout our first few years of life. Initially, Bowlby (1969) speculated as to whether this caregiving system was related to physiological survival alone – providing food and physical protection. However, he argued that, given the endurance of attachment needs across the lifespan, attachment relationships were likely to be fulfilling more of a psychological and social function as well, fulfilling our need for social bonds and connectedness. Attachment relationships are now understood to provide physiological, emotional, cognitive, behavioural, sense of self and interpersonal (or relatedness) regulation (Padykula & Conklin, 2010).

Security and regulation

Bowlby (2005, pp. 29–30) defined attachment behaviour as

> any form of behaviour that results in a person attaining or maintaining proximity to some other clearly identified individual who is conceived as better able to cope with the world. It is most obvious whenever the person is frightened, fatigued or

sick, and is assuaged by comforting and caregiving .... Nevertheless, for a person to know that an attachment figure is available and responsive gives [them] a strong and pervasive feeling of security, and so encourages [them] to value and continue the relationship.

This 'safety regulation system' (Mayseless, 2005, p. 2) or 'felt security' (Kobak & Madsen, 2008, p. 32) is optimally fostered when the caregiver is attuned and responsive and able to attend to the child's physiological and emotional arousal. Both infants and adults actively engage in this attachment relationship, building a reciprocal, interdependent relational system. As Solomon and George (2011, p. 10) highlight, Bowlby

> considered the attachment system to be a component in the overall homeostatic system that regulates the organisms response to stress... the ongoing regulation of the infant's internal state depends upon maternal coregulation just as the infant's attachment behaviour must be supported by the complementary caregiving behaviour of the mother. This in turn requires that the mother's caregiving system ought to be organized to respond in an effective coherent way to infant cues and other environmental demands.

A brief but compelling example of this mutual regulation can be found in what is termed the 'still face' experiment (Weinberg & Tronick, 1996; an illustration of this experiment can be found on the Internet at http://www.youtube.com/watch?v=apzXGEbZht0). In one illustration, the initial part of the still face experiment, the mother and infant engage in a mutually responsive and attuned interaction. They laugh together, and the infant points out things in the room to her mother – responses are clearly in attunement with each other.

The mother is then cued to turn away from her infant and adopt a 'still face', that is, a non-responsive face. For the purposes of the experiment, she turns to face the infant again and is devoid of any interaction, physical, emotional or verbal. Immediately, the infant notices the difference and tries to elicit her mother's responsiveness again – she repeats the verbal, facial and physical expressions and gestures that had characterised their previous interaction. Then, she turns away from her mother, reaches out to her and screams a high-pitched scream. In just these few minutes of interaction, she exercises her communication repertoire in an effort to engage her mother. When it seems that it is failing, she becomes acutely distressed, and the experiment is ceased. What these few minutes show is the impact on an infant of a lack of responsiveness and attunement. While this change is in the context of a typically highly responsive and attuned relationship (and therefore the interaction is as much about a fundamental shift in an existing relationship, perhaps more so than the impact of a lack of responsiveness), nevertheless, it vividly portrays how quickly an infant becomes distressed and disorganised in her emotional regulation in an effort to elicit proximity within the relationship.

The physiological regulation pattern occurs through the attunement between the adult caregiver and the infant:

> Through visual-facial, auditory-prosodic, and tactile-gestural communications, caregiver and infant learn the rhythmic structure of the other and modify their behavior to fit that structure, thereby co-creating a specifically fitted interaction. (Schore, 2009, p. 192)

The attunement and subsequent regulation that occurs in these critical relationships with others in infancy has been shown to be setting down important neural pathways for our later emotional, physiological and relational interactions, as we shall see in Chapter 4. As Schore and Schore (2008, p. 10) note,

> Attachment communications are critical to the development of structural right brain neurobiological systems involved in processing of emotion, modulation of stress, self-regulation, and thereby the functional origins of the bodily-based implicit self.

Internal working models

Attachment security is built up through the mirroring that goes on in these relationships – the theory proposes that we learn to see others and ourselves based on how we have been mirrored in these early relationships:

> The end result is that a child can read the expression on another's face and know what that person is feeling without extensive conscious effort to figure out the meaning of the experience. (Allen & Fonagy, 2011, p. 127)

The ability to have our own minds and know that our thoughts and feelings are different to those around us and to know something of how to read the thoughts and feelings of those others is an essential survival skill. This is referred to as developing the capacity to mentalise (Allen, 2012). Children who have not been able to acquire this ability will misread their own experiences as well as the cues of others – studies show that neutral faces tend to be interpreted negatively and as hostile, for example.

Bowlby referred to the cognitive patterns or schemas as internal working models. He proposed that as individuals we needed two working models: 'If an individual is to draw up a plan to achieve a set-goal not only must [he] have some sort of working model of [his] environment, but [he] must have also some working knowledge of [his] own behavioural skills and potentialities' (Bowlby, 1969, p. 112). In this sense, internal working models are

> mental representations constructed during childhood and based primarily upon early experiences with significant caregivers...In addition to representational models of relationships, parallel but interactive models of the self are formed. (Main & Solomon, 1990, p. 345)

These internal working models become the foundation of our later expectations and attitudes towards others and the world around us. They enable a capacity to 'forecast the future' (Kobak & Madsen, 2008). As such, as Waters and Waters (2006) note, these internal working models become our internal scripts, our internal representations of ourselves and others. An important part of therapeutic work, described later in this chapter, is a focus on how these early internal working models or secure base scripts may be continuing to influence adult experience, consciously and unconsciously.

Attachment relationships: their distinctive qualities

An attachment relationship is distinguished from other relationships in three ways – by proximity-seeking behaviours when a child is under threat; by a 'secure base' effect, which enables the child to explore the world around them while experiencing the protective proximity of the caregiver; and the expression of separation protest or distress if the attachment figure is inaccessible. As illustrated above, even being physically present yet psychologically absent elicited a protest response from the attached infant. This display of behaviour on separation is indicative of the activation of the attachment behaviour system:

> It is when a figure is perceived as having become inaccessible and unresponsive, that separation distress (grief) occurs, and the anticipation of the possible occurrence of such a situation arouses anxiety. (Ainsworth et al., 1978, p. 21)

In attuned, responsive relationships, an infant develops both a physiological regulation pattern and, over time, a cognitive pattern of expectation about the world, its security and its predictability.

Attachment theory is therefore a theory of how we organise and regulate our internal states, not only from an emotional regulation perspective but also from a meaning-making one. As Solomon and George (2011, p. 3) note:

> Secure attachments are now understood to buffer the infant and child from toxic levels of stress and serve a critical role in the organisation of the neurophysiological substrates responsible for self-regulation.

However, as we shall see, these pathways remain open to ongoing influences and experiences throughout our lifespan. While the interest is primarily on attachment styles in infancy and early childhood and the foundations they create, the trajectory of our attachment styles and their expression within adult relationships has been of increasing interest also. Bartholomew and Horowitz (1991) proposed that romantic relationships in adulthood reflected earlier attachment styles – instead of three dominant styles, they identify four categories across the two dimensions of dominance and nurturance. People tend to display a style that was congruent with their own internal model and their model or image of others, such that a fearful and pre-occupied style was reflective of a negative self-image and a dismissing style reflective of a negative image of others. As with childhood experiences, the majority of adult study samples have shown a secure attachment style, persisting from earlier in the lifespan.

Attachment styles

From Bowlby's early description of his theory, researchers such as Ainsworth (1993) and Main and Solomon (1990) went on to study attachment styles between young children and their parents (typically mothers). Using Ainsworth's Strange Situation, a laboratory experiment that involved a series of separations and reunions between children and their caregivers, three main attachment styles were noted that were established in the first year of life. The Strange Situation enabled testing of what happened when an infant was separated from their caregiver and what attachment behaviour was exhibited both throughout the separation and when reunion occurred. An attachment style is now thought of as a

> systematic pattern of relational expectations, emotions, and behavior that results from internalization of a particular history of attachment experiences and consequent reliance on a particular attachment-related strategy of affect regulation. (Mikulincer et al., 2003, p. 79)

Most children (66%) displayed a secure attachment style in these initial experiments conducted by Ainsworth and replicated in later studies. Securely attached infants are generally less anxious infants, as their experiences in the world in relation to care needs have been typically predictable and stable in the context of nurturant, adult caregiving. Ainsworth and her colleagues noted that they were 'positive and unconflicted in their response to close bodily contact with the mother', and they used their caregiver 'as a secure base from which to explore an unfamiliar environment' (Ainsworth et al., 1978, p. 311). Importantly, 'Even when she is out of sight, he nevertheless usually believes she is accessible to him and would be responsive should he seek her out or signal to her' (Ainsworth et al., 1978, p. 312). As a result of this 'felt security', children with secure attachments 'tend to be more readily "socialized"', tend to be 'more positively outgoing to and cooperative with relatively unfamiliar adult figures' and 'tend to be more competent...explore more effectively and more positively, and thus they have a head start in learning about the salient features of the environment' (Ainsworth et al., 1978, pp. 313–314). An enduring characteristic is persistence (Ainsworth et al., 1978, p. 314), an important psychological trait, particularly in relation to the demands of coping with traumatic life events.

A secure attachment style is connected with resilience across the lifespan, both in the prevention of mental health issues and in recovery from traumatic life events. A secure attachment style has been associated with a person's ability to adapt in the face of adversity. In large part, this may be due to secure relationships ensuring that someone can 'foster a self-sustaining "circle of security"' (Hoffman et al., 2006, p. 38).

Another group of children (12%) were identified as having an insecure and anxious attachment with their caregiver. Ainsworth and her colleagues found that they

> do not seem to have confident expectations of the mother's accessibility and responsiveness. Consequently, they are unable to use the mother as a secure base from which to explore an unfamiliar situation. (Ainsworth et al., 1978, p. 314)

They were more likely to express 'immediate and intense distress' (Ainsworth et al., 1978) as a result of inconsistent responses from their caregiver.

The third group of children (22%) demonstrated insecure and avoidant attachment styles. Research has identified that where children exhibit insecure avoidant attachment styles, their mothers are more rejecting. As Ainsworth and colleagues noted (1978, p. 316), 'mothers themselves tended to find close contact with their babies aversive...tend more frequently to be angry with and irritated by their babies than other mothers'. The avoidant (often ignoring) behaviour of the infant has been understood as protecting them in the following way:

> Avoidance short circuits direct expression of anger to the attachment figure, which might be dangerous, and it also protects the baby from re-experiencing the rebuff that he has come to expect when he seeks close contact with his mother. It thus somewhat lowers his level of anxiety (arousal). (Ainsworth et al., 1978, p. 20)

Later, a fourth attachment style was added to the classifications, 'disorganised attachment' described by Main and Solomon (1990). This style of attachment was noted in children 'who appeared to have impaired organization of a response to separation (and other forms of adversity)', characterised by 'contradictory behaviour; misdirected or interrupted patterns' (Rutter, 2008a, p. 963) of interacting, sometimes with freezing or apprehensive responses. This style is still considered distinct from an attachment disorder as such. Attachment disorders were first incorporated into the *Diagnostic and Statistical Manual of Mental Disorders* in 1994 (APA, 1994) as reactive attachment disorder, discussed later in this chapter.

While attachment theory was initially focused on the relationship between an infant and their caregiver, an obvious interest is in how enduring these attachment styles are across a person's lifespan. The attachment styles evident in adulthood have been classified as autonomous, dismissing, preoccupied and unresolved (Hesse, 2008). The extent to which they relate directly to earlier attachment styles remains inconclusive. Some studies have shown that attachment styles are relatively enduring (Hamilton, 2000; Waters, Hamilton & Weinfield, 2000; Waters et al., 2000). However, a recent meta-analysis of attachment studies (Pinquart, Feussner & Ahnert, 2013) found evidence of only a moderate stability of attachment from childhood to adolescence. There was no evidence of stability over 15 years, and the attachment stability varied when younger age was included.

This is an important finding in relation to interventions – if problematic attachment styles are fixed and not open to change, attachment-focused work might not otherwise be worthwhile. Similarly, if negative life events are strongly associated with increases in attachment insecurity, then early intervention and support are strongly indicated.

Attachments to place and culture

While infants and children are the focus in relation to their attachments to caregivers, they are also attaching to place and to culture. Thus, attachment theory is in many ways generalisable to attachment to these broader dimensions – emphasising the importance of cultural attachment and place-based attachment and providing a way of understanding how culture and place provide security and protection, not only physiologically but also psychosocially. Our experiences of culture and place can provide regulation and familiarity, through our routines and predictable experiences of the worlds in which we live.

In the United States, for example, Susan Kemp (2011) has researched place-based child removal decisions and highlighted that often children are being moved not only into protective custody with unfamiliar caregivers but also to different geographic locations. This can lead to the loss of relationships with neighbours, peers and teachers, for example, as well as a loss of familiarity with their physical neighbourhoods and home environments, leading to a loss of sensory and relational familiarity. For children, attachment to place matters (Jack, 2010). This is arguably so across the lifespan, with transitions, both planned and unplanned, often creating major disruption and dysregulation for people, as the next section highlights.

Attachment explanations of trauma responses

Attachment theory has been applied in three major ways to understanding trauma experiences and responses.

Trauma and maltreatment within primary attachment relationships

Attachment theory's major impact has been on understanding the patterns and outcomes of attachment trauma; that is, trauma that occurs for young children in the context of their attachment relationships. 'Attachment trauma' is used to refer to 'trauma that takes place in attachment relationships' as well as 'the adverse, long-term impact of such trauma on your capacity to develop and maintain secure attachment relationships' (Allen, 2012, p. 163). It is seen to be 'a breakdown in the capacity to regulate internal states' (Van der Kolk, 2005, p. 403).

The link between trauma and attachment emerged in the early experiments with the Strange Situation (Ainsworth, 1978; Main & Solomon, 1990). While secure and insecure attachment styles were observed in the majority of children, as noted earlier, a number of children were not able to be consistently classified as belonging to one of these groups. Main and Solomon (1990) identified that within this 'unclassified' group, some children seemed to be exhibiting what could be termed 'disorganised' attachment styles. Children exhibiting a disorganised attachment style are characteristically inclusive of 'approach, avoidance or angry behaviours that are succeeded or interrupted by opposing displays or which are subsequently constricted' (Solomon & George, 2011, p. 6). They appear 'to lack observable goals, intentions or exploration. There are contradictory sequential or simultaneous behaviours and misdirected incomplete and interrupted movements' (Rutter et al., 2009, p. 531). The dissociation noted in these styles emphasises the traumatic responses underlying these behaviours.

Three conditions seem to be linked with the development of a disorganised attachment style. The first is where children's attachment in their home environments is with a caregiver who is disorganised themselves and therefore unable to provide the level of regulation needed. Maltreatment is not always a part of this attachment relationship – it may be that the caregiver is unable to provide an organised regulation because of their own experiences of unresolved significant personal loss of caregiver relationship and/or trauma. For other children, a disorganised attachment style is strongly associated with experiences of maltreatment (abuse and/or neglect) within the caregiver relationship. As Main and Hesse (1990, p. 163) describe it:

> Since the attachment figure is normally the 'solution' provided to the infant for dealing with stressful or alarming experiences, an infant who is frightened by the attachment figure is presented with a paradoxical problem – namely, an attachment figure who is at once the source of and the solution to its alarm.

Thus, Solomon and George (2011, p. 10) describe this is as 'fright without solution'. The infant experiences either ' "frightening or frightened" maternal behavior' (Solomon & George, 2011, p. 6).

For these infants, this early period of life is not characterised by attuned and responsive interactions with caregivers. For some infants, there is an absence of these attuned responses, while for others, there are stress- and/or terror-inducing ones from their caregiver. In these conditions, the infant faces an overwhelming dilemma. The one who should be providing the protection is both the source of fear or terror and simultaneously failing to provide protection. Therefore, attachment theory has been able to provide important understandings of complex trauma – where complex trauma is 'defined as experiences of multiple traumatic events within the caregiver system, in place of the safety and stability that is normally provided therein' (Jaycox et al., 2009, p. 339). As Allen (2012, p. 164) notes, these events can leave a child 'afraid and alone', two profoundly isolating experiences 'in the midst of unbearably painful emotion' (Allen, 2012, p. 163). As a result, shame can be a core outcome of relational trauma – 'chronically traumatized individuals feel shame not only for what has happened to them, but for who they are' (Dorahy et al., 2013, p. 73).

Childhood trauma within caregiver relationships is associated with poorer mental health in adulthood, including PTSD, anxiety and depression (see, for example, Spila et al., 2008). Poorer physical health is also well documented, with the increase in chronic illness attributed both to increased stress load from earlier in life and often poor health prevention behaviours associated with low self-esteem (see, for example, Schafer & Ferraro, 2013). From an attachment theory perspective, these outcomes are explained in terms of the fundamental loss of trust and stability within relationships, a loss of attunement to emotional needs and a loss of a sense of positive internal working models or cognitive schema. The heightened 'vulnerability to PTSD is associated with a failure of mentalising in attachment relationships in the aftermath of a stressful experience' (Allen, 2012, p. 256)

There are important explanatory links to be made here with the way in which intergenerational trauma is understood. Allen has proposed that intergenerational trauma may be transmitted as an unresolved disorganised attachment style (Allen, 2012, p. 165). Thus, not only is a dyadic relationship of parent/carer and child influenced by this, but multigenerations of the same family, with little recognition of this ongoing loss of trust and stability within core relationships.

Researchers and clinicians have noted that for children experiencing this violation and failure of protection, when fear is activated and protection is not available through this external attachment system, dissociation can be seen as an adaptive response in the immediate situation of threat.

For children faced with trauma within the caregiver relationship, the availability of effective family intervention and support is critical. When immediate family systems cannot provide the necessary attachment security and physical safety, alternate caregivers who can provide attunement and regulation are essential. For many infants and children, alternative caregivers in the form of grandparents and/or other kinship carers provide attachment relationships to buffer them from the overwhelming absence or violations occurring within their primary caregiver relationship. For example, one UK study of 80 children living in informal kinship care arrangements found that, despite maltreatment experiences in earlier parental relationships, attachment scores for these children were similar to the general population (Farmer et al., 2013). Thus, alternative caregiving arrangements were able to provide secure attachment relationships for these children.

Reactive attachment disorder

A disorder of attachment, termed 'reactive attachment disorder' (RAD; APA, 2013), has also been noted in some children who have experienced extreme deprivation. RAD was considered to be of two distinctive types until the recent revision of the *DSM*, with both arising from 'pathogenic care'. In this sense, pathogenic care is where there has been

> persistent disregard of the child's basic emotional needs for comfort, stimulation, and affection; persistent disregard for the child's basic physical needs; or repeated changes of primarily caregiver that prevent formation of stable attachments. (APA, 2000, p. 118)

One form of RAD was termed 'inhibited' RAD and is evident when there is

> a markedly disturbed and developmentally inappropriate social relatedness in most contexts...manifest by excessively inhibited, hypervigilant or highly ambivalent and contradictory responses. (APA, 2000, p. 118)

The other form was termed 'disinhibited' RAD and is evident in 'diffuse attachments as manifest by indiscriminate sociability with marked inability to exhibit appropriate selective attachments' (APA, 2000, p. 118). With the reclassification into one form of RAD only, some significant features may be missed, as the following case example highlights. Michael Rutter (Rutter et al., 2007) and others (Smyke et al., 2012) have noted that these reactive attachment disorders were a feature of some of the children who were adopted in the 1990s from Romanian orphanages into British homes, as outlined in this case example:

Case example: Attachment theory and neglect

British psychiatrist Michael Rutter has been leading a study of children who were adopted from Romanian orphanages in the 1990s into British and Canadian families (Rutter et al., 2007). In many ways, this study is one of the most extraordinary studies of attachment. In the 1990s, light was shed on the fact that hundreds of children had been placed in orphanages, given that their families were at breaking point with widespread poverty and famine. Under the political regime of the day, families were required to have at least five children, yet were unable to provide even the most basic of resources as a consequence.

The orphanages were exposed by Western media as places of extreme physical and emotional deprivation. Images on current affairs programmes showed three shelf trolleys laden with swaddled babies. The poor health and emotional status of these children, many of whom were chained to cots, with other children sharing the same space, was apparent in the audiovisual footage. Many, if not most, of these children were deprived of access to regular, attuned caregivers. With the media attention came a determination to rescue these children from their experience of deprivation. Several hundred of these children were adopted into British families under a government initiative. Following their adoptions, 144 of these children who were reared in institutional settings have been part of a longitudinal study of their well-being, which has charted the developmental impact of their transition from early, chronic deprivation in an institutional care context into generally supportive and nurturing family- and home-based care. The study has provided an in-depth focus on the pathways of attachment.

Key findings:

- Children who had a disinhibited attachment style did not show responsiveness to a new home environment.
- Children who had an inhibited attachment were no longer likely to show a reactive attachment disorder once they returned to or came into contact with good care.

Case example: (*Continued*)

These findings have been confirmed in another study of Romanian children, where children with early foster care placements following institutional care with inhibited RAD had better longer-term outcomes than children with disinhibited RAD (Smyke et al., 2012). It is important to note, however, that RAD is a rare diagnosis. It has a very low prevalence even among populations of institutionalised children who have experienced the pathogenic care referred to earlier (APA, 2000).

Trauma when faced with the loss of attachment relationships

Separation from attachment figures was the initial focus of Bowlby's work and others who followed in his footsteps. Attachment theory provides a way of understanding the distress and often trauma that such separations present, particularly when through death. In looking at complicated grief reactions, Shear and her colleagues (2007, p. 454) note that

> the death of an attachment figure presents a decisive and temporarily irreconcilable mismatch between an unrevised mental representation of a loved one and a dramatic change in the ongoing relationship with that person.

Four processes that are seen as occurring in these instances are outlined (Shear et al., 2007, p. 454):

(1) The unrevised working model produces a continuing sense of the presence of the deceased.

(2) The stress of bereavement activates attachment proximity seeking, triggering a strong sense of yearning and longing for the deceased, as well as activation of thoughts and memories of the person.

(3) Effective functioning of the working model is temporarily disrupted, leading to loss of regulation emotion, attention and physiological process.

(4) Strong activation of attachment is associated with inhibition of the exploratory system, resulting in loss of interest in the world and inhibition of goal seeking.

This description of what happens for people in the wake of the loss of an attachment figure is consistent with many of the trauma reactions outlined in Chapter 2.

Traumatic life events and the role of secure attachment

Attachment theory can also be usefully applied to understanding the loss of regulation that can occur through exposure to traumatic life events in both childhood and adulthood. As noted in Chapter 1, even for the most securely attached person responses to traumatic experiences are typically characterised by an initial period of dysregulation. With many people exhibiting secure attachment styles throughout their lives, these traumatic experiences can be accommodated, often quite rapidly.

A 20-year follow-up study of 50 out of 60 original participants provided unique insights into the impact of traumatic events occurring from infancy into adulthood (Waters et al., 2000). The aim of the study was to find out whether attachment styles changed over a person's life, and if so, what influenced these changes. The findings of this study indicate that attachment styles can change in relation to life experiences – both from secure to insecure/disorganised and from insecure/disorganised to secure, depending upon the exposure or not to multiple traumatic events. Negative life events (defined as the death or divorce of a parent, a life-threatening illness, parental mental health problems and/or abuse by a family member) did impact on later attachment style – for those infants whose mothers reported negative life events, eight out of 18 showed changes in attachment classification compared with seven out of 32 who had not experienced negative life events. This showed that 44% of those who had experienced negative life events experienced a change in attachment classification compared with 22% who had not. Importantly,

> stressful life events were significantly related to the likelihood of a secure infant becoming insecure in early adulthood (66.6% if mother reported one or more events versus 15% if she reported none, $p = .01$) in secure infants. (Waters et al., 2000, p. 687)

In contrast: 'Stressful life events were not significantly related to classification changes in insecure infants' (Waters et al., 2000, p. 687).

Implications for practice

Drawing on the theoretical concepts outlined so far, attachment-based approaches in the aftermath of trauma focus on intrapersonal processes – regulation, internal working models of an individual – and, where relevant, interpersonal processes – including improving parent–child communication and their cue reading of their child (Rutter, 2008a).

There are commonalities with other trauma theories that encourage relationship-based practice – particularly, with psychodynamic approaches encouraging the establishment of a strong positive working alliance as part of the therapeutic work and person-centred approaches whereby the therapist provides conditions of warmth, genuineness and unconditional positive regard. There are specific areas of focus, however, within attachment-based approaches to trauma interventions.

In summary, attachment-based practice approaches, therefore, focus on three specific areas of intervention:

1. The establishment of a secure base – a reliable, responsive, consistent 'caregiver' substitute

2. The provision of physical and emotional attunement and regulation within a therapeutic relationship

3. Assistance with building healthy 'internal working models' from which a traumatised person can understand their own reactions and the reactions of others

The overall purpose of engaging in these tasks is to translate relational qualities of a secure, responsive, supportive and attuned therapeutic environment into internal states of being and working models. These ways of thinking, however, have also translated more widely into family-focused interventions and into broader frameworks within child welfare, health and educational systems.

Individual therapy contexts

Building a secure attachment within the therapeutic relationship

The aim of attachment-focused interventions is to either restore or introduce an external experience of secure attachment within the therapeutic relationship in order to reinstate or introduce an internal experience of secure attachment within the person themselves. The therapeutic relationship intentionally provides a responsive, attuned relationship, providing the necessary containment and mirroring that was missing or lost from earlier caregiver relationships, so that a person can establish these relationships in their everyday lives. Bowlby (2005, p. 159) describes the therapeutic work as follows:

> In providing [a] patient with a secure base from which to explore and express [their] thoughts and feelings the therapist's role is analogous to that of a mother who provides her child with a secure base from which to explore the world. The therapist strives to be reliable, attentive, and sympathetically responsive to [the]

patient's explorations, and, so far as [they] can, to see and feel the world through [their] patient's eyes, namely to be empathic.

Revisiting the 'fright' (and finding ways of self-soothing)

Once this first therapeutic task is under way, the second task is to encourage the person to

> explore the various unhappy and painful aspects of [their] life, past and present, many of which [they] find it difficult or perhaps impossible to think about and reconsider without a trusted companion to provide support, encouragement, sympathy, and, on occasion, guidance. (Bowlby, 2005, p. 156)

If the trauma creates an experience of 'fright without solution', the goal of therapeutic work is to tolerate fright *with* solution – to come to experience and tolerate intense emotional reactions of fear and anxiety, to develop a new internal working model of self, or secure base script, and of others and to gain a sense of physical, emotional and cognitive control and coherence. As Allen (2012, p. 253) notes, 'understanding *is* the treatment'. In this sense, there are strong parallels with other theoretical approaches such as narrative approaches that we explore in Chapter 6.

A very controversial aspect of attachment therapy, however, is one that moves beyond psychological and relational insight building and relates to 'holding therapy'. Proponents argue that 'non-directive interactions will simply elicit no engagement' (as discussed in Sudbery et al., 2010, p. 1540) and therefore that directive, physical holding techniques are advocated for use in the context of therapeutic support to contain (physically and psychologically) disengaged, poorly attached children and young people. There is little evidence to support these practices where attachment difficulties have arisen in the context of earlier maltreating family relationships. They have attracted robust and justified criticism in relation to the coercion and restraint they typically involve (Mercer, 2012; Shardlow & Sudbery, 2014).

Establishing new internal working models

The third task is to focus on the therapeutic relationship into which, as with psychodynamic thinking, the internal working models of self and others would be imported. The fourth task relates to reviewing and tolerating these ideas and internal working models. In a significant departure and perhaps criticism of psychodynamic approaches, Bowlby (2005, pp. 157–158) saw the fifth task as enabling a person

> to recognize that [their] images (models) of [themselves] and of others, derived either from past painful experiences or from misleading messages emanating from a parent, but all too often in the literature mislabelled as 'fantasies', may or may not be appropriate to [their] present and future; or indeed, may never have been

justified. Once [they have] grasped the nature of [their] governing images (models) and [have] traced their origins, [they] may begin to understand what has led [them] to see the world and [themselves] as [they do], and so to feel, to think, and to act in the ways [they do].

This insight-oriented approach can then assist in being proactively engaged in thinking and acting differently.

Optimising family functioning where there has been maltreatment

Not surprisingly, much of the application of attachment-based approaches has been within the context of child welfare practice, where there has been parental abuse and neglect of children. Attachment-based interventions in this context focus primarily on parents, encouraging them to become attuned to their child's cues and enabling them to respond to these cues in appropriate and nurturant ways. Many studies have identified that maltreating parents were themselves maltreated. One argument for the difficulties in subsequent parenting is that their own disorganised attachments are reactivated when they find themselves in the stressful context of parenting an infant. As a result, they are unable to accurately read the cues of the infant, as their own unmet needs cloud their perceptions. This results in 'distorted perceptions of the infant, lack of attunement and insensitive care' (Cicchetti et al., 2006). Interventions that focus on building adaptive relationships have shown success, with Cicchetti et al. (2006), for example, demonstrating that children at 26 months and their parents had more secure attachment styles when there had been interventions that focused on the infant–parent relationship attunement and cue reading when compared to a control group who received no intervention. This was a considerable gain, given that at the start of the study the infants of maltreating parents had shown significantly higher rates of disorganised attachment behaviour.

These are often intensive programmes using audiovisual feedback and supportive therapeutic relationships to provide focused feedback and training to parents. It often requires insight-oriented work (as outlined above) with parents as to the origins of their own trauma experiences and subsequent parenting and attachment styles.

Optimising child welfare, hospital and education systems

In addition to the more specific therapeutic work outlined above, within many child welfare systems, and particularly in relation to placement and foster care practices, attachment theory has informed decision-making processes in at least two ways. The first way is in relation to whether or not a child should be placed outside of parental care in the first place. As Goldsmith et al. (2004, p. 1) note:

> In keeping with the best interest of the child, decisions about child placement must look beyond maltreatment as a single risk factor, giving additional consideration to the emotional costs of separation on a child's developing attachments and examining how system responses and legal decision making may help or harm the child's attachment system. Thus, both maltreatment and attachment concerns are critically important factors in child placement decisions, which may have long-term consequences for a child's overall life adjustment.

The second way is in relation to how foster parents come to relate to children who may have experienced traumatic attachment relationships, with some evidence suggesting that the older the child, the more difficult it is for a foster parent to establish a secure attachment with them (Barth et al., 2005).

Within hospitals and schools, too, attachment theory has drawn attention to the acute distress that children can experience. In the hospital context, this has meant that far more sensitive alignment has occurred with parental visiting rights with children, with many paediatric hospitals supporting 24-hour parental presence to allay the separation concerns of their children. In the school context, there is greater awareness regarding the important role teachers and other school staff can play as important attachment figures and, also, regarding the importance of 'secure base' environments (see, for example, Riley, 2010).

A case scenario

How would you go about working with George, his mother and/or the hospital staff in attachment-oriented ways?

George is five years old. He was admitted to hospital with gunshot wounds to his scalp and leg. He was shot by his father at home during an argument his father was having with his mother. His father turned the gun on himself and died as a result. George had been conscious throughout all these events. George's mother comes to visit occasionally and wants him discharged as soon as possible. George is highly anxious and will not talk with anyone. He refuses to play with the other children on the ward, instead watching them silently from his bed. A case conference is being organised to discuss his progress.

Critically reflecting on attachment approaches

While attachment theory was very strongly criticised throughout the 1960s and 1970s in favour of behavioural approaches, it has come into central focus, supported by neurobiological development theories. It is seen to be an important bridging theory between inner and outer worlds.

A major criticism of the theory was the initial focus on maternal behaviours, not only in relation to the gendered implications of the theory but also in relation to the singularity of the relationship. This thinking has been considerably expanded to acknowledge that most children have multiple attachment relationships and that these continue and change into adulthood. The ability to engage in multiple secure attachments is again adaptive and of a protective capacity. If this singularity was true, the current practices within day cares around Western countries would be causing major psychological harm with prolonged separations, whereas, consistent with attachment theory, where there are high-quality day care arrangements, good ratios of staff to children and therefore good opportunities for responsive attunement to children's needs, there are good psychosocial outcomes (Vandell et al., 2010).

Feminist critiques question the essentialist and biological determinism inherent in attachment theory (Knudson-Martin, 2012). While Knudson-Martin and others acknowledge that 'the focus of attachment theory on relational bonds is consistent with feminist values', concerns are raised about the absence of understanding these bonds in 'the larger societal context, such as gender, culture, and power' (Knudson-Martin, 2012, p. 299). Attention to these influences, which become reflected in the context of private relationships, is critical.

Another major criticism has been the belief that it only spoke to a Western culture and therefore was a culturally specific theory. Ainsworth went to extensive lengths to look at attachment behaviours in other cultures, in Uganda, for example, to test the cultural specificity of the theory. She found, as others have later, that attachment relationships exist in all cultures and that relations with significant attachment figures, whether in individualistic or collectivist cultures, were important for well-being in all these contexts. Variation occurs, however, in the cultural expectations and norms about the expression of attachment behaviours, rather than whether they exist or not. For example, Fiona Ryan documents the Aboriginal concept of 'holding', expressed in the term 'kanyinyinpa', whereby attachment experiences can easily be identified as occurring – however, she documents the Aboriginal expressions of this through the use of eye contact, the containing of distress before it occurs and the many different layers of non-verbal communication that non-Aboriginal people do not typically see or understand (Ryan, 2011). Thus, cultural expression differs but the core human need of attachment behaviours does not.

Another enduring criticism is of attachment theory's breadth and lack of specificity (see Fonagy, 2001, for discussion). Studies have shown that maternal sensitivity is not the key quality determining later adult functioning – with very small correlations shown between the role of maternal stability and the stability of attachment styles – 'the bottom-line message is that on its own, attachment security in infancy constitutes a very weak predictor of adult functioning, accounting for only some 5% of the variance' (Rutter, 2008a, p. 966). As Rutter (2008a, p. 959) notes, 'attachment does not constitute the whole of social relationships'.

Conclusion

Attachment theory builds bridges across inner and outer worlds in a unique way, as the first approach to provide a link between biological, psychological and relational systems of both an individual infant and their caregiver. Attachment approaches provide an explanation of how we draw on the relationships around us early in life to make sense of ourselves and others and how we continue to draw on these internal working models as well as realities of social relationships throughout adulthood. They also provide explanation of the internal dysregulation that is created when these relationships are inherently traumatic rather than nurturant. These understandings have now come to be linked strongly with the ideas that we look at in the next chapter, relating to the neurobiology of traumatic stress responses.

4

Symptom Approaches: Reducing PTSD

Introduction

In this chapter, we look at the ways in which trauma responses are understood as a particular psychiatric disorder, post-traumatic stress disorder (PTSD), with its specific set of symptoms identified by the American Psychiatric Association (2013). PTSD is a relatively rare outcome for survivors of trauma, yet it occupies a dominant space in the research literature. In this chapter, we look at current understandings of PTSD in terms of its prevalence and its aetiology. We look at how neurobiological research is shedding light on the role of the amygdala and stress responses, in particular, for the cause and maintenance of post-traumatic stress symptoms. We examine the practice implications, which focus on cognitive behavioural and neurosequential strategies.

Post-traumatic stress disorder as a trauma response

As highlighted in Chapter 1, in 1980 PTSD was recognised for the first time as a psychiatric disorder in the third edition of the *Diagnostic and Statistical Manual of Mental Disorders* (APA, 1980), marking a key turning point in understandings of trauma. The diagnosis was included following intense lobbying by two particular survivor groups – Vietnam War veterans and women who had survived family violence and/or sexual assault (Burstow, 2003). Recognising that an event could cause a psychiatric disorder, rather than primarily characteristics of a person's inner world, was a major shift in thinking. For all the controversy it has raised since, critically, the labelling of the disorder allowed for legal, political and medical acknowledgement of and intervention following trauma. For many survivors, this has meant that often inexplicable symptoms suddenly had a language and coherence, enabling them to make sense of overwhelming intrusion, avoidance and hyperarousal symptoms. A diagnostic label has enabled them to access focused treatments and support. This identification has enabled extensive study of these symptoms arising as a result of trauma experiences and the development of new clinical interventions. In these next few pages, we look at these particular symptoms. We focus on the *DSM V*, acknowledging that the International Classification of Disorders (ICD; World Health Organisation, 2010) also addresses PTSD and is undergoing significant revisions for the new ICD-11 due for publication in 2015.

Revisiting the definition of traumatic exposure

The definition of traumatic exposure for a PTSD diagnosis has attempted to capture what the nature of these traumatic events is. According to the *DSM V* (refer back to Box 1.1 in Chapter 1), trauma exposure is now defined as exposure to 'actual or threatened death, serious injury, or sexual violence' through either direct experience, witnessing others or learning of close family members or friends encountering these events.

The definition of trauma exposure has, not surprisingly, been the source of significant debate over the years (see, for example, Weathers & Keane, 2007 and Friedman et al., 2011a; Friedman et al., 2011b). With the recent revision to the criteria, serious consideration was given to removing the criterion altogether, given the difficulties in establishing a workable definition across so many diverse experiences. The criterion was retained, however, given its relationship with the subsequent criteria firmly established in studies of PTSD. Friedman and his colleagues (2011a, p. 754) concluded, for example, that, 'the traumatic experience is usually a watershed event that marks a major discontinuity in the life trajectories of individuals affected with PTSD, unless the onset of the disorder is delayed'. In defining traumatic exposure, challenges emerge, however, given the political and legal context of trauma work.

In the first (*DSM III*) definition of exposure (Criterion A), for example, the trauma exposure was defined as being 'outside the range of usual experience' (APA, 1980). This became a very problematic definition, particularly in relation to those who experienced sexual assault. Given the estimates of prevalence, according to which one in three women experiences sexual assault during a lifetime, lawyers in the United States argued that women could not be experiencing PTSD as a result of a sexual assault because it was so common. As per the outrageous argument, PTSD could not be considered outside of the range of usual experience (Brown, 1995), thus denying women appropriate recognition of their suffering and distress.

As discussed in Chapter 1, in the new criteria, the 'trauma exposure' definition has been refined to focus very specifically on the (actual or perceived) threat to the self – through death, injury or sexual violation. This relatively narrow scope of what constitutes traumatic exposure continues to be an area of critique and concern. For example, feminist theorists see this focus on physical trauma as only part of the picture – 'feminist models attend as well to relational and process components of trauma' (Brown, 2004, pp. 465–466).

The ICD-10 (WHO, 2010) words the traumatic exposure somewhat differently to the APA, seeing that PTSD

> arises as a delayed or protracted response to a stressful event or situation (of either brief or long duration) of an exceptionally threatening or catastrophic nature, which is likely to cause pervasive distress in almost anyone.

This definition highlights the extremity of the event as the cause of distress rather than characteristics of the person who experiences it, and resonates with early APA (1980) definitions of traumatic exposure.

An important addition to the definition of an exposure is to highlight that the fourth criterion of exposure to details of an event 'does not apply to exposure through electronic media, television, movies or pictures, unless this exposure is work related' (APA, 2013, p. 6). In a meta-analysis of 28 international studies, Berger, Coutinho et al. (2011) found that rescue workers do have higher rates of PTSD than the general population, consistent with other studies (Chang et al., 2003; Alden et al., 2008). Questions have arisen as to what exposures contribute to these outcomes, including exposures beyond the work role itself in the media. The new definition of PTSD exposure, in making a link with media witnessing as impactful only with workers, not the general public, has arisen following research after 9/11 in particular, which found that general exposure through these media forms did not result in PTSD (Breslau et al., 2010). This was despite initial reports that suggested the general public was experiencing probable PTSD as a direct result of media exposure to 9/11 (Schlenger et al., 2002).

The symptoms of PTSD

Following exposure to traumatic events, PTSD is diagnosed if there is persistence over time of a cluster of three symptom types – intrusion, avoidance and hyperarousal. Very recently, a fourth symptom category has been added into the disorder's definition (APA, 2013), which we will explore later.

In the context of extreme stress situations, these responses have a highly adaptive function, as will be highlighted below. Once the threat has passed, however, and symptoms persist, they become maladaptive, interfering with people's capacity to function well in so many areas of their lives. For this reason, PTSD has come to be seen as 'a failure of mechanisms involved in recovery and restitution of physiological homeostasis' (Yehuda & LeDoux, 2007, p. 19).

The first symptom indicative of a failure to restore homeostasis is that of intrusion. It makes sense that we keep trying to cognitively process what has happened into a manageable memory, with memory fragments intruding into our waking and sleeping life. At the extreme, these become problematic symptoms of intrusion – intrusive thoughts and memories that are unexpected, unwanted and distressing. Flashbacks, when it seems as if something is recurring in the present from the past, with all of their physical and emotional intensity, are commonly experienced. Box 4.1 shows the *DSM V* definition of these intrusion symptoms.

Box 4.1 Intrusion criteria for post-traumatic stress disorder

Presence of one (or more) of the following intrusion symptoms associated with the traumatic event(s), beginning after the traumatic event(s) occurred:

1. Recurrent, involuntary and intrusive distressing memories of the traumatic event(s)

2. Recurrent distressing dreams in which the content and/or effect of the dream are related to the event(s)

3. Dissociative reactions (e.g., flashbacks) in which the individual feels or acts as if the traumatic event(s) were recurring (such reactions may occur on a continuum, with the most extreme expression being a complete loss of awareness of present surroundings)

4. Intense or prolonged psychological distress at exposure to internal or external cues that symbolize or resemble an aspect of the traumatic event(s)

5. Marked physiological reactions to internal or external cues that symbolize or resemble an aspect of the traumatic event(s)

Source: American Psychiatric Association (2013).

At the same time as experiencing unexpected intrusive reminders of trauma, avoidance symptoms can be experienced, which are both conscious and unconscious efforts to avoid reminders of what has happened. This avoidance may be cognitive, emotional and/or behavioural as we try to forget or move on from what has occurred. Box 4.2 outlines the current symptom description, which now only includes active avoidance experiences, not passive ones.

Box 4.2   Avoidance criterion for post-traumatic stress disorder

Persistent avoidance of stimuli associated with the traumatic event(s), beginning after the traumatic event(s) occurred, as evidenced by one or both of the following:

1. Avoidance of or efforts to avoid distressing memories, thoughts or feelings about or closely associated with the traumatic event(s)

2. Avoidance of or efforts to avoid external reminders (people, places, conversations, activities, objects, situations) that arouse distressing memories, thoughts or feelings about or closely associated with the traumatic event(s).

Source: American Psychiatric Association (2013).

This avoidance of internal and external reminders can link theoretically with defence mechanisms, outlined in Chapter 2.

We also stay acutely alert at a sensory level for the recurrence of the event(s). Hyperarousal is a way of trying to prepare for what was previously unanticipated. Again, from a survival perspective, it is logical to stay alert for future dangers, if previous ones have been so threatening (Ellard, 1997; Burstow, 2003). Box 4.3 outlines the specific behaviours that are linked with this hyperarousal state.

Box 4.3   Hyperarousal criteria for post-traumatic stress disorder

Marked alterations in arousal and reactivity associated with the traumatic event(s), beginning or worsening after the traumatic event(s) occurred, as evidenced by two or more of the following:

1. Irritable behaviour and angry outbursts (with little or no provocation) typically expressed as verbal or physical aggression towards people or objects.

2. Reckless or self-destructive behaviour

3. Hypervigilance

4. Exaggerated startle response

5. Problems with concentration

6. Sleep disturbance (e.g, difficulty falling or staying asleep, or restless sleep).

Source: American Psychiatric Association (2013).

The traumatic stress experience for many survivors often involves all three of these symptom clusters, and PTSD-based research has provided a strong evidence base for this. Importantly, a new set of criteria has been included in the latest version of the PTSD diagnosis. Dissociation has been long iden-tified as a key traumatic stress symptom, as discussed in Chapter 2. To recap, dissociation is the experience of a disconnection between emotional and cognitive realities. It is as if events are happening in a suspended reality, as if someone cannot feel what they are thinking. It is often accompanied by a sense of depersonalisation – as if it is not actually happening to the person themself at that time. In the new criteria, there is far greater elaboration of dissociative experiences along with a range of negative behaviours, such as anger, for example. Therefore, a new category of symptoms relating to changes in cognition and mood is now included. This includes some of the passive avoidance criteria that were formerly in the avoidant cluster. Box 4.4 outlines these symptoms:

Box 4.4   Criterion D for post-traumatic stress disorder

Negative alterations in cognitions and mood associated with the traumatic event(s), beginning or worsening after the traumatic event(s), as evidenced by two or more of the following:

1. Inability to remember an important aspect of the traumatic event(s) (typically due to dissociative amnesia and not to other factors such as head injury, alcohol or drugs)

2. Persistent and exaggerated negative beliefs and expectations about oneself, others or the world (e.g., 'I am bad,' 'no one can be trusted,' 'the world is completely dangerous', 'my whole nervous system is permanently ruined')

3. Persistent distorted cognitions about the cause or consequences of the traumatic event(s) that lead the individual to blame himself/herself or others

4. Persistent negative emotional state (e.g., fear, horror, anger, guilt or shame)

5. Markedly diminished interest or participation in significant activities

6. Feelings of detachment or estrangement from others

7. Persistent inability to experience positive emotions (e.g., inability to experience happiness, satisfaction or loving feelings)

Source: American Psychiatric Association (2013).

In the *DSM V* definition of PTSD, there is widespread recognition that trauma impacts differently on adults and children. Therefore, a differentiation of responses for children is provided, highlighting behavioural responses more than cognitive ones. For example, in relation to children's intrusion experiences, 'there may be frightening dreams without recognizable content', and in relation to dissociative experiences, 'trauma-specific reenactment may occur in play' (APA, 2013).

Consistent with earlier versions of the diagnostic criteria, symptoms within all these four categories must persist for more than one month and must cause 'clinically significant distress or impairment in social, occupational, or other important areas of functioning'. The symptoms must also be distinguished from those 'due to the physiological effects of a substance (e.g., medication or alcohol) or another medical condition' (APA, 2013, p. 7).

It is important to highlight that a post-traumatic stress response, as distinct from PTSD, is a highly adaptive and normal human response in the immediacy of a traumatic experience. Confronted by extreme and overwhelming circumstances, it makes adaptive sense that we are immediately shocked and numbed by what has occurred. Something unexpected and overwhelming has taken place that does not fit into a person's experience of the world. Remembering, forgetting, avoiding and staying alert to possible future threats are extraordinary survival mechanisms in the immediacy of overwhelming, unfamiliar and unpredictable circumstances. It is widely recognised that many people experience these 'symptoms' in the first few weeks following a traumatic event. For most people, these symptoms are experiences that tend to oscillate during this time and then resolve (Horowitz, 1992). The oscillation of avoidance and intrusion symptoms allows the integration over time of sensory and cognitive information that was unable to be processed (Horowitz, 1992). This oscillating allows a new experience to be slowly incorporated into a new coherence and understanding. This gradual tolerance of the new realities of post-trauma and post-loss experiences enables a restoration of functioning to occur for most people.

For a small number of people, they are experienced profoundly enough in the first month post-trauma to be considered an acute stress disorder (APA, 2013). The symptoms become maladaptive when both the threat is no longer a part of daily life and/or a person stays in this high-energy state over a prolonged period of time, such that an acute stress state becomes a chronic one. This is where the diagnosis of PTSD comes into play, when, after at least one month following a traumatic experience, these symptoms impact on a person's distress and overall ability to function: 'In short, it appears that PTSD reflects a failure of adaptation, whereby normal acute reactions to extreme stress do not correct themselves over time' (Friedman et al., 2011a, p. 751). The critical questions therefore become who is at risk of developing PTSD and what can be done to both prevent and treat it?

Prevalence

A relatively clear set of symptom criteria has given researchers a framework for establishing the prevalence of PTSD following a variety of trauma experiences. This has enabled researchers over three decades now to focus on the prevalence of PTSD in the general community and following specific traumatic events, as well as focus on PTSD outcomes following treatment interventions.

In terms of prevalence, broadly speaking, PTSD is a relatively rare outcome, with the majority of trauma-affected people demonstrating resilience in the studies that have been undertaken. Estimates vary enormously across trauma experiences and contexts, and are limited by a range of methodological challenges. To illustrate, four different regional studies are very briefly overviewed to highlight the diversity of findings across different contexts.

In the American context, Kessler and colleagues studies continue to provide an important benchmark (Kessler et al., 1995; Kessler et al., 2005). They report on the National Co-morbidity Survey Replication (NCS-R) 2003, which assessed for a number of *DSM IV* disorders. For PTSD, the PTSD checklist (PCL-C) and the Impact of Event Scale – Revised were used with 5,692 of this nationally representative sample of 9,282 English-speaking Americans who were aged 18 years and older (Kessler et al., 2005). A lifetime prevalence of PTSD was found to be 6.8%. Significant gender differences were noted – among men, a prevalence rate of 3.6%, and among women, 9.7%. The 12-month prevalence rate was 1.8% among men and 5.2% among women.

In the Australian context, in a stratified sample of 10,641 participants, as part of the Australian National Survey of Mental Health and Well-being, the estimated 12-month prevalence of PTSD was found to be 1.33% (Creamer et al., 2001), a rate that is considerably lower than that found in the lifetime prevalence estimates of the above-mentioned North American study. While this study also found women to be at higher risk of PTSD than males, these differences were less pronounced than in other studies (Creamer et al., 2001).

In the European context, a recent study (Darves-Bornoz et al., 2008) found a similar 12-month prevalence rate of 1.1%, with 0.5% in men and 1.7% in women across representative samples from Spain, Italy, Germany, the Netherlands, Belgium and France.

In the Northern Ireland context, a study found that 'around 60% of the adult population experienced a traumatic event', with 39% experiencing trauma directly related to conflict associated with the Troubles (Bunting et al., 2013). An overall prevalence rate of 5.1% was found, much higher than many other studies.

PTSD outcomes have been studied in relation to different traumatic events – in terms of acute compared with chronic traumatic stress situations and also natural compared with interpersonal traumatic events. The study by Darvez-Bornoz and colleagues (2008), cited above, did find that six traumatic events were more likely to be linked with higher prevalence rates of PTSD – rape, an undisclosed private event, having a child with a serious illness, being beaten by a partner or caregiver and/or being stalked. In the context of our discussions in Chapters 2 and 3, the explanation may well lie in the degree of relational abandonment and violation that occurs. In the chapters ahead, it may well be because of the degree of social betrayal also that can occur or the difficulties in forming a coherent narrative that is externally rather than internally focused. Or, as the latest PTSD definition highlights, it may well be due to the profound threat to physical integrity that occurs during sexual assault.

As noted in this discussion, men and women's different exposures to traumatic experiences and different recovery experiences have long been areas of enquiry. Some studies have shown women to be at more risk of developing PTSD (Tolin & Foa, 2006; Breslau, 2009, p. 99; Lilly & Valdez, 2012; Moser et al., 2007), although others have shown only minor differences (Creamer et al., 2001). Some of the arguments for the higher rates of PTSD for women are that women are exposed to more potentially traumatic events (Kessler et al., 1995) and that these traumatic events are often relationally based (Kendall-Tackett, 2005). The link is difficult to understand fully, as it is interconnected with so many other factors. Norris, Perilla, Ibanex and Murphy (2001, p. 7), for example, highlight that 'sex, the biological factor, becomes utterly confounded with gender, a sociocultural construction'.

Given the often hidden nature of traumatic life events and the methodological challenges in researching traumatised populations, it is not surprising that there are many gaps in the research on PTSD prevalence.

What causes PTSD?

While first and foremost a PTSD diagnosis is driven by exposure to an external event, studies continue to show that outcomes differ for individuals exposed to the 'same' event. This leaves the actual cause of PTSD relatively unknown (Yehuda & LeDoux, 2007). Despite several decades of extensive research, the quest continues to find the cause of PTSD. In the ICD-10 definition of PTSD (WHO, 2010), for example, it is stated:

> Predisposing factors, such as personality traits (e.g. compulsive, asthenic) or previous history of neurotic illness, may lower the threshold for the development of the syndrome or aggravate its course, but they are neither necessary nor sufficient to explain its occurrence.

This is evident in the high comorbidity rates of PTSD with other psychiatric diagnoses – alcohol and drug issues, major depression and other anxiety disorders (Breslau, 2009; WHO, 2010; Kessler et al., 1995).

The cause of the PTSD response has been the focus of much research over recent decades – the extent to which it is caused by an overwhelming of the cognitive and emotional processing systems is seen to be the core 'wound' of PTSD and then maintained by other cognitions and meaning structures.

Neurobiological approaches, in particular, have attempted to provide explanations of the systems that cause and maintain PTSD. While it is beyond the scope of this book to explore these in extensive detail, some of the leading causal explanations are now overviewed – including the hypothalamic pituitary adrenal (HPA) axis and the role of the amygdala.

The HPA system maintains our daily rhythms of hormone production as well as enabling us to respond to stress when needed. From infancy, if we are functioning in situations of relatively infrequent and regulated levels of stress, we develop a capacity to manage these occurrences in the context of our everyday relatively homeostatic state of being. That is, we can accommodate and recover from stressful experiences. We develop an adaptive capacity for infrequent stress responses, followed by periods of regulation of emotional and sensory arousal. Cortisol is a key stress hormone, responsible for regulating this arousal and is released during these stressful experiences. Contrary to what would be expected, studies have consistently shown that those with PTSD have lower cortisol levels, and therefore may be unable to activate their stress reducing systems in times of high stress demand (Solomon & Heide, 2005; Yehuda & LeDoux, 2007; Dozier et al., 2006).

A major area of interest has been in relation to traumatic stress in infancy, when psychological homeostasis is first developing. The growth of our neural pathways in our first year of life is rapid (Schore, 2001, 2002a, 2002b, 2009). Neural pathways are the connections that form in our developing brains to enable increasingly complex and coordinated functions to be performed, such as those associated with our motor, cognitive, emotional and verbal skills. The ways in which these neural pathways form influence the type of pathways we develop. This understanding provides new insight into why childhood trauma seems to impact in very different ways from those experienced in adulthood.

Neurobiological understandings emphasise that '[d]uring development the brain organizes itself from the bottom up, from the least (brainstem) to the most complex (limbic, cortical) areas' (Perry, 2009, p. 242). Our brains develop more complex, cognitive and limbic functions as we move through the early years of our lives. Thus, early development is sequential and foundational. This means that if a child is encountering extreme stress, their brains are being organised from a chaotic base. The 'organising and orchestrating role' of monoamine systems does not occur in the same way as for children growing up under safe and predictable circumstances. As Perry (2009, p. 242) notes:

> If the patterns or incoming neural activity in these monoamine systems is regulated, synchronous, patterned, and of 'normal' intensity, the higher areas will organise in healthier ways; if the patterns are extreme, dysregulated, and asynchronous, the higher areas will organize to reflect these abnormal patterns.

Neurobiologists have highlighted the use-dependence of neural pathways in early development: 'in a child who has experienced chronic threats, the result is a brain that exists in a persisting state of fear' (Perry & Hambrick, 2008, p. 40). This is resonant of the discussion in Chapter 3 about trauma as 'fright without solution'. The plasticity of the brain, that is, its ability to change and adapt positively, despite earlier trauma experiences, has become a key focus. To what extent could a child's neural pathways be negatively influenced by trauma and then positively influenced by interventions? The findings about the plasticity of the brain, that is, its ability to be 'rewired' after trauma, has provided a scientific rationale for the investment in intensive early childhood trauma support and intervention. Reports such as *From Neurons to Neighborhoods* (National Research Council and Institute of Medicine, 2000), set a new mandate for active and different interventions.

What this has meant, for example, is that previously, cognitive behavioural approaches with children emphasised the need for them to be able to narrate their experience coherently and, similarly, experience a reduction in trauma symptoms. However, what neurobiological findings have supported is that 'therapeutic efforts must activate the neural systems that mediate that particular child's symptoms' (Perry & Hambrick, 2008, p. 42). This is a very different approach, whereby

> Any efforts to change the brain or systems in the brain must provide the experiences that can create patterned, repetitive activation in the neural systems that mediate the function/dysfunction that is the target of therapy (Perry, 2009, p. 244)

Perry and others have been instrumental in arguing that interventions, particularly with children, must attend to these processes to be successful. Rather than using interventions that focus on the cognitive or relational regions of the brain, interventions need to engage with 'lower stress-response networks' (Perry, 2009, p. 244), such as through music, art and physical relaxation techniques. These enable the reprogramming of neural networks, so that children can then learn to function in safe and predictable environments.

The extent to which a neurobiological understanding can explain adult trauma experience, and therefore interventions, is less well established. By adulthood, neural pathways are laid down, although still able to adapt (Doidge, 2010). Some studies have suggested that there is an immediate impact upon the adult brain through experiencing adulthood trauma (Woon et al., 2010).

The focus of neurobiological understandings of adult trauma has been on the role of the amygdala. The amygdala was identified as the particular site in the brain linked with the coding of and re-experiencing of traumatic memory. What the research on the amygdala has shown is that it functions in a pre-reflective way – that is, without cognitive processing. The advantage of this is that information that threatens our survival can be processed immediately. However, it also means that it is a

> pre-reflective memory trace that can operate as though the past dangers were present. The amygdala function knows nothing of place and time and is also a center for instinctive memory. (Scott, 2009, p. 118)

PTSD is characterised by the flashbacks, and the sense of events happening currently – the 'amygdala attack' of PTSD acting as if past dangers are still present. In non-traumatic circumstances, the amygdala works in tandem with higher order cognitive function. As noted by Scott (2009, p. 118):

> The hippocampal function, on the other hand, provides spatial and temporal contexts for events. As long as there is cooperation between these two functions a person experiences a traumatic event as past and can remember its emotions in spatial context as well. It was then at that place.

This transforms the all-pervasive sense of 'here and now' to a sense of 'then and there'. The physiological, emotional and cognitive regulation is synchronised.

Research shows that the amygdala encodes and stores traumatic memory in very different ways from non-traumatic memory, given it was encoded and stored when a person is under extreme stress. It is proposed that the 'dissociation during the event prevents elaboration during encoding, which disrupts both memory storage and retrieval, consequently leading to PTSD' (Bedard-Gilligan & Zoellner, 2012).

This finding has transformed understandings of traumatic memory. In Chapter 2, psychodynamic understandings of traumatic memory were examined. A psychodynamic approach emphasised that a person represses or suppresses traumatic memory because it is intolerable and anxiety provoking. The implication is that the total memory is processed and stored, but that fragments, when they can be tolerated, emerge into consciousness.

The cathartic release and conscious acknowledgement of the memory is the intended outcome of psychotherapy. However, these neurobiological findings suggest that traumatic memory is more typically partial, and likely to be encoded in emotional rather than cognitive ways, therefore not readily translatable into verbal memory form.

Other research seeks to locate the aetiology of PTSD in genetic and molecular sources (McCrory et al., 2010; Yehuda et al., 2011). These areas of research remain in their infancy, with findings too inconclusive to date to inform therapeutic interventions.

Resilience and recovery from post-traumatic stress

As noted in Chapter 1, recovery is broadly seen to occur when a person no longer experiences all of the symptoms of PTSD. Through the processes of oscillating between confronting the new reality and at times avoiding it, the resolution of symptoms occurs because the new experience is gradually accommodated into an understanding that at least does not cause the same degree of psychosocial difficulty described earlier. Over time, for most people, the hyperarousal settles as a sense of safety returns. Such notions of recovery do not mean that a person will be symptom free as such. They may continue to live with post-traumatic stress symptoms but will no longer experience the full range of symptoms and/or with the same intensity.

Resilience, therefore, can perhaps be best described within this approach as the capacity to be exposed to stressors and to be able to restore physiological homeostasis, emotional and cognitive functioning, and maintain a sense of self, in the aftermath of traumatic events. The aim of PTSD-focused interventions, therefore, is to promote symptom management and reduction through a variety of techniques.

Implications for practice

In both research and practice, distinctions are made between interventions that focus on the immediate or acute stress phase of traumatic experiences and on the longer-term therapeutic phases.

Short-term interventions for reducing immediate distress and restoring a sense of safety

Two key practice approaches have been consistently promoted within the literature in relation to reducing the immediate distress of traumatic experiences – debriefing and Psychological First Aid (PFA). These interventions, as distinct from therapy interventions, are typically offered through assertive outreach means rather than waiting for people to engage in help-seeking behaviours. In this way, they are uniquely aimed at reaching out to people either in the midst or early aftermath of trauma encounters.

Since the 1990s, debate has continued as to the efficacy and role of debriefing following traumatic events. This is in relation to debriefing people who have been involved in traumatic events and those who have been involved in a professional capacity – for example, emergency service workers or counsellors.

Formal debriefing is an activity that was proposed by Geoffrey Mitchell (Robinson & Mitchell, 1995), who was working in the United States with fire-fighters. It was therefore set up as an operational support process. Debriefing was part of a suite of interventions provided after a critical incident and is typically a seven-stage process of group discussion with those affected by the incident. The steps are as follows: (1) introduction; (2) the facts; (3) thoughts and impressions; (4) emotional reactions; (5) normalisation; (6) planning for the future; and (7) disengagement (Mitchell, 1983; see Rose et al., 2002, for a Cochrane Collaboration review).

In the early days of the debriefing efforts, it was proposed by some that debriefing was a useful way of screening for those likely to go on to experience PTSD, and also of preventing PTSD. Research focused extensively on the outcomes of debriefing processes, whether they used the formal Mitchell Model or other techniques. The findings were mixed. Some studies found that there were benefits with debriefing interventions, particularly in relation to subjective reports of satisfaction with the process (Robinson & Mitchell, 1995). Some studies actually found that debriefing was harmful, with an increase in PTS symptoms being reported by those who had participated in them (see Gist & Lubin, 1999, for a robust discussion). While it may have been the case that the debriefings increased people's experiences of traumatisation, one counterargument to this was that people were more informed about the symptoms of PTSD and therefore more likely to report them when asked, thus leading to higher reporting, not necessarily higher prevalence. Other studies have simply found that there is insufficient evidence for their efficacy (Wethington et al., 2008).

Formal debriefings are used more cautiously now. In particular, consideration is given to the appropriate group composition of participants, taking careful note of power and political issues. However, their use throughout the 1990s changed practices considerably – much more care is now taken with people in the immediate aftermath of traumatic incidents, in that the importance of information is recognised, both relating to the incident(s) itself and about the expected trauma responses. The wider public is much more informed as a result about psychological reactions to trauma. The use of the term 'counsellors' is common now in media reports of traumatic incidents, such as school shootings or natural disasters, even if the primary involvement is for the purposes of psychoeducation not counselling.

PFA is now the immediate intervention used during and in the days after a traumatic event. It is an intervention that recognises the traumatic stress response people are likely to be experiencing. It is focused on restoring a sense of safety and functioning, with the aim of 'reducing the initial distress people experience and promot[ing] early and longer term adaptation' (National Child Traumatic Stress Network and National Center for PTSD Center for PTSD, 2016). It is, therefore, an acute traumatic stress intervention.

PFA plays on the metaphor of physical first aid – it is a first response to manage immediate trauma 'wounds' from a psychological point of view. It is based on the following assumption:

> Immediately after the trauma, the emphasis needs to be on self-regulation and on rebuilding. This means the re-establishment of a sense of security and predictability, and active engagement in adaptive action. (Van der Kolk et al., 2004)

The tasks involved in PFA are outlined in Box 4.5:

Box 4.5   Tasks involved in Psychological First Aid

Psychological First Aid

- *Preparing to deliver PFA* – this preparation task involves careful planning in relation to who is affected by the trauma, preparing yourself as facilitator for entry into the setting and being sensitive to the particularities of the trauma situation, including cultural.

- *Contact and engagement* – these tasks involve introductions, active outreach and the setting of any required ground rules such as confidentiality.

- *Safety and comfort* – these tasks involve attending to the immediate physical safety and emotional support of survivors, attending to immediate concerns relating to the safety of others and, if needed, beginning to address immediate issues relating to deaths of others, assisting with practical location, identification and/or funeral arrangements.

- *Stabilisation* – this task focuses on supporting emotionally overwhelmed survivors with appropriate orienting strategies.

- *Information gathering: current needs and concerns* – this task involves a comprehensive psychosocial assessment, exploring a survivor's disaster experiences, their immediate and pre-existing mental health concerns, their current psychosocial functioning and support networks.

Box 4.5   (Continued)

- *Practical assistance* – this task focuses on identifying immediate needs and appropriate resources for addressing them.

- *Connection with social supports* – this task focuses on activating available support networks and/or establishing new ones.

- *Information on coping* – this task is one of primary psychoeducation in relation to stress and trauma responses, with particular attention paid to the developmental needs of survivors and their families. Strategies for coping with anger, sleep, negative emotions, substance use and other emotions and behaviours are discussed appropriately.

- *Linkage with collaborative services* – referrals to ongoing support services if appropriate are discussed and provided as needed.

Source: National Child Traumatic Stress Network and National Centre for PTSD (2016).

PFA should more accurately be referred to as *psychosocial* first aid, in that it is an intervention that attends to a person's psychological well-being in the context of their social resources. It is about mobilising personal and social resources to support psychological distress.

Longer-term interventions

Therapeutic work in the longer term with PTSD is focused primarily on symptom management and restoring affect regulation and then moving towards more meaning-focused re-integrative work. With an extensive evidence base emerging about the nature and prevalence of PTSD, many studies have now been conducted into the clinical efficacy of different interventions. The most common interventions are trauma-focused cognitive behavioural therapy (CBT) interventions, and in many countries now guidelines have been developed for PTSD interventions that focus primarily on these CBT approaches. For example, in the United Kingdom, the National Institute for Health and Clinical Excellence Clinical Guidance 26 on PTSD recommends that 'the first line treatment is trauma-focused cognitive behavioural therapy (TF-CBT) that includes techniques of eye movement, desensitisation and reprocessing (EMDR)' (Joseph & Murphy, 2014, p. 1097). A key centre of influence on the UK guidelines in recent years is the Northern Ireland Centre for Trauma and Transformation, which has developed an evidence base for the trauma-focused CBT interventions outlined below. In Australia, the National Centre for Post-traumatic

Mental Health recommends cognitive behavioural interventions also in the *Australian Guidelines for the Treatment of Adults with Acute Stress Disorder and Post-traumatic Stress Disorder* (Australian Centre for Post-traumatic Mental Health, 2007). In the United States, Foa et al.'s (2009) *Guidelines* have become profoundly influential in outlining the range of theoretical approaches and clinical interventions with post-traumatic stress disorder and highlighting the centrality of CBT approaches. Thus, trauma-focused CBT has come to dominate current practices.

At this point, it is important to revisit a cautionary note from Chapter 1. Evidence for PTSD interventions exists because of the tightly prescribed symptoms of PTSD and the tightly structured interventions that are used. Many of the 'gold standards' of medical clinical research can be met with this approach, for example, through randomised control trials. The lack of evidence of other interventions for PTSD does not mean that these interventions are unsuccessful. The lack of evidence is purely a lack of evidence, given the difficulties in measuring outcomes in the same way.

With CBT established by randomised control trials as an effective intervention method and given the focus within a PTSD diagnosis on cognitive symptoms, trauma-focused or PTSD-focused approaches to CBT have emerged in the past decade. Ehlers and Clark's (2000; 2008) model of PTSD has been widely adopted, for example, emerging from their work at the Northern Ireland Centre for Trauma and Transformation. The approach is further described in studies by Ehlers et al. (2005) and by Ehlers et al. (2010). Their model of PTSD proposes the following:

> People with PTSD perceive a serious current threat that has two sources: excessively negative appraisals of the trauma and/or its sequelae and characteristics of trauma memories that lead to re-experiencing symptoms. (Ehlers et al., 2010, p. 387)

PTSD is maintained by cognitive strategies and behaviours that are intended to reduce the sense of current threat, but that maintain the problem by preventing change in the appraisals or trauma memory, and/or by increasing symptoms.

Within their intervention, three major treatment goals are outlined (Ehlers & Clark, 2008) – to modify the negative appraisals, reduce re-experiencing by developing an understanding of memories and triggers, and develop new coping strategies. These goals are relatively consistent across most trauma-focused interventions currently practised; for example, Perry (2009) advocates for distress reduction and affect regulation training, along with a focus on emotional and cognitive processing.

Modifying negative appraisals

Looking more specifically at these areas of intervention – the first goal is to 'modify excessively negative appraisals of the trauma and sequelae'.

Addressing this goal, a person is supported to re-examine and modify unhelpful negative appraisals of experiences – with Ehlers and Clarke (2008) advocating for the provision of information, Socratic questioning and behavioural experiments. A focus is built around re-evaluating the sense of permanent change since the trauma; 'reclaiming your life' assignments are discussed in each session and usually done as homework. In achieving this first goal, a person is encouraged to 'reclaim' their former lives by reinstating significant activities or social contacts they have given up since the trauma.

Reducing the re-experiencing of trauma symptoms

The second goal is to reduce the re-experiencing of trauma symptoms by elaborating on the trauma memories and developing a capacity to discriminate specific symptom triggers. The goal is to address the exposure aspects of the experience and can involve imaginal reliving of the events, writing out detailed narratives of the event, revisiting trauma sites and, again, building a cognitive understanding and an ability to discriminate different triggers.

Importantly, these exposure aspects of the therapeutic process do seem to require emotional responses *and* cognitive integration – that is, the exposure process does rely on a process of activation of traumatic stress symptoms, whereby activation

> refers to the conditioned emotional responses (such as fear, sadness or horror) that are triggered by trauma memories, and trauma-specific cognitive reactions (such as intrusive negative self-perceptions or sudden feelings of helplessness). (Briere & Scott, 2006, p. 132)

All treatment approaches, whether written as in journaling or letter writing (Pennebaker & Seagal, 1999), verbal or Eye Movement Desensitization and Reprocessing (EMDR) oriented, discussed further below, highlight that 'in order to extinguish emotional-cognitive associations to a given traumatic memory, they must be (1) activated, (2) not reinforced, and, ideally, (3) counterconditioned' (Briere & Scott, 2006, pp. 132–133). That is, it is not adequate to merely react emotionally. A cognitive reworking is required. By directly confronting the fear-inducing aspects of the traumatic event, the emotional and cognitive fear reactions can be integrated and defused.

Another specific technique developed for PTSD is EMDR (Solomon & Shapiro, 2010; Shapiro, 2001). It is proposed as an information-processing model, integrating aspects of all the major psychological traditions (Shapiro, 2002). The core component of EMDR is the engagement of the client in some form of bilateral movement (such as eye movements) at the same time as recalling traumatic material, over an eight-phase process. Studies have shown that these bilateral and rapid eye movements are correlated with shifts in cognitive content (Shapiro, 2002). These exposure therapies have been found to be effective in reducing PTSD symptoms (Powers et al., 2010).

Developing new coping strategies

The third goal is to do away with dysfunctional behaviours and cognitive strategies that may have emerged in the trauma aftermath in an attempt to cope with the distress. In this area of work, a person is encouraged to discuss the problematic consequences of their current behaviours and ways of thinking. Survivors are encouraged to talk through the advantages and disadvantages of their rumination and devise ways of dropping or reversing the problematic strategy.

This exposure and integration-focused work requires careful attention to distress levels and an ability to tolerate such exposure. In order to do this work, Briere and Scott (2006) advocate staying within the 'therapeutic window', whereby the therapeutic window is

> the psychological midpoint between adequate and overwhelming activation of trauma-related emotion during treatment. It is a hypothetical 'place' where therapeutic interventions are thought to be most helpful. (Briere & Scott, 2006, p. 125).

He and his colleagues propose that there can be an undershooting or an overshooting of the therapeutic window in therapeutic practice.

Throughout such trauma-focused work, a number of techniques can be used to maintain the work within the therapeutic window (Briere & Scott, 2006). Grounding techniques can be used. They include reminding people of their immediate physical and emotional safety and grounding them in the present moment and realities of their physical surrounds, the 'here and now'. This moderates a person feeling the fear state of the 'there and then'. Similarly, reminding people of their efficacy and normalising their PTSD responses can enable them to remain focused and able to engage in problem solving (Briere & Scott, 2006, p. 127).

One specific approach to working with PTSD is Perry's Neurosequential Model of Therapeutics, which emphasises the importance of assessment of a child's developmental history. This includes taking details of the timing, nature and severity of the challenges a child has faced, which provides an understanding of their trauma load. An assessment is taken of their relational history also. This information is drawn together with a functional brain map, developed by neuroimaging. Only when all this information is brought together is a specific intervention plan drawn up, given that the neurobiological sequence is so important. Once a functional brain map has been developed, therapeutic efforts 'start with the lowest (in the brain) undeveloped and/or abnormally functioning set of problems and move sequentially up the brain as improvements are seen' (Perry, 2009, p. 252). What this has encouraged is a focus on the use of 'patterned, repetitive somatosensory activities such as music, movement, yoga (breathing) and drumming or therapeutic massage' (Perry, 2009, p. 252) to facilitate reorganisation of what may have been a 'poorly organised brainstem' (Perry, 2009, p. 252). As improvements are seen in self-regulation, therapeutic efforts can move to more relational-related problems (limbic system) – play or music therapy improving dyadic skills and eventually to cognitive behavioural or psychodynamic approaches.

As well as symptom reduction and eradication through therapeutic techniques such as those described above, medication is used in some instances to assist people with their stress, anxiety and depression responses (Yehuda & LeDoux, 2007). Medications for post-traumatic stress reactions have been found to be useful in conjunction with psychotherapeutic approaches, but there is insufficient evidence available to support medication approaches alone (National Research Council, 2008; Foa et al., 2009). Given our focus on the psychosocial aspects of trauma, it is beyond the scope of this book to explore these issues extensively.

In comparison with other approaches, there is noticeably less emphasis on the therapeutic aspects of the relationship, although grounding and trust are important components of the intervention.

A case scenario

How would you go about working with Rosa based on your understanding of PTSD?

Eleven months ago, Rosa was raped by her employer one late afternoon at the back of the shop where she worked. She has told no one at work or at home about what happened, but she is finding that she is edgy and teary. She is screaming at her children more often. She cannot sleep at night, scared she will have nightmares about what happened. She listens to every noise in the house. Any door noises trigger her particularly, taking her back to the moment when he locked the door behind her, trapping her in the back office. When her husband tries to be affectionate with her, she takes herself off to the bathroom and bolts the door. Sometimes, she rocks herself on the bathroom floor to try to stop the memory of the incident.

Critically reflecting on symptom approaches

Alongside the prominence of this psychiatric or PTSD approach to trauma research and practice, there is extensive critique. The criticisms relate to two key areas – a specific concern with the limits of the diagnosis of PTSD and a general disagreement with the 'psychiatrization' and 'medicalisation' of trauma (Davis, 1999).

Many note that PTSD, while often seen as the essence of a trauma response, only relates to the 'tip of the iceberg' of trauma responses (Norris, 1992, p. 416). While speaking of the 1994 definition of trauma, Drozdek's (2007, p. 9) observation could still hold:

> The PTSD concept...is a reduced one. It does not take into account the whole spectrum of post-traumatic damage, including core belief changes (Janoff-Bulman, 1985), dissociative moments, ruptures in growth and development of victim's personality, and co-morbidity like depression or substance abuse.

PTSD has been seen by many to be a very narrow cluster of post-traumatic symptoms – its usefulness has been to provide a common language in very complex human territory (Joseph & Murphy, 2014, pp. 1096–1096). Yet those diagnosed with PTSD are highly likely to be diagnosed with other conditions – particularly anxiety, depression and drug and alcohol problems (Joseph et al., 1993; Foa et al., 2009). Given this, the question is raised as to whether PTSD is a distinct diagnosis, leading others therefore to critique the entire diagnostic categorisation of a psychiatric disorder. For example, Ellard (1997, p. 87) proposed:

> Post-traumatic stress disorder is one of this generation's epidemics, and the growing wave of enthusiasm for it as a diagnosis may disadvantage many whose suffering is real.

While stated in 1997, many would claim this statement still holds as strongly as ever.

The PTSD diagnosis has been seen as privatising and stigmatising individuals by giving a label of a psychiatric disorder for experiences that have occurred within their social environments and that they have had very little control over. Davis (1999) refers to this as the 'psychiatrization' of trauma. The focus on the impact and a neglect of the cause therefore means that human distress is seen as a psychiatric illness or disorder (Sanders, 2005). The sociopolitical, cultural layers that encompass a person's suffering are neglected, and a persons' experience is isolated from their context. Factors such as poverty or place-based vulnerability are seen as descriptive and associated, for example, rather than causal, when a psychiatric diagnosis predominates. Where this becomes potentially problematic is that interventions focus only on an individual's intrapsychic experiences rather than on broader sociopolitical concerns. In Chapter 1, it was highlighted that, 'What happens after a trauma has been shown consistently to have the biggest impact on whether a person develops PTSD' (Allen, 2012, p. 256). The lack of appreciation of this aftermath context in treating PTSD alone is seen to be problematic.

Many view PTSD as a Western concept that bears little relevance outside of these contexts (Tummalla-Nara, 2007). This is critical if we are looking at trauma experiences and responses in a global context, perhaps most importantly in the context of refugees and asylum seekers – millions of people are displaced by civil wars and seek refuge in countries around the world. It is essential that trauma interventions are culturally appropriate rather than culturally appropriating. The PTSD model tends to infer that PTSD arises as a result of exposure to a single incident, rather than addressing the response to chronic and pervasive contexts of high fear, alarm and uncertainty. In Chapter 8 we look at this in more detail.

A final criticism that is raised consistently is that with the proliferation of PTSD-based research and practice, there must be following recognition:

> The professions which have popularized PTSD are not disinterested parties. Rather, they are stakeholders in a process which constructs specialist knowledges, and within which professional groups compete for territory. (Davis, 1999, p. 755)

The language of PTSD and the research and practice it drives undeniably generate their own industry and professional contestations. We revisit these themes in Chapter 8.

Similar to many of the criticisms of the concept of PTSD are criticisms of the neurobiological approach. As one author notes, 'the results of neuroscience show nothing more than the underlying physiological correlates of behaviour' (Norton, 2007, p. 61). Its critics see it as providing a reductionist and deterministic view of trauma impacts, which do not eventuate in people's experiences. In the same way that the PTSD approach is criticised for offering a medicalised view of trauma's impact, neurobiology is seen all the more to be focusing on the physical and medical aspects of trauma, with the risk being that interventions will increasingly focus in this area, rather than remaining primarily psychosocial.

Noted three decades ago by the developmental psychologist Kagan, the following statement still arguably holds:

> The belief that experience produces a permanent change in the brain, wedded to the premise that the brain directs thought and behaviour, implies that since the structures first established are likely to direct the later ones, early experience must be important, even though most modern research on the brain also indicates inconstancy. Many synapses vanish; some are replaced; and new ones are being established throughout the life span. (Kagan, 1984, p. 87 cited in Norton, 2007)

This view is shared by some of the most prominent trauma researchers such as Michael Rutter (2008b). Thus, while its appeal is in the certainty and 'scientific' orientation of thinking about trauma, in reality, the science is in its infancy. Much still remains unknown about the specifics of the neuroscience of trauma's impact (Rutter, 2008a,b; Yehuda et al., 2011).

Conclusion

The PTSD diagnosis is borne out of the observation of a cluster of severe symptoms some survivors experience in the aftermath of trauma, documented now over centuries of human experience. A diagnosis of PTSD can provide many survivors and their families with useful frames of reference and links with appropriate interventions. However, such a diagnosis has also been widely criticised as a concept that is without sociopolitical and cultural context.

Neurobiological understandings have strengthened insight into trauma's impact at physiological levels. They have drawn attention to the importance of the developmental stage of trauma survivors and the ways in which trauma will impact so differently as a result of this developmental capacity. The processing of traumatic memory has also become clearer as the role of the amygdala has been better understood.

Notwithstanding the many criticisms that are made in relation to the psychiatric rather than more socio-cultural and political emphasis of these approaches, interventions based on these theoretical understandings have demonstrated successful outcomes, supporting people to live more effectively with their trauma memories and sensory experiences.

5

Person-Centred Approaches: Recreating Congruence

Introduction

In this chapter, we look at person-centred approaches to trauma. Person-centred (or 'client-centred', as initially termed) approaches originated from the work of Carl Rogers (1965, 2007 [1957]) and provide a way of thinking about both human functioning and therapeutic intervention based on humanistic and existential assumptions.

We explore how resilience is conceptualised within a person-centred approach, with the emphasis on our human actualising and growth tendencies. Then we look at person-centred approaches to understanding trauma responses – particularly in light of the self-structure proposed by Rogers and the challenge of incongruence that trauma presents. This approach builds on important foundations from psychodynamic and attachment approaches, but incorporates some fundamentally different core beliefs. Rogers' writings predate the language of trauma used today and tend to focus on human concerns of a more general nature. Notwithstanding this, his theorising and practice have laid down important foundations for trauma-specific theorising. Trauma recovery becomes a process of re-establishing congruence and engaging in actualising our potential and growth.

Person-centred approaches provide both a way of thinking about individual uniqueness and adaptation and a way of thinking about the therapeutic relationship. The six core conditions of the therapeutic relationship, which place survivors at the centre of the pace and direction of therapeutic interventions, will be explored in this chapter.

Person-centred approaches to resilience and recovery

Core to Roger's writing and practice was a radically different belief about human tendencies and psychology from those we have explored in earlier chapters. He proposed a theory of the fully functioning human being, arguing for our innate tendency towards actualisation and growth. This view – that we move towards our potential rather than towards our incapacity – was a profoundly different view from the dominant psychological views of the time (Joseph, 2005, p. 197) and arguably remains so today in the trauma field. The principle of actualisation

> points towards an organismic appreciation of humanness (the person as an organism in process), with growth (or adaptation) and flourishing as metaphors for change. It militates against an instrumental appreciation of humanness (the person as machine), with manualised repair and adjustments as metaphors for change. (Sanders, 2005, p. 31)

In this way, the distinction between the PTSD approach outlined in the previous chapter and person-centred approaches to trauma begins to emerge, which we return to in the next section.

Rogers highlighted the importance of the social-environmental conditions in enabling this potential to be reached; that is, he recognised the importance of our outer world contexts for our capacity to grow, develop and function optimally. As Joseph and Murphy (2012, p. 4) summarise:

> person-centered theory suggests the tendency to proactively grow, develop, and move toward autonomous functioning, when the social-environmental conditions are optimal. Importantly, it is a biological tendency, not a moral imperative.

Thus, a person-centred approach highlights our tendency to move towards growth and development. Rogers proposed that when there was congruence between our internal and external alignment of our actualising potential, authenticity and flourishing could be achieved. In the face of adversity, resilience can be seen as the ability to sustain or restore this congruence.

For this capacity to be reached, people need to have a self-structure that is congruent with their experiences. That is, a self-structure that is congruent between inner and outer worlds – the psychological and the social environment. This psychological self-structure is maintained by processes of defence, such that when anxiety arises, we can continue to try to maintain a sense of congruence. When this anxiety is too great or the defences break down, there is a breakdown of congruence. So, there are parallels here with psychodynamic thinking in that the role of defence mechanisms in everyday life is an important one and cognitive approaches in emphasising the importance of our meaning structures. The difference with the approaches lies in how we go about restoring a sense of congruence.

Rogers argued that we seek an 'accurate symbolisation' of our experience in order to re-establish a sense of congruence between our self-structure and our experiences. Anxiety arises as a result of tension when our symbolisation is not congruent with who we are and want to become and/or is not congruent with the context in which we find ourselves. In particular, traumatic experiences frequently shatter this ability to form an accurate symbolisation, when there is no existing frame of reference or self-structure. Thus, incongruence is experienced, which Rogers (2007 [1957], p. 241) defined as

> a discrepancy between the actual experience of the organism and the self picture of the individual insofar as it represents that experience.

Importantly, the self picture, or this 'accurate symbolisation', is recognised as unique to each person, another distinguishing feature of person-centred approaches:

> Each individual, for Rogers (1951, p. 483), 'exists in a continually changing world of experience of which he is the center'; and, given that this ever-changing phenomenological experiencing will be unique to the individual, the very essence of each human reality is distinct. (Cooper & McLeod, 2011, p. 213)

This is a critical departure from other approaches to trauma and resilience – person-centred practitioners generally reject the need for diagnostic approaches to counselling, seeing the use of reductionist categories (of PTSD, for example) as missing the essence and uniqueness of a person's experience.

The conditions in which this congruence can be established form the foundation of person-centred approaches. In a seminal article, Rogers (2007 [1957], p. 241) set out six necessary and sufficient conditions for counselling, arguing that if these conditions were in place, psychological change could be achieved. In this sense, these conditions become the foundation for growth-promoting work. Box 5.1 shows these six conditions.

Box 5.1   The six necessary and sufficient conditions

The six conditions necessary and sufficient for counselling

1. Two persons are in psychological contact.

2. The first, whom we shall term the 'client', is in a state of incongruence, being vulnerable or anxious.

3. The second person, whom we shall term the 'therapist', is congruent or integrated in the relationship.

4. The therapist experiences unconditional positive regard for the client.

5. The therapist experiences an empathic understanding of the client's internal frame of reference and endeavours to communicate this experience to the client.

6. The communication to the client of the therapist's empathic understanding and unconditional positive regard is to a minimal degree achieved.

Source: Rogers (2007).

An empathic understanding is critical to promote resilience and understanding of a person's distress and their potential. Rogers (2007 [1957], p. 243) described this empathic understanding as the ability to do the following: 'To sense the client's private world as if it were your own, but without ever losing the "as if" quality – this is empathy, and this seems essential to therapy'.

In person-centred practice, Rogers proposed that people respond positively to therapeutic practice when the therapist themselves engages with a person and their world with three conditions – warmth, unconditional positive regard and genuineness. This engagement in the therapeutic process in this way was a radical departure from usual psychotherapeutic practice during the 1950s and 1960s. It focused attention on the importance of the attitude of the practitioner and how this influences the co-creation of a person's sense of themselves. In one of the most provocative paragraphs, the values that Rogers brought to the counselling encounter are raised in the questions he asks:

> How do we look upon others? Do we see each person as having worth and dignity in their own right?...Do we tend to treat individuals as persons of worth, or do we subtly devalue them by our attitudes and behaviour? Is our philosophy one in which respect for the individual is uppermost? Do we respect [their] capacity and [their] right to self-direction, or do we basically believe that [their] life would be best guided by us? (Rogers, 1965, p. 20)

This attitude of the practitioner, not from a position as expert but as colleague or ally, is seen as modelling attitudes that in turn the client can internalise. There is an inherent respect for the dignity of the person articulated in this paragraph – a belief in the worth and the capacity of a person. In adopting this attitude, insight into the client's realities and world views could be possible, stepping out of our own worlds to try to

> perceive the world as the client sees it, to perceive the client....as....seen by themselves, to lay aside all perceptions from the external frame of reference while doing so, and to communicate something of this empathic understanding to the client. (Rogers, 1965, p. 29)

This empathic engagement is not dissimilar to the positive conditions required for secure attachment outlined in Chapter 3 – the importance of responsive, positive and, most importantly, accurate attunement to an infant's distress and experience. Through this sensitive and responsive relationship, while attachment theory proposes this enables regulation of our physical and emotional worlds, person-centred approaches propose that a new self-structure can emerge and congruence can be restored.

Person-centred approaches to trauma

While person-centred approaches have been used in practice for more than 50 years, only relatively recently have they been incorporated more explicitly into trauma-focused therapies. In part, this was due to their general bypassing, given the rise of behavioural approaches over the 1960s and 1970s (Neville, 2009), followed by the rapid rise of neuroscientific approaches. This, on the one hand, could be seen as a result of person-centred approaches per se having lost a strong presence or alternatively, as Barrett-Lennard and Neville (2010, p. 269) note, a result of their integration into a broad range of approaches:

> Over time, Rogers' theory of the necessary and sufficient conditions for therapeutic change (especially the therapeutic significance of empathy) went from being a revolutionary idea to being largely taken for granted as the foundation of effective counseling.

The core conditions of person-centred therapeutic approaches have become well entrenched as the successful conditions of many other approaches.

Person-centred approaches contribute in at least two distinct ways to thinking about trauma responses – first, in relation to thinking differently about the nature of the trauma response, and second, in relation to focusing on post-traumatic growth. In this way, person-centred approaches provide explanations for both post-traumatic stress and post-traumatic growth experiences. Each of these is now examined.

The impact on the self-structure

Rogers (1944) wrote specifically about trauma in only one paper, in the context of veterans returning from the Second World War. As distinct from all the approaches we have looked at so far, Rogers was known for 'speaking out against the medicalisation of distress and professional expertism' (Sanders, 2005, p. 25). He rejected the idea of 'human distress as an illness' (Sanders, 2005, p. 22), as the person-centred approaches continue to do.

In this one paper, he wrote about the psychological adjustments that were required in returning to civilian life. Already a future focus is evident in the language that emphasises the *'returning* to civilian life', rather than being defined by the nature of being a veteran (past). These seven adjustments are outlined here in Box 5.2 as they connect with Rogers' core thinking about the traumatic damage that is done and the pathways to recovery that emerge.

Box 5.2   The seven areas of adjustment to civilian life

The seven areas of adjustment to civilian life

(1) Vocational readjustment

(2) Hostilities – identified as 'one of the deeper problems' (Rogers, 1944, p. 690). Rogers saw that 'hostility and aggression may rather rapidly be dissolved by permitting free expression of these attitudes in an understanding atmosphere, in which such bitterness and hatred is accepted, without approval or disapproval, as a part of the individual' (Rogers, 1944, p. 690).

(3) Disturbances of self-esteem – understood as 'a sense of loss of status' (Rogers, 1944, p. 691).

(4) Uncertainty of purpose and goals – understood as the impact of traumatic experiences shattering a person's core beliefs and their sense of meaning. This can be seen as a cognitive or narrative approach as we have looked at in earlier chapters or can be seen in more philosophical and existential terms – that is, not reduced to cognitions but a way of finding meaning and purpose.

(5) Combat residuals of combat stress – understood as 'increased restlessness, disturbed sleep and a tendency to be hyper-emotional' (Rogers, 1944, p. 692). Links are clear here with the hypervigilance aspects of PTSD.

(6) Marital and family adjustments – recognising 'the community of interests which existed before the war is likely to be sharply reduced' (Rogers, 1944, p. 693). This can be likened to the loss of libido noted in the psychodynamic approaches.

(7) Adjustment to handicaps – identifying the physical damage of combat incorporates an emphasis on the physical as well as psychological nature of war trauma.

There are clear similarities with many of the PTSD 'symptoms' as they later came to be identified. However, the seven dimensions give consideration to much broader relational and social factors. They highlight the way in which trauma creates tension in an extreme and overwhelming form and leads to an inability to re-establish a sense of congruence. For some, this includes a loss of a sense of self and a loss of a self-structure that carries meaning. Trauma is experienced as major and disruptive incongruence between the self and the world. As Turner (2012, p. 31) suggests:

> it is the gap between the clients' former understanding of their selves and/or the world, and the world that they are now confronted with, that results in incongruence. 'Processing' is the task of accurately symbolising the new information and incorporating it into the new model – of making sense of what has happened. In most cases that gap between the existing self-structure and the traumatising experience is narrow enough to enable the experience to be

assimilated into the self-structure fairly readily ... However, in some cases the gap between self-structure and the traumatising experience is currently too great for assimilation.

Central to recovery is the need to re-establish congruence. Person-centred approaches see traumatic responses as occurring when there is an incongruence between what we hold as core assumptions and what we have experienced. The work of Janoff-Bulman is highly relevant to understanding these assumptions, as noted by Joseph (2011). She argues that we develop a narrative of core assumptions about ourselves and the world around us that helps us build a sense of security and safety in order to function each day. This is the world view we establish, our core existential map that we live by. These assumptions become the fundamental assumptions of our self-structures as long as our experience matches them. As she states:

> Traumatic life events involve reactions at life's extremes. By understanding trauma we learn about ourselves, victim and non-victim alike, and begin to become aware of our greatest weaknesses and our surest strengths. (Janoff-Bulman, 1992, p. 4)

Depending upon where we are living in the world and our past and present circumstances, we will experience different levels of safety and security, but still hold these experiences within a set of core assumptions.

The first assumption is that the world is benevolent. This means, 'A benevolent world is not only one in which good things happen, but one in which people are good' (Janoff-Bulman, 1995, p. 77). The second assumption is that the world is meaningful:

> A meaningful world is one in which events 'make sense' because they predictably follow certain accepted 'social laws ... In Western cultures, events are meaningful if they follow principles of justice. (Janoff-Bulman, 1995, p. 77)

The third assumption is that the self is worthy (Janoff-Bulman, 1992, p. 6). This 'involves seeing oneself as decent and worthy and thereby as deserving of good outcomes' (Janoff-Bulman, 1995, p. 77).

Post-traumatic growth

In Chapter 1, the concept of post-traumatic growth was introduced. While PTG is often thought of as part of a cognitive approach, in many ways this concept can be seen to reflect the actualising processes after trauma, the efforts to re-establish a new congruence and self-structure. PTG could be termed 'post-traumatic actualisation', enabling connections with the possibilities for the full self, the positive possibilities that are new and now present. For these reasons, we look at PTG as part of a person-centred approach.

The experience of growth is different from a return to a pre-trauma baseline experience. It is more wholly aligned with Roger's notion of actualisation and the reaching of full human potential:

> The individual has not only survived, but has experienced changes that are viewed as important, and that go beyond what was the previous status quo. Posttraumatic growth is not simply a return to baseline – it is an experience of improvement that for some persons is deeply profound. (Tedeschi & Calhoun, 2004, p. 4)

The relationship between the traumatic experience and growth is not always clear. Some propose the following:

> It is the individual's struggle with the new reality in the aftermath of trauma that is crucial in determining the extent to which posttraumatic growth occurs. (Tedeschi & Calhoun, 2004, p. 5)

Developing a self-structure that can accommodate the new reality is a critical part of recovery (Joseph, 2005, p. 199).

However, a careful distinction needs to be made between a positive symptoms approach and a person-centred, growth approach. A positive symptoms approach can be associated as much with a medical model of trauma as a negative symptoms approach (Joseph & Murphy, 2012). Growth following trauma is not about medicalising in the other direction – it is about transformative processes that many people report after trauma experiences.

The positive changes in self-perception include an increased sense of self-reliance and of being a stronger person (Tedeschi & Calhoun, 1995). This leads to self-evaluations of greater competence in difficult situations and therefore greater confidence. A study by McMillen et al. (1997) identified different personal changes again, with the aspects of personal growth including the perceptions of becoming a nicer person, stronger, more spiritual and making changes in life priorities. The commonality of these perceived changes is that they highlight a deeper sense of self-awareness or capacity for self-reflection, experienced as positive changes or gains. These changes in self-perception have been conceptualised (Schaefer & Moos, 1992) as occurring in two ways – through enhanced personal resources and enhanced coping skills. In relation to enhanced personal resources, the following factors have been identified – more cognitive differentiation, assertiveness, self-understanding, empathy, altruism and maturity. It then follows that enhanced coping skills include such factors as the ability to think through a problem logically, to seek help when needed and regulate affect (Schaefer & Moos, 1992).

The enhanced relationships with others include an increased closeness to others, as in becoming closer to family and friends, as well as experiencing an increased sense of community closeness. Schaefer and Moos (1992; Tedeschi et al., 1998) view enhanced social resources as relating to better relationships with family and friends and to building new support networks and confidant relationships. Often, the network of support available to trauma survivors is expanded, for example, by the meeting of other survivors in the formal recovery settings or therapeutic groups.

The area that resonates very strongly with person-centred approaches is that of experiencing an enhanced philosophy of life. Many people talk about their experience of trauma as being like a 'wake-up call' or a major turning point in their life. As a consequence, this crisis causes them to confront issues of their own mortality and their life's purpose and meaning. In doing so, people frequently report positive changes in their priorities and their sense of appreciation of life. For many, this involves questioning issues of religion and spirituality (McColl et al., 2000) or a general philosophy of life or world view that provides new meaning (Silver et al., 1983). It often leads to making changes in employment or relationships.

Maslow (1968, p. 206) argued that 'the state of being without a system of values is psychopathogenic' in that all people need a 'framework of values, a philosophy of life, a religion or religion-surrogate to live by and understand-by'. Growth is considered to have taken place when these beliefs about the world, the self and transcendent aspects of daily life, are strengthened. Enhancement or the perception of enhancement in this area is seen as a buffer against the ongoing disorganisation and distress of trauma, in that it provides a stable self-structure.

A more specific area of growth is an awareness of the need to attend to physical health needs – in terms of diet, exercise and other aspects of physical and mental health, such as meditation and relaxation. Affleck et al. (1987) reported, for example, that men who had experienced heart attacks reported being 'taught a lesson' about the importance of health behaviour practices to live a long life. They found that those who perceived benefits seven weeks after their initial coronary episode were more likely to have avoided further coronary episodes at a follow-up eight years later. This benefit may well connect then with the perceived benefit of appreciating life more, and thus the cycle of growth begins.

These experiences have been surprisingly strongly critiqued in the literature with many researchers questioning the accuracy of these reports of growth. This seems somewhat ironic, when people can report that things have negatively changed for them but somehow cannot report positive changes simultaneously. Consistent in many ways with a strengths perspective:

> To make these observations is not to callously disregard the real pains and trauma that individuals, families and communities confront; nor is it to blithely turn away from the realities of abuse of all kinds inflicted on children; nor is it to deny the tenacious grip and beguiling thrall of addictions. It is, however, to forswear the ascendancy of psychopathology as society's principle civic, moral and medical categorical imperative. It is to denounce the idea that most people who experience hurt, trauma and neglect inevitably suffer wounds and become less than they might be. (Saleebey, 1997, p. 4)

It is to see that despite these experiences, people can continue to find ways to flourish and to find their human potential.

These positive outcomes depend upon two criteria (Tedeschi & Calhoun, 1995). The first is that an event is perceived as a formidable challenge; that is, that there is incongruence that needs to be resolved. The second is that a person's personality is characterised by persistence, determination, confidence, an ability to make emotional connections with others and the acceptance of the limitations of circumstances where necessary (Tedeschi & Calhoun, 1995, p. 43). Thus, the person who is able to adopt a growth focus needs both 'the willingness to take up the challenge' (Tedeschi & Calhoun, 1995, p. 55) and 'a persistently active approach to experiences and problem-solving' (Tedeschi & Calhoun, 1995, p. 55).

Seven principles have been proposed in relation to growth in the aftermath of trauma. These are set out in the first column of Table 5.1, with linkages with person-centred ideas made in the second. From this conceptualisation of post-traumatic growth, they have proposed a seven-stage model of post-traumatic growth, whereby the individual, prior to the traumatic event, has a range of personality characteristics and potential for growth and creativity. When encountering the traumatic event, an initial response takes place, whereby affect, cognition and behaviour mechanisms, which are normally functional, are overwhelmed. The secondary response over time is for rumination to take place, which eventually leads to a revision of the cognitive scheme and emotion-focussed coping. The first steps of growth take place, according to the model, after this secondary reaction process, when initial growth and coping successes are experienced in the areas of affect (distress becomes manageable), cognition (revised schemas are comprehensible) and behaviour (new goals are manageable). Further growth may take place, called wisdom, whereby the affect of the individual is one of serenity, cognitions involve the development of meaningful life narratives and dialectical thinking and behaviour is manifested

Table 5.1 The seven principles of post-traumatic growth

Post-traumatic growth principles	Person-centred principles of trauma and growth
1 Growth occurs when schemas are changed by traumatic events.	Self-structures are disrupted by trauma, resulting in incongruence.
2 Certain assumptions are more resistant to disconfirmation by any events and therefore reduce the possibilities for schema change and growth.	Incongruence continues when self-structures cannot accommodate the reality of the trauma event.
3 Reconstrual after trauma must include some positive evaluation for growth to occur.	Actualisation promotes growth and flourishing.
4 Different types of events are likely to produce different types of growth.	Each person is unique in their circumstances and in their actualisation experiences.
5 Personality characteristics are related to possibility for growth.	Everyone experiences their own potential and actualisation differently.
6 Growth occurs when the trauma assumes a central place in the life story.	Accurate symbolisation of trauma experiences leads to a new congruence and sense of purpose.
7 Wisdom is the product of growth.	Actualisation is the product of trauma and growth.

Source: Adapted from Tedeschi and Calhoun (1995).

in self-efficacy and creativity is meaningful. Tedeschi and Calhoun (1995) underpin this model of unanticipated change with the support offered by others in terms of emotional support, ideas for new schemas and behaviour.

Implications for practice

In Roger's (1944, pp. 695–696) article relating to war veterans, he outlined five principles for practice. These five principles translate well into core statements about person-centered principles for trauma interventions. While they are only briefly presented in the 1944 article, and were developed early in his thinking, they are elaborated below to draw links with other trauma approaches and highlight the person-centred nature of these principles. In a contemporary context, trauma-focused, person-centred work has two core tasks (Cooper & McLeod, 2011, p. 216):

> The first is to specifically orientate the therapeutic work around the client's goals, and the second is to develop the degree of negotiation, metacommunication and collaboration in the therapeutic relationship.

As highlighted in this chapter, person-centred approaches are founded upon core conditions for change, which in turn translate into practice implications and skills.

Creating an authentic therapeutic relationship

The recognition of the counsellor's role in the co-creation of therapeutic work is a profound contribution of person-centred approaches. In many ways, a corrective emotional experience, similar to that proposed in psychodynamic approaches, is the goal of this therapeutic relationship – in this case, mirroring and/or re-establishing congruence. However, in many ways, person-centred approaches see a metaprocess as occurring within the totality of the relationship, for both involved, given the intersubjectivity. As Sanders (2005, p. 35) highlights, a core value and skill are brought to the fore in therapeutic work to promote resilience, which is that of the therapeutic relationship itself:

> A further departure from medically-orientated psychopathologies arises when CCT theory proposes that the experience of resolution of the distress may not be due to the instrumental effects of the techniques of empathy, unconditional positive regard (UPR) and congruence, but rather as a result of the totality of the relationship – a unique, co-created healing moment where complex human contact is the curative factor.

Congruence and co-created moments then become the aim of the therapeutic encounter also – between the client and their world and that of the practitioner and their world.

Rogers' identified the first principle as treating a trauma survivor as 'a whole individual, not in atomistic fashion'. This integrative approach recognises the full humanity of each person. Within the relationship, warmth for the human condition and appreciation of the dilemmas that are being encountered is then emphasised.

A non-expert position is adopted through the condition of genuineness – that is, an openness and authenticity in the relationship. The expertise is in listening to the person and in being aware of the predicaments of their lived experience. This genuineness is shared openly, highlighting moments of incomprehension, or misunderstanding, or highlighting incongruities that are heard in the discussion, between thoughts and behaviours, between real and desired ways of being. This genuineness of presence, in Rogers' view, often emerges when the practitioner is 'close to the transcendental core of [their] being' (Rogers, 1986, p. 198).

Unconditional positive regard is particularly important in the aftermath of trauma experiences:

> It involves the therapist's genuine willingness for the client to be whatever feeling is going on for [them] at that moment – fear, confusion, pain, pride, anger, hatred, love, courage or awe. (Rogers, 1967, p. 62)

Being able to give voice to the incongruities that arise between the person we would like to be and the way in which we may have behaved at a particular time is a challenging task, reliant on a deep sense of trust with another person. Survivors can experience guilt, blame and shame for their role and/or responses during their experiences. Being able to provide a space where these are heard and accepted reflects what Rogers saw as the quality of unconditional positive regard, valuing or prizing the person in a total way.

Fundamentally, these core conditions translate into deep listening to a person's story and suffering, listening carefully for the ways in which change is needed and desired, from their perspective. It translates into listening for the incongruities a person is experiencing as distressing and problematic.

Practice focuses on understanding the uniqueness of the person's experience and what it is like through their eyes, not anyone else's. It does not seek to normalise the experience in the same way of other approaches (e.g., normalising the experiences of post-traumatic stress symptoms). The emphasis is on listening to the very unique and particular aspects of what it is like for this person to be living with these past and present realities. This is critically important, given that part of the difficulty of people's aftermath experiences is often that others do not want to or cannot listen to the trauma experiences they have encountered.

Understanding the incongruence and symbolisation created by traumatic experience

The second principle is to 'recognise the importance of emotionalised attitudes', recognising that trauma creates distress that is expressed in high arousal, anger, hostility, sadness and a range of emotions that become, in turn, attitudes. The third principle is to 'recognise the importance of release of feeling and acceptance of feeling'. This resonates with the exposure focus of many approaches, the need to integrate the expression of feeling with a cognitive acceptance and recognition of it. In this sense, the reworking is about establishing a new and trauma-inclusive symbolisation. As Rogers (1965, p. 41) highlights:

> In the emotional warmth of the relationship with the therapist, the client begins to experience a feeling of safety as he finds that whatever attitudes he expresses is understood in almost the same way that he perceives it, and is accepted.

This brings to light the core value and skill of empathic listening. Person-centred approaches use the skill of empathy (Egan, 2014). This involves a very active engagement in the listening process, and many argue that what has been heard must be actively reflected back to the person somehow. Thus, it is not a passive listening, but an active process of actively confirming with a person what they have heard and in particular what they have heard by way of congruities and incongruities with what matters to that person.

While there is an active reflective process, it is a non-directive style of listening and participation (which is distinct from the assertive outreach interventions we looked at in Chapter 4). With the focus on actualisation, a person-centred approach has a particular understanding of the therapeutic relationship:

> there is no need for the therapist to push the client because the client will be intrinsically motivated to increase congruence between self and experience, and to accurately symbolise their experiences in awareness when the right social environmental conditions are present. (Joseph, 2005, p. 196)

Restoring a congruent self-structure

The fourth principle is to 'build on their ability to readjust themselves, once they have come to see their situation more clearly', recognising the tendency of people to orient towards their potential, towards actualisation. This connects very strongly with the idea of people being able to grow and learn from their experiences. It highlights an emphasis within person-centred approaches on 'reorganisation of the self and more integrated functioning of the self are thus furthered' (Rogers, 1965, p. 41).

Rogers (1944, p. 696) highlighted that if there could be 'adequate release of pent-up feeling, and thorough-going acceptance of that feeling on the part of the psychologist, then it will be found that the individual has many psychological resources for dealing with the situation itself'.

Promoting actualisation and growth

The fifth and final principle is to 'assist them in discovering satisfying purposes', demonstrating the inclination people have towards finding new meaning and purpose to move towards their full humanity. The aim of therapeutic intervention is to 'to facilitate the actualization of the client's unique potential in the way that best suits the individual client' (Cooper & McLeod, 2011, p. 213). For many people, this is realised in the five dimensions of post-traumatic growth described earlier.

A case scenario

How would you go about working with Ben in person-centred ways?

Ben is a 27-year-old veteran, who served two tours of duty in the Middle East. Since coming home, he cannot reconnect with everyday life. He goes out with his army colleagues whenever he can, often for several days of binge drinking. After these binges, he often finds himself extremely depressed and despairing about life. He remembers two particular, vivid incidents from his military service: one, where he was hiding behind a wall with gunfire all around him and being terrified for his life, and the other, when he and his comrades shot at a car, killing all three occupants. He cannot believe he was capable of these acts, even though he knows they are the realities of war. He is proud of serving his country and feels he learnt a lot about who he is while he was away from everything that was familiar to him, but he cannot reconcile the world of war and his life back at home since.

Critically reflecting on person-centred approaches

From the early days of Rogers' articulation of person-centred approaches, criticisms have been raised. Here, we consider the criticisms of its lack of evidence base, lack of addressing political concerns and overall positive human assumptions.

The criticism of a lack of an evidence base is shared with many of the approaches in this book – there is little evidence to demonstrate the efficacy of the approach in the form of an empirical evidence base. It is important to note that, even though the lack of an evidence base is noted for person-centred approaches, in the United Kingdom a survey of 13 specialist trauma services showed that person-centred practice approaches were incorporated in trauma work (Murphy et al., 2013). This is despite the NICE guidelines supporting the use of trauma-focused CBT as the preferred intervention.

The criticism of a lack of political emphasis is similarly shared by other approaches. While it is clearly stated in person-centred approaches that the social environment is a critical component in human growth and flourishing, the extent to which the oppressive aspects of the social environment are integrated into therapeutic work is questioned. This raises the question:

> is it the person that should change, mending human flaws and shortcomings in order to best fit in with the world, or should we change our world and its structures in order to best support our striving for fulfilment? (Neville, 2009, p. 66)

This dilemma is faced by many practitioners in the context of providing individual counselling support.

The third area of criticism is in relation to the belief in our actualising tendency. As highlighted earlier in this chapter, many have questioned Roger's proposal of the positive inclination humans have in relation to growth and adjustment. There have been strong critics of this assumption, suggesting that human beings are not innately driven towards actualisation. The whole movement of salutogenics was born out of this divide of opinion, which continues today.

Associated to this are two more specific criticisms – relating to the non-directive assumptions that are associated with this belief and to the concept of PTG. 'Person-centred therapy' is named as such because it places the person at the centre of the process and of the concerns. Thus, a core belief is that practitioners do not need to be directive in a therapeutic context but, rather, open to the concerns and pace of the client. Some would argue that the nature of traumatic distress, with its often self-destructive elements such as suicidal ideation and its characteristic fixation on experiences that continue to overwhelm, does not lend itself well to responding with this approach.

Criticism of the concept of PTG occurs both in the context of person-centred approaches and in its own right. As with the actualisation critique, the research into positive consequences of trauma has been consistently challenged in a number of ways. Firstly, growth is questioned on the basis that it is an illusion. Taylor and Brown (1988, 1994, p. 21) proposed that people exhibit positive illusions in three important domains: (1) we view ourselves in 'unrealistically positive terms'; (2) we believe we have 'greater control over environmental events than is actually the case'; (3) we hold 'views of the future that are more rosy than base-rate data can justify'. The question as to what is an illusion and what is reality continues to be debated (Block & Colvin, 1994; Taylor & Armor, 1996) in view of the difficulties when one is dealing with peoples' interpretations or 'subjective perceptions of stimuli and events that do not have a sure, physical basis' (Brown, 1991)' (Taylor & Brown, 1994, p. 22). However, given the importance of subjective perceptions in well-being, it is vital that they be examined further rather than be dismissed.

Secondly, the question arises as to whether growth leads to adaptation. There is evidence to suggest growth or positive outcomes are connected to longer-term adaptation. As Affleck and Tennen (1996, p. 903) note, these positive adaptational outcomes have been observed in studies with cancer patients, stroke victims, women dealing with infertility and mothers caring for acutely ill newborn babies. The latter study, for example (Affleck & Tennen, 1996), was a longitudinal study with mothers in neonatal units. Asked if there were benefits from hazardous deliveries and periods of prolonged hospitalisation, 75% of the women reported at least one benefit. The mothers who did not identify any benefits were found to have more mood disturbance and psychological distress at both six and 18 months later.

Not all research that has examined the issue of post-traumatic growth, however, has supported the existence of positive consequences of trauma as influential on adaptation. Lehman et al. (1993), in examining the positive and negative life changes following bereavement and their relations to adjustment, found that 'the number of positive life changes reported was unrelated to reports of psychological symptoms and well-being' and that 'statements of personal growth may not be reliable indicators of adjustment' (Lehman et al., 1993, p. 90). Many studies have found a relationship between ongoing traumatic stress and growth (Levine et al., 2009).

Thirdly, the relationship between positive and negative consequences of trauma is called into question. This involves examining whether they are independent dimensions or whether growth is an outcome from the persistent rumination and search for new meanings caused by ongoing experiences of distress (Calhoun & Tedeschi, 1998, p. 360).

Finaly, positive consequences are challenged by viewing benefit-finding as a proxy for denial (Affleck & Tennen, 1996, p. 902). Cross-validation studies have found subjective and objective reports of growth to be consistent (Weiss, 2002). On this note, it is curious that growth reports are always critiqued negatively for their subjective bias and their lack of validation in objective, observable terms, yet negative reports of psychological symptoms are rarely questioned as to their validity and reliability in the same manner. Thus, reports of intrusion and avoidance symptoms, for example, are accepted at face value and reports of growth or perceived benefit are dismissed or, at least, regarded as questionable.

Conclusion

Person-centred approaches focus on the growth and potential of people. They focus on the existential and meaning-making dilemmas of trauma and the ways in which they can block the flourishing potential of a person. Post-traumatic growth has been included under this umbrella as a result, given its emphasis on the restorative mechanisms after trauma. This chapter has explored how these issues are addressed in the context of an authentic, therapeutic relationship with another person. Fundamentally, person-centred approaches are about instilling hope (Hobfoll et al., 2007) and promoting resilience, in that they focus principally on promoting and mobilising the worth and dignity of a person and their struggle towards wholeness.

6

Narrative Approaches: Re-authoring for Meaning and Coherence

Introduction

As we have seen in earlier chapters, a sense of coherence and meaning is fundamental to our well-being. This chapter brings together many of those threads to look at how meaning can be constructed or reconstructed in the aftermath of trauma within narrative approaches. Narrative approaches are based on different theoretical foundations from those in earlier chapters. They draw on feminist, family therapy, political, cultural and social theories. In this chapter, we explore the unique contribution of narrative approaches to understandings of trauma and resilience.

Narrative approaches are concerned with understanding the narratives we internalise about ourselves and others, how these in turn influence our experience of ourselves and others, and how they can be transformed into new ones, both for ourselves and our broader social contexts. Narrative approaches are therefore focused on understanding the stories and scripts we develop and come to live by. These narratives shape how we think, feel and behave as individuals as well as how we see ourselves belonging in a wider context. Critically, narrative approaches are also concerned with the interconnectedness between our self-narratives and the wider social, structural and cultural contexts in which we live. Attention is therefore paid to analysing and challenging social and cultural narratives, and thus the approaches are political as much as personal.

So, we look at some of these understandings of narrative identity formation and resilience before we look at the impact of trauma and the practice implications. The chapter concludes with an exploration of some of the points of tension within narrative approaches.

Narrative understandings of resilience

From a narrative perspective, resilience is an interactive process. It is interactive in that resilience can also be regarded as 'the outcome of experiences, identity stories, and connections with others' (Yuen, 2007, p. 5). Three tenets of narrative approaches address these resilience possibilities.

Firstly, narrative approaches are concerned with the stories that reflect our beliefs, knowledge, values and wishes, which combine to form a sense of who we are, a sense of 'myself'. As narrative therapist and author Michael White explains:

> This is the sense of self that is associated with the internalisation of a language of experience that is narrative in form and that characterizes what William James called the 'stream of consciousness'. (White, 2011, p. 124)

A narrative identity emerges for each one of us from these streams of consciousness, formed by what we tell ourselves and others and have others tell us. A person's narrative identity is indicative of 'the kind of commitments a person has, what is of importance to him or her, and ultimately what kind of person he or she becomes' (Ward, 2012, p.251). Studies have shown that physical and mental health is associated with narrative identities that have coherence of structure, meaning and emotion (Pennebaker & Seagal, 1999).

Within narrative approaches, this sense of 'myself' is seen as shaped profoundly by the second tenet of resilience, our sense of time – past, present and future – as we build a narrative coherence (or not) throughout our individual lives. Time can be seen as

> one of the most basic regulatory processes that lend order to experience and without which a sense of self would be impossible. Lacking the ability to order experience chronologically, for example, no coherent personal narrative could be assembled. (Brothers, 2008, p. 34)

In researching people's experiences of a diagnosis of life-threatening illness, for example, Crossley (2003, p. 292) found that people experienced a crisis in their narrative identity, particularly their profoundly threatened sense of future time. She notes:

> we orient towards the world with an implicit sense of temporal coherence, connection, order and experiential unity during the course of everyday practical life.

Thus, our self-narrative gives us a sense of unity and predictability (even if it is not necessarily a positive one). It is our familiar sense of 'myself' and temporal coherence that enables us to function in our daily lives.

Thirdly, these narratives form not only in a particular time context but also in particular socio-cultural and political ones. Narrative approaches view context as the critical aspect of influencing the narratives of individuals, families and communities – that is, our narratives are dialogical and co-created. We internalise and generate self-narratives based on our social experiences. In this sense, Arthur Frank (2010, p. 665), who focuses particularly on illness narratives, suggests:

> Stories enjoy an exceptional place in human lives, first, because stories are the means and medium through which humans learn who they are, what their relation is to those around them (who counts as family, as community, and as enemies), and what sort of actions they are expected to perform under which circumstances. Stories teach which actions are good and which are bad; without stories, there would be no sense of action as ethical.

Many of these stories are so embedded in our sense of who we are that we rarely question them or where they came from, until we encounter traumatic experiences that bring them into sharp focus.

If 'the self is socially achieved' (Thomas, 2010), narrative approaches regard the social-cultural aspects of our experiences as a critical determinant of what our narrative self looks like. Thus:

> Narratives provide structures of meaning that allow the person to understand both the role and the wider social or cultural plot of which it is a part. (Neimeyer & Stewart, 1996, p. 361)

This is where the socio-cultural and political aspects of context become a key and differentiating focal point. In this process of externalising, what can be seen as the central tenet of narrative approaches is upheld – whereby, 'The problem itself is externalized so that the person is not the problem. Instead, the problem is the problem' (White, 1987, p. 52). This moves the focus away from individuals alone to look at what maintains a problem in a person's life. Thus, it becomes possible to re-author our personal stories and identities, a process that 'requires moving beyond simply telling and retelling stories to an active deconstruction of oppressive and unhelpful discourses' (Brown, 2007, p. 3). This supports us in re-establishing power and control over traumatic experiences – that is, demonstrating resilience.

Narrative approaches have been embraced in practice and research by many Aboriginal and First Nations people, seeing this valuing of story and cultural context as speaking to their experiences of well-being and resilience and therefore providing a relevant therapeutic lens. The strength of oral traditions that underline their communities and well-being resonates well with the strengths of a narrative approach:

As Aboriginal people, we have always told stories about our lives, and we know how important it is for people to be connected to their own stories, the stories of their family, their people, their history. These stories are a source of pride. When people become disconnected from them, life can be much harder to live. (Wingard & Lester, 2001, p. v)

For Canadian First Nation people, narrative approaches similarly resonate, given their capacity to address

the ruptures of cultural continuity that occurred with the systematic suppression and dismantling of indigenous ways of life that resulted in a profound sense of dislocation and despair. (Kirmayer et al., 2011, p. 86)

This emphasises the importance of 'a communal or collective dimension, maintained by the circulation of stories invested with cultural power and authority' (Kirmayer et al., 2011, p. 86). This works at both individual and collective levels to build a sense of strength, identity, voice and value.

These three tenets – a sense of myself, time, and socio-cultural context – are important aspects of thinking about well-being and resilience. Based on these tenets, resilience can be seen as the processes of authoring and re-authoring our sense of self after traumatic experiences in ways that are empowering and life enhancing. It is also evident when larger cultural or collective narratives are socially just and humane, supportive of people's realities and recovery needs.

Narrative understandings of trauma

Many of the approaches we have already explored have a strong focus on the loss of meaning as a result of trauma experiences. Narrative approaches, in emphasising both individual and socio-cultural contexts, bring a unique focus to meaning making in the aftermath of trauma.

Disrupted narratives

Many narrative approaches argue that trauma disrupts or fractures our narrative identity. As Neimeyer and Stewart (1996, p. 362) note:

The traumatic experience not only disrupts or damages the victim's narrative stream of consciousness, but may also fundamentally challenge the unity of the victim's selfhood.

A new trauma narrative and a traumatised self emerge, leaving a person in a 'traumatised world' (Neimeyer & Stewart, 1996, p. 362).

Survivors must both incorporate what has been physically and emotionally experienced into a new narrative and revisit core values that have often been challenged or shattered. People find themselves generating a new sense of role and plot about themselves and the world around them. In this sense, Janoff-Bulman's (1992) work has been profoundly influential in thinking about the narratives we carry with us and which become shattered in traumatic experiences – narratives of ourselves as worthy and the world as good and/or predictable, as described in Chapter 5.

Rebuilding a new self-narrative after traumatic experience is about re-establishing experiences and narratives of safety and of these core assumptions. This resonates with Michael White's (2004, p. 48) observation: 'Even in the face of overwhelming trauma, people take steps to try to protect and to preserve what they give value to.' In this way, a central tenet is as follows:

> The traumatized person is not without a narrative as much as he or she is faced with a traumatic narrative that, by definition, is very different from the primary, coordinating story. (Neimeyer & Stewart, 1996, pp. 362–363)

This is similar to the ideas of incongruence explored in Chapter 5.

Narrative Exposure Therapy is one approach that actively incorporates this narrative rebuilding. A person is encouraged to establish a 'lifeline' representing 'the life "story" of a person in a ritualized and symbolic way' (Schauer et al., 2011, p. 43). On the floor, a person lays out a rope to show the flow of their life and punctuates it with 'flowers for happy major events and good times in life' and stones 'as symbols for fearful and in particular for traumatic events', giving an opportunity to talk through all events in a single session of contact (Schauer et al., 2011, p. 43).

Beyond narrative

Another view is that the state of being traumatised is a state of being without a narrative – either because the trauma itself is beyond words, description and meaning or because the social or cultural narrative differs so profoundly from the one they carry with them or are trying to develop. In this sense, traumatic experience is seen to be beyond words – that this quality actually distinguishes traumatic from stressful experiences.

If 'language is the digestive juice of the psyche' (Gordon, 2007, p. 14), many survivors report that experiences are so beyond anything familiar or anything that can be described that traumatic realities cannot be easily spoken of, for fear of re-experiencing them and/or fear of traumatising others, among many other possible reasons. Therefore, it may well feel as if these experiences cannot be digested in this sense into our psyche if they cannot be voiced. In the therapeutic context, Gordon (2007, p. 15) notes this moment when traumatic experiences become too much to narrate:

> The first manifestation of damage is evident when the traumatised person tells their story spontaneously. If we do not interfere, their account is fragmentary. They begin at some point of significance and narrate a sequence that suddenly halts...the pause indicates a point in the narrative of intense threat – they pause at a peak of arousal...they are suspended in the moment of threat.

Bringing words to the 'moment of threat' is a critical component of healing, as people come to be able to recount a more coherent narrative without experiencing the emotional intensity associated with this recounting.

This is along the same lines as the view of psychiatrist, Viktor Frankl (1984, p. 95), who survived concentration camp experiences, who noted the words of Spinoza (the philosopher): 'Emotion, which is suffering, ceases to be suffering as soon as we form a clear and precise picture of it.' Naming and voicing experience is a critical part of forming such a clear picture. Without naming, the problems of isolation, alienation and meaninglessness as an experience of self and of others can persist.

Social silencing

For other reasons, the realities of trauma may not be able to be spoken. Many traumatic experiences confront us with the extremes of human behaviour, particularly the extremes of evil and cruelty. Accounts of these experiences can traumatise those listening to them, as well as those who have experienced them. As a result, many survivors report a wish to protect others from what they have endured and survived themselves (Caruth, 1995). This can silence survivors from putting into words with others what they have witnessed.

Others are silenced by the nature of the trauma that they have experienced and the pressures upon them to remain so. Globally, sexual abuse within families and more broadly in institutions such as the church, schools and sports clubs has been more widely recognised (Middleton et al., 2014). At the time of writing, the Australian Royal Commission into Institutional Responses to Child Sexual Abuse is under way, seeking to uncover the systematic sexual abuse of children that has occurred in any private, public or non-governmental organisation that is, or was in the past, involved with children, including government agencies, schools, sporting clubs, orphanages, foster care and religious organisations (Australian Government, 2013).

The media reports to date of this commission reveal the horrific extent of abuse that has occurred over past decades and along with that the extensive processes of personal and broader social denial of such trauma and abuse. Many children who tried to speak to those in authority about their experiences were not believed and, in some instances, punished further for their efforts to break the silence. For children experiencing abuse, the silences have been reinforced because,

> A number of myths have been used to minimise the problem: children were said to lie or to fantasise; they were said to be sexually provocative or seductive; the intervention was said to be more harmful; strangers were said to be the real danger; and mothers were said to be collusive. (Goddard & Hunt, 2011, p. 417)

Many traumatic encounters and their aftermath can be characterised by intense experiences of anger, shame, loneliness, guilt, meaninglessness, self-loathing and hatred. Experiencing the safety to name these experiences is a critical component of recovery, and these broader social silencing processes work against this safety being achievable.

Socio-cultural and political contexts

From the three points made above, you can see the critical intersection of individual and our broader social contexts. Laub sums up the dilemma that is created when he states:

> This imperative to tell and to be heard can become itself an all-consuming life task. Yet no amount of telling seems ever to do justice to this inner compulsion. There are never enough words or the right words, there is never enough time or the right time, and never enough listening or the right listening to articulate the story that cannot be fully captured in thought, memory and speech. (Laub, 1995, p. 63)

He highlights the alienation and helplessness of traumatic memory and narrative. Up until this point, you can no doubt hear a lot of similarities with the approaches we have looked at in the earlier chapters. Giving voice to trauma is ideally about seeking a resonance between past and new narratives and building future narratives based on these past and important values. This focus on the internal narratives that we hold is a critical part of therapeutic process and has formed a major focus within clinical and research work with illness narratives and within mental health generally.

However, narrative approaches take another critical step and explicitly link these internal narratives with their socio-cultural and political contexts. Thus, problems are not within individuals or as a result of their internal psychopathology. Rather, narrative practitioners have emphasised the importance of externalising problems, to see them as part of a much wider relational and social context, as described earlier.

Given that traumatic experiences are seen to be external problems in the first place, this is all the more pertinent (yet often lost) in trauma work. This is quite different to the PTSD emphasis, which, while an external traumatic stressor is central to the diagnosis, sees the problem of PTSD as an individual's inner world predicament and disorder. Focusing on PTSD, we find:

> The problems caused by the trauma remain located within the person and not with the regimes responsible for the abuses they have suffered. As long as the silence is maintained, human rights atrocities continue to go unchallenged. Very often bearing witness to these horrific events can break the silence and restore people's capacity to go on with their lives. (Blackburn, 2005, p. 99)

By relocating problems in wider social and cultural context, a new resistance and empowerment can occur in relation to trauma's aftermath. Thus, narrative approaches have a strong political and social justice thread running through them.

This is reflected in Betrayal Trauma Theory (Freyd et al., 2007). From her work with survivors of sexual assault primarily, Freyd and her colleagues have proposed a theory that incorporates the dimension of social betrayal in considering a person's trauma experience and recovery. We look at this in greater detail in Chapter 8. However, it is important at this point to note that this theory addresses the importance of the intersection of the individual trauma-inducing elements of a trauma experience with the broader degree of social betrayal or support. The theory demonstrates how women's post-trauma experiences are influenced by the absence of broader narratives of recognition (Tang & Freyd, 2012).

The importance of these social or collective narratives has been highlighted also in disaster work (Chamlee-Wright & Storr, 2011). These narratives have been shown to influence the level of social capital that can be leveraged post disaster. For example, if we see ourselves as part of a tight-knit, resilient community, we are likely to think and act in ways that reflect this sense of connection and support. In this sense, 'public narratives' structure 'individual narratives' (Somers, 1994, in Chamlee-Wright & Storr, 2011, p. 270). As Chamlee-Wright and Storr (2011, p. 270) note:

> social capital in the form of shared narratives helps communities to (a) make sense of their circumstances; (b) assess their capabilities and prospects for recovery; and (c) decide on and sustain a course of action.

In the absence of supportive collective narratives, where people's experiences are rendered taboo and/or unacceptable, the consequences have been shown to be devastating. For example, as noted in Chapter 1, the very high rates of suicide of veterans after the Vietnam War was attributed in large part to the broader social views of the war and the subsequent marginalisation of returning soldiers (Figley, 1978; Lester, 2005). Once home, not only were veterans struggling with the traumatic experiences that they had been a part of – they were confronted by an angry, unsympathetic community. Therapeutic work with Vietnam War veterans highlighted the importance of these wider social narratives (Figley, 1978). The many layers of the veterans' aftermath experiences of PTSD could not be seen outside of this broader social narrative. This drew attention to the importance of placing trauma reactions in a much broader context of understanding.

Implications for practice

While many of the elements of practice may seem similar to those described in earlier chapters, particularly in relation to finding new meaning in the aftermath of trauma, a narrative approach differs quite significantly. From a narrative perspective:

> The primary therapeutic task in addressing the effects of trauma on people's lives is then to provide a context for the development or redevelopment of the sort of personal reality that gives rise to the sense of self that is referred to as 'myself'. (White, 2011, p. 124)

In providing a context for the development or redevelopment of a new personal reality, the key aspects of practice can be seen as involving an articulated politicised stance within the therapeutic relationship, asking questions in particular ways to listen to particular aspects of people's stories, witnessing of survivors' stories in non-psychologised ways and, by forming testimonies, engaging in advocacy and social change.

Articulating a politicised therapeutic stance

Within narrative approaches, the nature of the therapeutic relationship is similar to person-centred and anti-oppressive approaches in that the client is seen as the expert in their own lives, and there is a profound respect for, and belief in, the strengths and rights of the survivor. However, narrative practitioners will typically adopt more of role that is exemplified in the metaphor of an investigative journalist, whose task is to 'develop an exposé on the corruption associated with abuses of power and privilege' (White, 2011, p. 27).

Seeing the therapeutic setting as a place where narratives are co-created between a practitioner and trauma survivor or a researcher and interviewee is central. There is typically acute attention paid to the inherent power within these relationships and efforts to minimise power disparity in professional processes wherever possible. Critical reflection is a core component of a practitioner and researchers' work. White's own reflections demonstrate this: 'I believe that if one is not tripping across abuses of power in one's therapeutic practice, it means that one has gone to sleep' (White, 2011, p. 31). It is a powerful reminder to keep listening to our work, through both external and internal means.

There is also a profound belief in overtly addressing the injustices someone has experienced. In this sense, trauma is not understood solely in terms of a survivor's narrative but in term of real conditions and experiences. Thus, addressing inequalities, promoting social justice and engaging in collective action are part of the work, as we explore later. In this sense, narrative approaches to both practice and research are inherently situated in political standpoints.

Witnessing survivors' stories in non-psychologised ways

At the individual level, witnessing stories in non-psychologised ways supports the task of internal redevelopment and reorganisation. Given this explicitly and inherently political and cultural focus, narrative therapy

> largely bypasses psychological explanations and interventions, and instead seeks to help people by working with the ways in which they talk about issues, and the ways in which they participate in social life. (McLeod, 2006, p. 207 cited in White, 2011)

The first step in working with trauma narratives is to support survivors in the witnessing of their own trauma. This involves listening together to the ways in which a survivor is constructing their story by way of actors and plot and silences, listening to the internalising of problems and to the broader socio-cultural context. Listening in this way supports the creation of a more coherent narrative and an internal witness 'who substitutes for the lack of witnessing in real life' (Laub, 1995, p. 71).

An essential element of practice is that survivors are supported to tell their stories over time 'in a way that will be restorative for them' (Blackburn, 2005, p. 98). In many ways, this may not seem dissimilar from the principles underpinning other approaches. Safe therapeutic and research environments are critical. However, the restorative element of telling stories is particular to narrative approaches in that it involves particular styles of questioning and interviewing, based on the centrality of broader socio-cultural narratives.

Using a particular style of questioning

The restorative work of narrative therapy is focused on naming and reframing experience, of reconnecting with what is valued and hoped for. Thus, giving voice to trauma experiences is an important way of maintaining

> a constant relationship with all of those purposes, values, beliefs, aspirations, hopes, dreams, visions, and commitments held precious – to their refusal to relinquish or to be separated from that which was so powerfully disrespected and demeaned in the context of trauma, from that which they continue to revere. (White, 2011, p. 126)

From this commitment, the intention of various narrative techniques is to

> provide a foundation through my questions that gives people an opportunity to resurrect and to further develop a preferred 'sense of myself' and to identify how they responded to the trauma they were being put through'. (White, 2004, p. 48)

Processes of enquiry focus on externalising problems and on developing alternate or preferred stories, listening for unique outcomes and exceptions in people's situations. For example, with women who had survived sexual abuse (McPhie & Chaffey, 1999, p. 51), practitioners asked them the following four questions, which focus on the aftermath of their sexual trauma:

- Think of a time when terror wasn't travelling with you.
- What was different about this time?
- How did you feel?
- What were some of the things you felt when terror wasn't with you?

The intention of these questions is to enable women to be in touch with their strengths and their moments of resistance. Rather than being problem-saturated questions, they are strength-saturated, focusing on externalising the experience in new and empowering ways.

Another technique is to explore the 'absent but implicit' in a person's story. This aspect addresses the observation that we typically define experience by what is missing, yet we may not explicitly articulate what is missing. Listening for the absent but implicit is about listening not only to the nature of the problems as articulated by someone but also to what values, wishes and hopes are embedded behind them. It is about drawing out these issues that may be absent from the conversation but implicit in the narrative of the problem. An example of this is given in these sorts of questions: 'What does this pain speak to in terms of important beliefs about life that have been subjugated or violated?' (Carey et al., 2009, p. 321) or 'What might these tears testify to about what it is that is held precious?'

Narrative therapy involves the intentional relating of narrative, that is, not just the telling of stories but also a focus on this being restorative. This is consistent with other approaches that we have looked at that emphasise it is not just the relating of narratives but the transformation of them, or in this sense, the restoration of them. In working with refugees in the UK context, Blackburn (2005, p. 100) identifies four themes that she has found central in 'creating a context for restorative tellings'. These four themes relate to considerations of safety; considerations of shame, guilt, humiliation and anger; considerations of power and trust; and ways of re-invigorating the 'sense of myself'. These themes reflect understandings of the core damage that trauma can create and the core areas where narrative restoration can occur.

Many narrative theorists and practitioners, however, emphasise that it is not just the telling of an individual narrative within a therapeutic relational context, although this is an important step in the process of recovery. There are other significant aspects in the telling that are proposed, such as testimony formation and advocacy.

Forming testimony for advocacy and change

While conversation is a key aspect of the therapeutic process, some narrative approaches engage in other forms of externalising and validating of people's experiences, both at individual and collective levels. This constitutes the important task of forming a testimony of what has occurred, affirming the experiences that people have survived.

Sharing and documenting traumatic experience is seen as an important restorative intervention – at individual, family or community levels (Denborough, 2005, 2012; McKinney, 2007). At an individual level, the sharing can occur in the context of an individual process of journaling or letter writing. The importance of this is evident in the extensive amount of literature giving autobiographical accounts of surviving traumas, in both published and online formats. However, the therapeutic aspect of narrating in this way is related to the meaning-making processes that are being undertaken in documenting in this way – that is, it is not just documenting events, but it is documenting the meaning of these events that is also therapeutic (Boals et al., 2011). This genre of writing contains the story for someone and gives it an authority of voice (Denborough, 2012). Pennebaker (1995; Pennebaker & Seagal, 1999) and others have extensively researched this form of intervention, with three meta-analyses providing support for the weak to moderate effects of such disclosure on health and well-being (Smyth, 1998; Frattaroli, 2006; Frisina et al., 2004).

Another method of documentation is the testimony method (Blackburn, 2005). This has been used to develop formal statements that provide a detailed record of traumatic events, written over time by survivors and sometimes in their community context as well. These statements of the survivors' experiences can form an important part of formal proceedings, such as court cases and hearings, or remain a more private exercise, but one that nevertheless validates and narrates a survivor's story. To go through this process of forming a single document that contains, both practically and metaphorically, the story of a person's traumatic experience can be enormously beneficial. This enables a restoration of control, the very thing that traumatic experience takes away from people.

Collective narrative therapy

More public forms of testimony formation occur at various levels within our societies, within the legal contexts of court cases, commissions and enquiries. The Nuremberg Trials in Germany after the Second World War and the Truth and Reconciliation Commission in South Africa are perhaps two of the most well-known instances of this occurring. National enquiries or, in many contexts, Royal Commissions, can provide these testimony-forming opportunities. As described earlier in this chapter, the Australian Royal Commission into Institutional Responses to Child Sexual Abuse (http://www.childabuseroyalcommission.gov.au/) is giving many people such an opportunity through gathering both confidential and public accounts of the sexual (and therefore also physical and psychological) abuse encountered by children in a range of care situations. The commission's website states: 'People may want to tell their stories for different reasons. For many, having their voices heard will help with healing and rebuilding their lives' (http://www.childabuseroyalcommission.gov.au/tell-us-your-story). The second sentence captures the essence of narrative approaches.

Another example is the landmark report, *Bringing them home*, from the National Inquiry into the Separation of Aboriginal and Torres Strait Islander Children from their Families (1997). This report documented the experiences of Australia's Aboriginal and Torres Strait Islander Stolen Generations, the forced removal of Aboriginal children from their families and communities. In documenting the trauma of individual children, a broader national awareness of their experiences was established, leading to a national apology in 2008 by the then prime minister, Kevin Rudd. Symbolically, these acts of acknowledgement, accountability and apology marked a significant change in the relationships between Aboriginal and non-Aboriginal Australians.

Findings have been mixed about the benefits of this public testimony process, in part because they are not contained and predictable processes. Some studies have shown that publicly narrating personal experiences, witnessing others' stories and having your own story witnessed is extremely therapeutic with positive outcomes. Other studies have shown that engaging in these experiences can lead to a loss of control of information, processes and outcomes, with subsequent long-term harmful effects for some people. Others have argued that regardless of outcome, participating in these public processes give voice to people's experiences, and while there may be no control over the final outcome or findings of such processes, engaging in the process is the important, validating step (Herman, 1992). We look at this issue again in Chapter 8.

Other non-legal forms of ceremonies and rituals of all kinds are also consistent with narrative approaches' emphases on naming publicly the experiences that people have survived. The therapeutic qualities of people coming together to share experiences, to remember collectively and to form a continuing story of what has occurred have been well noted.

In forming a link between our own narratives and those shaped by broader social and collective narratives, narrative practices can include active engagement in social change so that these broader social stories are transformed. This is consistent with the belief that

> changing these stories often involves challenging larger social stories within people's problem-saturated stories about themselves and their lives. All individual stories are social stories. (Brown & Augusta-Scott, 2007, p. xvii)

In this sense, narrative approaches have addressed the fact that trauma is not just about individual memories and difficulties in the aftermath but also about real conditions and realities for people that need to be prevented in the future. It has advocated addressing the social injustices at the core of trauma experiences, seeking collective action and promoting human rights at much broader socio-cultural levels – it is not an individual therapy approach only but a socially transformative one. This is particularly so in relation to gender and violence, for example.

A case scenario

How would you go about working with the Hasan family and the community in narrative ways?

The Hasan family arrived in the United Kingdom after six years of living in a refugee camp. Their four children range in age from 5 to 16. Before they moved to the refugee camp, Mr Hasan had disappeared for three weeks when he was taken by the local militia and tortured, given his political affiliations. When he was released, he returned home to his family. Then, they all fled, reaching the refugee camp after weeks of travel. Life there was not easy, with the girls living under constant threat of rape and food shortages leading to massive tensions in the camp. Now settled, the children are going to school. Settling into their new community is proving difficult for all of them. Neither do they speak to each other about their experiences nor to anyone outside their family. Child protection services received a notification of protective concerns, but the case was closed. Recently, though, Mrs Hasan has connected with a local women's group from her community. She is hearing stories very similar to her own and feels that it is important to share them broadly. When a community day is announced, where storying activities will be offered, she is keen for all of her family to come along.

Critically reflecting on narrative approaches

The strength of narrative approaches lies in the fact that they prioritise the subjective dimensions of a person's distress and seek to find the causes to this distress in the narratives that are formed between the person and their social world. That is, to reiterate, the person is not the problem. The problem is the problem, and so new narratives are sought that establish this distance between problematic self-narratives and broader socio-cultural narratives. Recovery from trauma is in the restoration of meaning and narrative identity. The social and cultural context is as much a part of the problem as the individual and, similarly, as much a part of the solutions.

One of the questions raised within and outside narrative approaches is that of 'truth telling' – whether it is solely a person's individual subjective narrative that matters and/or is there an objective, and perhaps different, 'truth'? How do people's accounts that may differ of a shared traumatic experience come to form a coherent narrative? Behind this questioning sit major philosophical beliefs relating to the nature of subjectivity and self, of relativism and reality in our daily contexts. This is not just an important philosophical discussion. After many traumas, legal and compensatory processes can occur, where the veracity of people's accounts is challenged. Very heated debates rage within the literature regarding the nature of the 'truth' (Crossley, 2003; Atkinson, 2009; Frank, 2010).

Perhaps not surprisingly, given the emphases of narrative practice, research has not established an extensive evidence base for therapeutic outcomes. Randomised control trials cannot be implemented in the same way when therapeutic interventions are not emerging from guidelines and standardised treatment protocols. In fact, narrative practitioners have resisted empirical ways of valuing outcomes – the value of the work is understood through subjective and qualitative evaluations. Narrative approaches are considered more of an art of human engagement and the release of suffering, rather than a science of intervention and symptom control. Thus, they do not fit, nor should they, within the context of medicalised approaches to trauma treatment. Indeed, narrative approaches have been situated outside many of the mainstream contexts of practice, providing important political critique to many social issues. Yet, they are seen by many within the mainstream contexts of practice to be integral to interventions such as cognitive behavioural therapy and integral to promoting subjective well-being and social change. Creatively establishing an evidence base that is consistent with the beliefs of the practice is an immediate challenge and opportunity.

Conclusion

Whereas the PTSD and neurobiological approaches of earlier chapters emphasise the scientific and objective aspects of people's trauma reactions, narrative approaches emphasise the qualitative and subjective aspects. Narrative approaches value the deeply personal aspects of human suffering and survival and seek to find solutions in the strengths of individuals and in wider communities of recovery. Using a justice focus in much of the work, narrative approaches are therefore deeply respectful of human predicaments – how people come to experience the oppression of their circumstances, including perpetrators, and how transformative listening and externalising problems can be. They provide culturally respectful and sensitive approaches to practice in the aftermath of trauma.

7

Social-Ecological Approaches: Rebuilding and Sustaining Systems

Introduction

In this chapter, we look at social-ecological understandings of trauma, resilience and recovery. We look at how these system approaches can help us understand individual-level coping and adaptation through a focus on the interface between people and their social and environmental contexts. We look at how resilience is conceptualised and then at how the impacts of trauma are understood, at both individual and community levels, before focusing on the implications for practice. Social-ecological understandings of resilience relevant to this discussion have emerged most prominently from two quite distinctive fields of practice – from child and family welfare and from disaster response and recovery work. In this chapter, disaster experiences form the main focus, given that they illuminate the systems-level thinking that is necessary. However, these ideas are just as applicable in many other trauma circumstances.

Social-ecological understandings of resilience

Social-ecological approaches differ from the other approaches we have considered in two distinctive ways. Firstly, they shift our focus to a systems level of thinking. In one sense, all of the approaches that we have considered draw implicitly and often extensively on systems thinking. However, the systems-level conceptualisation of social-ecological approaches draws from even wider disciplinary bases than those we have looked at so far. These bases include community development theories, from social geography, economics, development, urban planning and family therapy theories as well as the many psychologically derived approaches we have considered so far. Social-ecological approaches place the interaction of systems at the centre of their focus and, in doing so, decentre the attention on individuals. These systems can include family or household, extended family, friends, school, workplace, hospital and/or education systems, to name just a few. Secondly, they are oriented more towards understanding processes of resilience and the promotion of recovery than specifying the negative impacts of trauma.

In essence, social-ecological approaches seek to understand the resources and processes that influence the adaptation of people and their environments (Bronfenbrenner, 1979; Adger, 2000; Adger et al., 2005). Three core aspects of these approaches are as follows: (1) people and their environments are systems in constant interaction; (2) theoretical approaches at this level attempt to capture the adaptive and maladaptive processes and outcomes occurring at both individual and family or community levels; (3) particular capacities, resources and processes can facilitate resilience.

People and their environments are systems in constant interaction

Social-ecological approaches draw attention to the many social and relational aspects of our well-being (Bronfenbrenner, 1979), seen as systems that are constantly in interaction. Family therapist Froma Walsh (2006, p. 12), for example, highlights that

> systems theory expands our view of individual adaptation as embedded in broader transactional processes in family and social context. It attends to the mutuality of influences over time.

Systems theorists propose that we exist within many complex adaptive systems, which are in turn influenced 'in simple and complex ways at specific scales, but they are also subject to external processes or perturbations' (Gunderson, 2010, p. 2). Bringing a systems perspective to individuals, families and/or communities and the ecosystems in which we live means that we can think of these systems as 'being comprised of structures and processes at specific spatial-temporal scale ranges (Gunderson, 2010, p. 1). Our service systems, be they statutory child protection systems, hospitals or counselling services, should also be included in this thinking.

In terms of the structure of these systems, some of the dimensions we can look at are boundaries, diversity, resources and history. For example, in thinking about a geographic community or township that is affected by a disaster, there may be a strong sense of identity built up over many years by many residents, who have shared many life experiences and come to see themselves as a tight-knit community. This may mean that they are quite a closed system to newcomers to that community – they have a distinctive boundary regarding who is an insider and who is an outsider. The open or closed nature of a system is an important dimension to assess. If there is little diversity within a system that is closed, for example, there can be strength in commonality. However, trauma can present a need for diversity, and thus such a closed, homogenous system may be less able to be adaptive under such circumstances. In child protection work, a family that is closed to support from outsiders, perhaps because of interventions in the past, may be extremely challenging to engage with unless this history and boundary is fully appreciated.

A network analysis of the types of links can highlight the extent to which these links promote or inhibit resilience:

> networks composed of 'bridging' links to a diverse web of resources strengthen a community's ability to adapt to change, but networks composed of only local 'bonding' links, which impose constraining social norms and foster group homophily, can reduce resilience. (Newman & Dale, 2005, p. 1)

In terms of their processes, we can analyse a system's roles, function and their capacity for change. How resourced is a system such as a family or community by way of roles – of leadership, of active participants in decision-making, for example? How do they see their roles and functions, and do these perceptions differ from those who are intervening? These roles and functions in turn lead to an overall identity emerging – which for some families and communities may be relatively stable and for others rapidly changing. Does a family or community see itself as functioning well, as able to cope with challenges?

Adaptation as a constant process

Social-ecological approaches understand processes of adaptation as constant, whether the system is at individual, family and/or community levels. This is one of the key differences in explanatory focus. Outside of high-stress or trauma contexts, it is argued that we make adjustments to accommodate relatively minor changes, but we learn to function within the various systems of which we are a part. For example, many age-related transitions within a family, such as a child moving from kindergarten to school, are accommodated after a period of adjustment. When trauma occurs, more complex processes of adaptation are required to restore functioning and a sense of equilibrium (Germain & Bloom, 1999). One of the core tenets of crisis theory is that systems, faced with unpredictability, are more amenable to finding new ways of functioning in order to restore a sense of equilibrium. This means that individuals or families can be more open to doing things differently because there is recognition that existing ways will not work under the circumstances. This malleability or flexibility of systems serves an important survival function.

There are different views about this process of adaptation, with some arguing that, 'Adapted functioning is not necessarily superior in level or character or effectiveness to pre-event functioning: it is simply different' (Norris et al., 2008, p. 132). Others, however, do argue that adaptation is about growth or better outcomes, as reflected in the following statement about community resilience following disasters:

> Achieving resilience in a disaster context means the ability to survive future natural disasters, with minimum loss of life and property, as well as the ability to create a greater understanding of place among residents, a stronger, more diverse economy; and a more economically integrated and diverse population. (Berke & Campanella, 2006, pp. 192–193)

In this sense, resilience is also seen as tapping into a future focus, which becomes an important aspect of preparedness to prevent damage from future disasters. This resonates with the idea of resilience as 'bouncing forward', referred to in Chapter 1.

Resilience is therefore seen as the adaptive capacity of a system – be that a family, a community, an institution or community. Thus, resilience is not an outcome in and of itself but a process, leading to adapted outcomes. Outcomes are typically thought of in terms of wellness (physical and mental) at individual and community levels (Norris et al., 2008) or re-establishing a sense of equilibrium. Others would also see family well-being as an important outcome (Walsh, 2006; Ungar, 2010).

Adapted function can be seen to be present when a system (be that a family, a school, a community) can remain responsive to demands and stressors placed upon them, while still retaining a sense of identity, wellness, purpose and structure. Thus the attributes and resources within systems become critical to understand. Bringing wider systems into the equation of understanding and assessment means that a focus is on what resources and capacities (formal and informal) are available at these broader levels, as well as at the individual level. For example, for refugees settling in a new country, the availability or absence of family or social networks, has a strong link with health and mental health outcomes.

Attributes and resources in resilient systems

Resilience attributes or properties

There are many ways of theorising resilience at systems rather than personal levels, as the literature highlights. These are relatively new conceptualisations, with an emerging rather than well-established evidence base as to their ability to be operationalised and evaluated. However, they have provided useful conceptualisations for many interventions as we see later in the chapter.

Four key properties of systems have been identified as critical determinants of resilience (Bruneau et al., 2003): robustness, redundancy, resourcefulness and rapidity. Robustness is seen as the 'strength, or the ability of elements, systems, and other units of analysis to withstand a given level of stress or demand without suffering degradation or loss of function' (Bruneau et al., 2003, p. 737). Alongside this, redundancy is described as

the extent to which elements, systems, or other units of analysis exist that are substitutable, i.e., capable of satisfying functional requirements in the event of disruption, degradation, or loss of functionality. (Bruneau et al., 2003, p. 737)

The third property is the property of resourcefulness, primarily the

capacity to identify problems, establish priorities, and mobilize resources when conditions exist that threaten to disrupt some element, system, or other unit of analysis. (Bruneau et al., 2003, p. 737)

And the fourth property is that of rapidity: 'the capacity to meet priorities and achieve goals in a timely manner in order to contain losses and avoid future disruption' (Bruneau et al., 2003, p. 738). Together, these properties combine to promote resilience within a system.

Others have since refined these into three core attributes of resources rather than properties of systems. The rationale for refining them to three core attributes is that to talk about the resourcefulness of resources was redundant and is able to be encapsulated in the context of rapidity (Norris et al., 2008, p. 134). These are not dissimilar from the qualities of 'resistance' (robustness), recovery (rapidity) and creativity outlined by Boon et al. (2012, p. 387). The property of creativity in relation to community resilience, however, picks up on a key point of theoretical contention, whether resilience is about a higher level of functioning or a return to pre-trauma levels of functioning as described earlier. Boon et al. (2012, p. 387) define this process as the ability of a social system to maintain a constant process of creating and recreating, so that the community not only responds to adversity, but in doing so, reaches a higher level of functioning.

In relation to community resilience, the outcome of adaptedness is seen to be possible when the three core adaptive capacities (robustness, redundancy, rapidity) in turn influence the mobilisation of these sets of networked resources (Norris et al., 2008, p. 136): economic development, social capital, information and communication and community competence. These networked resources exist at both community levels and that of families or households, and we look at these community-level resilience resources in more detail later in this chapter.

Relatively neglected in much of the disaster literature is the family or household system, as a system of both resilience and vulnerability. Yet, it is one of the primary systems of recovery, arguably more important on a daily basis than community-level systems. The aim of studying family resilience has been to

> identify and fortify key interactional processes that enable families to withstand and rebound from disruptive life challenges. A resilience lens shifts perspective from viewing distressed families as damaged to seeing them as challenged, affirming their potential for repair and growth. (Walsh, 2006, pp. 3–4)

Three key interactional processes have been commonly identified that enable this rebounding capacity – processes relating to a family's belief systems (such as the meaning they make), organisational patterns (such as their flexibility or connectedness) and communication processes (Walsh, 2006, p. 26).

The focus within these system attributes is on how a family can achieve functional states in the everyday. These are common processes that are seen in families that cope well, according to Ungar (2010, p. 422).

Sets of networked resources

Social-ecological approaches see the availability and accessibility of sets of networked resources within and across systems as core to resilience (Ungar, 2010). These sets of networked resources support the overall 'wealth' of the system and provide a critical scaffolding effect around each of us in our lives (Gilligan, 2004, p. 95), in relation to ourselves as individuals, as members of families or households and/or as community members. The absence of such resources, as we see in this chapter, leads to vulnerability.

Conservation of resources (COR) theory, proposed by Hobfoll and colleagues (Hobfoll, 2001; Hobfoll et al., 2000), sets out four resource 'caravans' – personal, condition, energy and object resources – that are regarded as essential for our well-being. Examples of these resources are included in Box 7.1:

Box 7.1   Examples of Hobfoll's four resource 'caravans'

- Personal resources – for example, our sense of self-efficacy or self-worth, our intellectual capacities, our personality traits
- Condition resources – for example, our social networks, or our environmental conditions in which we live
- Energy resources – for example, the time we have available to commit to something
- Object resources – for example, a house, car or clothing

These provide an important map for some of the key areas of a person's life that may be affected in a trauma context. COR theory proposes that we are motivated to manage our resource availability, maintenance or loss so that we can conserve our resource access. Thus, we seek to protect against resource loss.

These resource categories have been identified in the context of individual trauma and stress experiences. At the community resilience level of analysis, different networks of resources have been identified. For example, Bruneau et al. (2003, p. 738) identify technical, organisational, social and economic resources as being critical domains influencing disaster resilience. Others such as Norris et al. (2008) identify economic development, social capital, information and communication and community competence as the four key networked resources. For this discussion, we focus on these latter four resources.

In referring to the first resource, economic development, reference is made to the 'fairness of risk and vulnerability to hazards, level and diversity of economic resources, and equity of resource distribution' (Norris et al., 2008, p. 136) within a particular community. Chapter 8 draws attention to these issues in particular, and, as we see, they are a critical resource for individuals, families and communities in relation to the impact of trauma. Sherrieb et al. (2010) tested measures for both economic development and the next resource we look at, social capital, and found good validation of these capacities as a broader measure of community resilience.

The second identified resource of social capital is perhaps the most commonly recognised resource for resilience, whereby it can be defined as the

received (enacted) social support, perceived (expected) social support, social embeddedness (informal ties), organizational linkages and cooperation; citizen participation, leadership and roles (formal ties); sense of community; attachment to place. (Norris et al., 2008, p. 136)

Trauma often precipitates major shifts in the social capital dimensions of a person's world post disaster, and thus a social networks lens is critical. From decades of child and family welfare practice and research, the following is now unquestioned:

> It is the provision of resources by the family and the state, not individual changes in the child per se, that most influence whether a child demonstrates resilience or remains vulnerable. (Ungar, 2010, p. 424)

Similarly, the literature supports the importance of social supports and resources, both formal and informal, as fundamental to adult resilience.

The third group of resources is that of information and communication, which is described as referring to the 'narratives; responsible media; skills and infrastructure; trusted sources of information' (Norris et al., 2008, p. 136). The ideas explored in Chapter 6 link very strongly with this area of resource capacity. Our social systems develop an identity and history, as well as being fluid and evolving. Narratives and core beliefs about systems emerge over time and are reinforced by external narratives – adaptation or maladaptation, language of victimhood or survivorship, our particular cultural contexts. The importance of being in control of information in order to make decisions and to re-establish security is well highlighted in all the trauma literature. However, for families and communities in a trauma context, where more systems of communication are activated, coordination and control become critical issues.

The fourth resource is that of community competence seen to be reflected in 'community action; critical reflection and problem solving skills; flexibility and creativity; collective efficacy, empowerment; and political partnerships' (Norris et al., 2008, p. 136). We revisit these four resource domains later in the chapter.

Before we do that, it is noteworthy that what is understated within these resource conceptualisations is the ecological resource dimension. This dimension refers to the physical environments in which people live, which are intimately connected with the issues outlined above and are profoundly affected in disaster contexts (Alston, 2013). This resource can be thought about in terms of the actual resources of shelter and physical safety for people or as a means of production, through to the aesthetics of place, attachment to place through familiarity. This resource critically influences health and well-being. This extends thinking beyond just our social systems – the links between our attachment to and our functioning in the physicality of place to well-being are often underestimated. As noted in a study of the impact of bushfires in Canada, 'Social relationships are both temporally and spatially located' (Cox & Perry, 2011, p. 396). This study noted

> the importance of the psychology of place to community and individual resilience when place is disrupted – not only through displacement, but as a result of the myriad economic, material and symbolic losses and changes associated with disaster events. (Cox & Perry, 2011, p. 395)

All of these resources create the pre-existing conditions of disaster and contribute to their aftermath. There is increasing recognition that many disasters occur in vulnerable contexts, geographically and socially, economically, with people forced to live in environments such as low coastal areas or fire-prone areas, given land prices, employment opportunities, pre-existing factors or conditions relating to lack of control, influence and resources.

By understanding a person's experiences in this way, a focus is placed primarily on resources and capacities at multiple levels within a social and environmental system – be that at family, local or wider community and national levels – rather than at the resources and capacities alone of individuals. A critical link with these attributes and resources, however, is how people mobilise and negotiate them in order to use them effectively. Thus, there is a vital individual motivational dimension, with wider family and community systems of resilience relying on the embedded resilience of individuals; in this sense, how people are able and supported to be 'navigators and negotiators' of these resources is key (Ungar, 2010). Thus, the following can be concluded:

> The better individuals and families are at navigating to what they need (and therapists at satisfying these needs), the more likely people are to experience themselves as coping well in stressful environments. (Ungar, 2010, p. 423)

The motivational aspect can be seen in understanding the appraisal processes therefore as the critical link:

> resources, including opportunities present in a person's environment, are important because they aid people in actualising their goals. To be useful, these opportunities must be recognised as such and taken advantage of. A lack of such resources has the opposite consequence by defeating the attainment of one's goals. (Lazarus, 2001, p. 383)

The profoundly interactive element of individuals and their social systems is highlighted. In Table 7.1, these individual-, family- and community-level resilience resources are summarised, showing some of the points of overlap and interaction.

Table 7.1 A comparison of individual-, family- and community-level resilience resources

Individual-level resilience resources	Family-level resilience resources	Community-level resilience resources
Condition resources: for example, our social networks, or our environmental conditions in which we live Object resources: for example, a house, car and clothing	Organisational patterns: 'flexibility, connectedness, social and economic resources'	Economic: 'fairness of risk and vulnerability to hazards, level and diversity of economic resources, and equity of resource distribution'
Personal resources: for example, our sense of self-efficacy or self-worth, our intellectual capacities, a sense of hope and optimism Condition resources: for example, our social networks, or our environmental conditions in which we live	Organisational patterns: 'flexibility, connectedness, social and economic resources'	Social capital: received (enacted) social support, perceived (expected) social support, social embeddedness (informal ties), organisational linkages and cooperation; citizen participation, leadership and roles (formal ties); sense of community; attachment to place
Condition resources: for example, our social networks, or our environmental conditions in which we live Personal resources: for example, our sense of self-efficacy or self-worth, our intellectual capacities, a sense of hope and optimism	Organisational patterns: 'flexibility, connectedness, social and economic resources' Communication processes: 'clarity, open emotional expression, and collaborative problem solving'	Information and communication: described as referring to the 'narratives; responsible media; skills and infrastructure; trusted sources of information'

Table 7.1   (Continued)

Individual-level resilience resources	Family-level resilience resources	Community-level resilience resources
Energy resources: for example, the time we have available to commit to something Personal resources: for example, our sense of self-efficacy or self-worth, our intellectual capacities, a sense of hope and optimism	Family belief systems: 'making meaning of adversity, positive outlook, transcendence and spirituality'	Community competence: reflected in 'community action; critical reflection and problem solving skills; flexibility and creativity; collective efficacy, empowerment; and political partnerships'

Social-ecological understandings of trauma

Conceptualising trauma exposures

In focusing more specifically on disasters in this chapter, as distinct from the more individualistic types of trauma exposure, this definition highlights the different nature of trauma exposure:

> A disaster is a sudden, calamitous event that seriously disrupts the functioning of a community or society and causes human, material, and economic or environmental losses that exceed the community's or society's ability to cope using its own resources (from http://www.ifrc.org/en/what-we-do/disaster-management/about-disasters/what-is-a-disaster/)

You can hear the centrality of systems thinking, in that resource loss within human systems is seen as core to the definition. Disaster is also defined as

> a situation or event which overwhelms local capacity, necessitating a request to a national or international level for external assistance; an unforeseen and often sudden event that causes great damage, destruction and human suffering. (Guha-Sapir et al., 2011, p. 7)

Traumatic events in disaster situations are compounded, given the exposure to another whole level of system chaos, creating secondary stressors and losses, at least, if not secondary traumas.

It becomes possible to appreciate that not only are individuals and their systems of relationships traumatised in disasters, but also 'Whole communities can be traumatised'. As Burstow (2003, p. 1297) explains, 'In making this claim, community theorists are not simply meaning that all people within the community are traumatized but that the community as an integral whole is traumatized'.

By their very nature, disasters typically disrupt social and ecological systems. The system, whether new or pre-existing, is in a state of shock or surprise (Holling, 2001; Folke, 2006), even if there has been some sense of forewarning. Systems will be in a state of attempting to restore functioning and to maintain identity (Folke et al., 2010).

Sometimes the scale of damage is so vast that social and/or ecological systems are not just disrupted but also destroyed. When this occurs, the systems are unrecognisable and unable to be restored. The 'structures, processes and identity of a community' (Gunderson, 2010, p. 3) are unable to be re-established into anything recognisable of the former state. Some communities experience so much change post disaster – with people dying or relocating that the concept of transilience, introduced in Chapter 1, may be more accurate a description – that identity is changed as a result of the disaster experience – so while there may be elements of a former community, its continuity has so fundamentally changed that speaking of it 'bouncing back' to a former state is less possible than resilience at an individual level.

With individual traumas, typically there is an ability to return to some sense of the familiar. After a car accident or assault, a survivor can return home to an environment that is physically, relationally familiar and often with a relatively similar routine. The structures and familiarities of the systems in which a person lives continue relatively undisrupted – it is the individual at the core who is changed. With disasters, typically the home base is completely or partially destroyed. The restorative routines and familiarities cannot be evoked to assist with the restoration. These stabilising factors are no longer accessible. At this level, attachment to people and place are profoundly disrupted, which often leads to disruption of all layers of experience – the loss of the familiar. People are directly affected by their own traumatic exposures and/or vicarious ones as well as the entity of their social and physical environments being disrupted.

Thus, trauma's capacity to overwhelm functioning is occurring at multiple levels. Whereas the approaches we have looked at to date imply relatively stable outer world structures and relationships, here the disruption and overwhelming nature of the trauma are multidimensional and profound. It is more conceptually challenging to understand the processes of impact and of recovery, given the scale of impact simultaneously on individuals, families and communities.

Traumatic impacts

Drawing on the conceptualisation of resources outlined earlier in this chapter, the impact of the trauma of disasters can be mapped accordingly across the economic-, social-, informational- and community-level resources available to individuals, families and their communities. The multiplicity of effects is profound. From a systems perspective:

> The capacity to deal with the types of uncertainties and surprises will require novel approaches, creative combinations of strategies, and the ability to adapt to a changing environment. (Gunderson, 2010, p. 7)

We now consider some of the ways in which these approaches and strategies, enabled by resources, have been understood.

Economic

The economic impact of disasters is typically vast for households, communities and governments. Some estimates suggest that it takes on average 11 years for regions to recover economically from fires and floods. The significance and strain of financial hardship at all social levels is often underestimated and overlooked (Hildreth, 2009). Interventions that focus on these types of ongoing stressors have been called for, with some claiming that there is more need to go beyond trauma-focused to psychosocial interventions to address well-being from more of a daily stressors perspective (Miller & Rasmussen, 2010). Studies consistently show that economic stressors are associated with poor mental health outcomes from disasters (Bryant et al., 2014).

Social capital

By virtue of disasters, pre-existing social capital resources inevitably change. This may be because within family and community systems, people have died, have been dislocated or have chosen to relocate. Some people are outside of the perceived social networks of the disaster, with many disaster-impacted people (e.g., bereaved relatives) not living in the geographic region of the disaster. The conceptualisation of the social system as geographic only is often problematic in terms of what the implications are for accessing social capital. In the case of some groups of people perceived to be a community, it may be forcing it to function for the first time as a community – a new system forms, with new social capital resources. Unlike the isolation that many survivors of individual traumas often face, survivors of disasters can find themselves overwhelmed with new social networks that require navigation and negotiation, particularly in relation to the formal response and recovery supports that are provided. People are often relying on external agencies to intervene and manage the actual incident either as occurring or in the initial aftermath.

Social support has been consistently identified in studies as a common and essential resilience resource (Rodriguez et al., 2013). The received and perceived social support available to people have been found to be critical influences in well-being post disaster (Hawkins & Maurer, 2011; Brewin et al., 2000). This support can be provided through both formal and informal systems. For example, after the Canberra bushfires in 2003, street barbecues and parties, as well as arts and environmental activities, were reported to be extremely effective ways of coming together (Winkworth et al., 2009).

However, social capital can be perceived to be damaged or destroyed in disaster situations. People frequently report disturbances to their prior social capital as a result of trauma experiences. The experience of increased community closeness, for example, was examined by Erikson (1976) in his follow-up of the Buffalo Creek community after a flood disaster that saw 125 people killed and 4,000 people relocated. He found a sense of community and social capital to be non-existent, challenging the notion that communities are often brought closer together through crisis. This conclusion has since been challenged, with subsequent research highlighting the ways in which various aspects of the community were not so negatively impacted (Schwartz-Barcott, 2008) and were able to engage in restorative processes. Such developments highlight the challenge of who is assessing the social capital and restoration processes, as well as when in time this is being done. Social systems are not static entities.

One of the continuing challenges in disaster responses is the degree to which assertive outreach psychosocial services should be provided as a new form of social capital. Studies continually reflect ambivalence about service use and the identification of personal need (McFarlane & Williams, 2012). For example:

> Experiences in Australia have repeatedly indicated that 'labeled' mental health services established in disaster zones are not accessed by the community: Rather, people shun them and prefer to use opportunities to talk over their experiences in settings that are not advertised as formal mental health services. (Rowlands, 2013, p. 23)

The challenge remains in these interventions in reaching the right people needing support in the right way. Consistent with the research we have looked at in previous chapters, most people make good recoveries from disasters in terms of their mental health outcomes. In disaster situations, help seeking and screening are understood very differently from the ways in which responding to individual traumas are.

Information and communication

Studies have highlighted the critical role of effective information flows and communication processes during and after disasters (see Muller, 2011). This information flow and transparency is at all levels – government, emergency services, community and family members.

With people often already perceiving themselves to have lost control as a result of a disaster, communication failures can compound a sense of disempowerment, anger and frustration. The media play a critical role in managing this information flow, and survivors often have to manage the media for the first time in their lives (Du Plooy et al., 2014). Building a collective narrative, whether in the context of families, communities and nations, begins during the disaster and influences the narratives of risk and resilience that evolve.

Community competence

Restoring a sense of family or community competence post trauma varies enormously. Studies suggest that the key to restoration is in promoting the sense of empowerment and efficacy of these systems (Winkworth et al., 2009). Some studies have described the overwhelming frustration that survivors have experienced in feeling taken over by these new systems of interventions (Crumpton-Cook, 1996). Subsidiarity principles, where decision-making is devolved to the lowest level possible within a system, when operationalised have shown good outcomes. This is inherently challenging within disaster situations, when a military-style response is typically adopted and required, and a social hierarchy is established, which can mitigate against such subsidiarity principles. Thus, rather than seeing the community as having the expertise necessary for managing its recovery, community-led recovery can be quashed. This has been shown to lead to experiences of secondary traumatisation due to the loss of autonomy and control. Some have gone as far as suggesting in instances of forced relocation there is evidence to suggest these processes can have more impact than the trauma itself. As examined in earlier chapters, themes of self-determination and autonomy remain key to resilience processes and outcomes.

Implications for practice

The implications for practice are many and address work with people as individuals, families and communities. As the focus of this book is primarily on individual trauma experiences and therapeutic interventions, the focus of this section is on how these social-ecological approaches inform practice that maintains a systemic focus. It is beyond the scope of this book to look at community level in detail, although we will look at some implications briefly as they are not dissimilar.

In many contexts, a range of psychosocial interventions post disaster are implemented (Rowlands, 2013), including case management, psychological first aid and longer-term, trauma-focused therapeutic work. Throughout this discussion, we look at interventions in terms of thinking systemically, rapidly engaging in a resourcing relationship, mobilising resources and capacities at individual, family and community levels and engaging in rebuilding, both emotional and practical.

Maintaining a systems focus of thinking

Within social-ecological approaches, preceding any intervention is a systems way of thinking:

> a social ecological understanding of resilience is congruent with systemic approaches to therapy that emphasize the need to change social interactions, environmental structures, and the availability of health resources (like access to health care, safety, education, and social support) rather than just changing individuals to adapt to the threats posed to them. (Ungar, 2010, p. 423)

This builds a strong focus into any interventions of a spectrum of responses – from prevention through to postvention responses:

> spanning both pre-event measures that seek to prevent hazard-related damage and losses and post-event strategies designed to cope with and minimize disaster impacts. (Bruneau et al., 2003, p. 735)

Thinking systemically involves thinking about the cycles of prevention, preparation, response and recovery involved in trauma experiences. It also involves thinking about the interactive nature of responses at individual, family, community and often state or national levels and any other systems that are impacted upon (Jackson et al., 2009, p. 203). It also involves thinking about the systems of responders that are involved, including government and non-government, across all these levels of the experiences of disaster (see, for example, Rowlands, 2013, p. 22, for an overview of Australian systems).

Rapidly engaging in a resourcing relationship

The therapeutic relationship at the individual and community level in these disaster contexts is typically seen as providing a new short-term resource in a system, with the intention of exiting after building capacity and brokering links back into the existing systems or newly emergent ones.

The five principles of mass trauma intervention (Hobfoll et al., 2007), introduced in Chapter 1, provide a map for the resourcing that is often needed for the restoration of functioning of individuals, families and communities. Planning and promoting active interventions in these five areas is strongly supported by the available evidence, as is incorporating these areas within the context of a therapeutic relationship:

- Promoting a sense of safety: the restoration of a sense of safety is seen as encompassing a personal level of physical and psychological safety, through to social systems levels.

- Promoting calming: reducing the emotionality of an initial post-trauma state is critical through strategies such as grounding and physical relaxation techniques.

- Promoting a sense of self and community efficacy: restoring a sense of control and efficacy is critical, however, and is clearly dependent upon the availability of resources in wider social networks. This is discussed more fully in Chapter 8.

- Promoting connectedness: however local the connections may be, linking with others in supportive ways and the restoration of social networks are well-established areas of early and important resourcing for people.

- Instilling hope: research affirms the key role that hope and optimism play in the aftermath of disasters. This is a critical component of any therapeutic relationship also, helping to establish a new sense of coherence in particular.

Consistent with the psychosocial first aid interventions outlined in Chapter 4, the focus is on supporting a person and their social systems in the restoration of functioning, balancing people's need for dependence, independence and interdependence (Trevithick, 2012; Du Plooy et al., 2014).

Mobilising resources and capacity at individual, family and community levels

If the argument is that systems have been damaged in structure and function as a result of disasters, restoring these systems through material and psychological resource provision is critical. This ensures that the right scaffolding is in place to support the systems or to prevent them from collapsing. The responsiveness of governments (and international aid) becomes a critical determinant of the availability of such resources, as does non-government organisation involvement. Practitioners have a key role in lobbying and liaising to ensure that individual, family and community systems are adequately resourced.

At local levels of practice, case management has proven to be an effective intervention in a number of major disasters in recent years. Following Hurricane Katrina in the United States, for example, case management was introduced and found to be problematic to implement, given resource difficulties and the challenges of individualising services to people with specific needs (Acosta et al., 2010). In Australia, following the Victorian bushfires in 2009, case management was implemented and found to be very well received by participants in the programme (Urbis Social Planning and Social Research, n.d.).

In the early stages of response and recovery, the resources systems require are often those at the most basic level of survival – shelter, food, health services and information. This affirms the following:

> In any such psychological intervention, it should not be underestimated that people's agitation and anxiety are due to real concerns, and actions that help them directly solve these concerns are the best antidote for the vast majority. (Hobfoll et al., 2007, pp. 292–293)

To be effective in resourcing disaster-impacted systems, a strong community-led focus is warranted, along with a strong social equity focus. In relation to the social equity focus, Breckenridge and James (2012, p. 246) note that problems of racism and socio-economic class inequalities emerge in the wake of disasters. They highlight research that showed within the American context of hurricanes Katrina and Rita that there was an 'utter disregard for black life'. Imposing culturally and structurally inappropriate interventions can lead to secondary traumatic stress and harm being done, as Chapter 8 highlights. Sensitive attention to inequality arising as a result of gender is also warranted:

> A gender perspective is required to ensure that men's and women's specific needs, vulnerabilities and capacities (set in the broader context of class, ethnicity, race and religion) are recognized and addressed (IFRC&RC, n.d.)

Rebuilding

The literature is rife with one key implication for the rebuilding processes of communities post disaster – they must be primarily community-led processes (Norris et al., 2008). A focus on rebuilding also enables a new focus on planning and building strengths and capacities to prevent against future disasters:

> communities must plan, but they must also plan for not having a plan; this means that communities must exercise flexibility and focus on building effective and trusted information and communication resources that function in the face of the unknown. (Norris et al., 2008, p. 143)

Having a disaster recovery plan in place and anticipating events has been found to be protective (Berke & Campanella, 2006). This perhaps exemplifies the 'bouncing forward' that Walsh speaks about. There is a natural human tendency to avoid thinking about disaster – within psychodynamic approaches seen as a defence mechanism. By building family and community strengths, we are better able to address future adversities.

A case scenario

How would you go about working with the community and/or community members in social-ecological ways?

A young man, with a prior history of arson and mental health difficulties, set fire to a row of shops and businesses in a small community on a Saturday night. Two families who lived upstairs in these dwellings died as a result of the fires, while many others were able to escape in time. One family included two parents and their three school-aged children. These children were very well-known locally. The whole school community was devastated by their deaths. Many children became extremely upset at the thought that it could have been them or their parents who had died. The other family was an older couple, very well connected in their business, social and religious networks. There was immense community anger about the deaths that had occurred, about the perpetrator's behaviour and about the major destruction to the property and infrastructure. A community meeting was called to address people's concerns.

Critically reflecting on social-ecological approaches

These approaches are arguably less theorised than earlier approaches we considered, in that they are seeking to understand the interaction of many more variables in adopting a community- and/or family-based lens. This means the explanatory mechanisms are more complex and diffuse between levels of interaction – often difficult to establish beyond description of variables, or more typically, explanation remains at only one level of interacting variables – the community level, for example, without accounting for individual processes of motivation and agency within that.

Three key criticisms of the strengths and limitations of social-ecological approaches are that they are largely descriptive rather than prescriptive approaches, they homogenise or conflate some dimensions of experiences and the subsequent interventions can disempower people. Each of these is briefly considered.

The first criticism, which is that social-ecological approaches have little explanatory power, has been an enduring criticism. Social-ecological approaches often incorporate a good map of and description of resources that influence well-being, but little research exists to support the predictive influences of these resources. Given this multiplicity and interactive nature of dimensions, it is extremely challenging to research the outcomes of interventions, for example. In this sense, these approaches are in their infancy in terms of having an evidence base.

The second criticism is that social-ecological approaches, particularly in relation to community resilience, homogenise the uniqueness of individual- and community-level interactions. Assumptions can be made about people by government, emergency or therapeutic services that do not reflect their own self-identification as a community member or the realities of that community.

The third criticism is that social-ecological approaches to disaster can disempower people. There is an extensive commentary in the disaster literature in relation to the disempowerment experienced by trauma survivors as well-intentioned, powerful bodies and people come in as part of the disaster response and take over, diminishing the capacity of people to exercise control and autonomy in their own lives (Crumpton-Cook, 1996). The involuntary nature of becoming part of disaster interventions and becoming a client without a voice has been well noted. Some have gone as far as critiquing the responses as patronising and patriarchal responses of hierarchies of government and emergency management responses. There is an inherent tension in exerting control and re-establishing order and enabling people to be autonomous and self-determining, ensuring survivors have a strong voice.

Conclusion

While social-ecological thinking is typically applied to disasters, it has enormous utility in work with individuals as well, in thinking about the resources and capacities at the interactive level of individuals and their contexts. With its focus on the interaction between our inner and outer worlds, it offers new insights into the conditions that support recovery and growth, as well as understandings as to why efforts at individual levels are thwarted. It requires thinking in much broader ways than the earlier approaches we have considered. While the focus throughout this chapter has been on the mass trauma experiences associated with disasters and communities, many lessons can be learnt for effective ways of thinking and practising with individuals and families as well as in relation to other trauma experiences.

8

Anti-oppressive Approaches: Recognising Rights and Redressing Oppression

Introduction

In this chapter, anti-oppressive ideas are presented, which originate from rights-based, feminist and other politicised approaches to trauma, resilience and recovery. As with earlier chapters, individual experiences of suffering and distress are central concerns and are a focus of therapeutic practice. However, these experiences are understood much more in the context of external events and conditions. In particular, anti-oppressive approaches politicise elements of the social-ecological understandings that we looked at in Chapter 7, and therefore practitioners often seek to address these as much as the individual experiences of suffering and distress.

In this chapter, we explore how anti-oppressive approaches help us to understand individual resilience and trauma responses. The implications for practice are examined, given the inclusion of a focus on the macro-determinants of human experience.

Anti-oppressive approaches to resilience

From an anti-oppressive perspective, as with narrative and social-ecological approaches, resilience and well-being are reflected in the qualities of both a person *and* their context. While other approaches that we have looked at also see this relationship as important, anti-oppressive approaches privilege this interaction far more so. They focus on the social inequalities and oppression that both cause trauma experiences and are the consequences of them. The uses and abuses of power become a central concern.

There are many extremely diverse theories of power based on, for example, the work of Marx (1959), Foucault (see Gordon, 1980), Young (1990), Bourdieu (1999), Butler (2003) and Castells (2011), varying in the extent to which they focus on relational, structural and/or cultural dimensions of power. Some theories see these dimensions of power as embodied and privilege subjective experiences, whereas others have much more economic understandings of power and disempowerment. As a result, and as is very well noted in the literature, there is an 'absence of a consensus on how best to understand the divergent and complex forms that inequality takes today' (Habibis & Walter, 2009, p. xv). These differences are challenging to articulate in the scope of one chapter alone, given the diversity of their theoretical understandings, including rights-based, feminist, philosophical and economic traditions.

The PCS model

Rather than focus at this deeper theoretical level, given this lack of consensus, a useful overarching frame of reference is the PCS model first articulated by Thompson (1993). This model proposes the interaction of personal-, cultural- and structural-level factors, all of which are determinative of the experiences of risk or resilience.

The personal level is concerned with how 'one's thoughts, feelings and actions at an individual level can have a significant bearing on inequality and oppression' (Thompson, 2003, p. 13). The focus here is on individual experiences and uses of power. This level provides insight as to how individual uses and misuses of power may lead to discrimination and prejudice, based on stereotypes. The explanatory mechanisms for why people oppress others are multiple – a large literature exists in relation to economic arguments and the attention to the distribution of scarce and/or limited resources (Marx, 1959; Maru & Farmer, 2012), and other literature addresses people's motivations at much more personal levels of conscious and unconscious levels of ignorance, stereotyping, superiority and/or fearing and hating difference (Thompson, 2006). Some argue that 'most oppression today is systemic and unintentional because it is built into our social institutions and carried out unconsciously in our day-to-day activities' (Mullaly, 2002, p. 41). However, many would argue that in many parts of the world oppression remains personal, intentional and conscious, as well as systemically embedded and unconsciously perpetrated.

While these are sometimes individual constructions, more often than not they arise in the context of cultural and structural relationships. As described in Chapter 1, the cultural level is concerned with 'sets of patterns shared across particular groups' (Thompson, 2003, p. 15). With these patterns often assumed to be the accepted ways of living, both explicitly and implicitly, many experiences of oppression, particularly marginalisation and discrimination, can occur at this cultural level. These socially patterned experiences of gender, ethnicity, religion, sexuality and class all come into consideration at this cultural level, influencing and influenced by the individual and structural levels of our contexts.

The structural level 'comprises the macro-level influences and constraints of the various social, political and economic aspects of the contemporary social order' (Thompson, 2003, p. 17). At this level, many of the individual- and cultural-level beliefs and behaviours become manifested in institutional structure and function and enshrined in economic and political decisions. A country's policies and practices around asylum seekers, for example, reflect the structural level. Mullaly (2002) uses the term 'structural violence' to refer to the violence that can be perpetrated through the flow-on from decisions that are made and the distribution of material resources at this level.

Despite the enormous diversity of thought, at their core, anti-oppressive approaches argue that individual resilience is enabled when we are free from oppression in our social contexts. Typically, this is manifested in us having access to material, social and symbolic resources in our environments and when we are able to experience justice, equality, empowerment and safety, for example. Thus, oppression is 'generally understood as the domination of subordinate groups in society by a powerful (politically, economically, socially and culturally) group' (Mullaly, 2002, p. 27). While groups or people can be dominant, they may not necessarily be oppressive. Therefore, for the purposes of our discussion, a focus on what oppression looks like at the individual level is an important consideration:

> When a person is blocked from opportunities to self-development, is excluded from full participation in society, does not have certain rights that the dominant group takes for granted, or is assigned a second-class citizenship, not because of individual talent, merit or failure, but because of his or her membership in a particular group or category of people. (Mullaly, 2002, p. 28)

Taking into account these sorts of assumptions, resilience therefore can be seen both in our capacity to exercise our rights and in our active resistance when we encounter the abuse of power by others. In this first section, we look at resilience in these two ways, as the mobilisation of rights and resistance. We conclude by looking at resilience as the expression of constructive power and control.

Resilience as the fulfilment of rights

Human rights traditions emerged strongly in the wake of the Second World War. That is, contemporary rights-based practice emerged from the profound traumas and atrocities that had been witnessed in so many parts of the world as a part of this conflict. The establishment of the United Nations (UN) and the Universal Declaration of Human Rights in 1948 were efforts to prevent the recurrence of such traumas (Alexander, 2012). While the UN and the Universal Declaration have been extensively criticised (Ife, 2012; Steel et al., 2009), they have been a cornerstone of ongoing collective peace and security efforts. They outline at a macro level critical trauma prevention strategies.

As stated by the preamble to the Declaration, 'recognition of the inherent dignity and of the equal and inalienable rights of all members of the human family is the foundation of freedom, justice and peace in the world' (United Nations General Assembly, 1948). Article 3 of the Declaration states: 'Everyone has the right to life, liberty and security of person.' At the very least, this declaration can be seen to be an effort to articulate these core rights and, perhaps more importantly, enable governments and the United Nations to attempt to uphold them for all citizens. Along with many other declarations and rights-based approaches more generally, it stands as an attempt by people to articulate the fundamental safety needs and rights of people, how they can be actualised and how they can be protected. These declarations articulate a view of the conditions necessary for optimal human and social well-being. Similar efforts to articulate and protect the rights of specific groups of people are reflected in the UN's Convention on the Elimination of All Forms of Discrimination against Women (CEDAW), the Declaration on the Rights of Indigenous Peoples and the Convention on the Rights of the Child. Given this,

> Putting people before profits and politics has been a powerful idea and is widely seen as a refreshingly positive view of human potential and human progress. (Chandler, 2002, p. 7)

Anti-oppressive approaches uphold the centrality of access to resources such as education, employment, health, religious and social resources. The capacity to be autonomous and self-determining and exert control over our bodies and our personal and social circumstances is strongly linked with physical and mental well-being (Antonovsky, 1998). These resources and capacities become particularly important in the aftermath of trauma as enablers of resilience.

Resilience as resistance

From an anti-oppressive perspective, therefore, resilience can be seen as the capacity to exercise freedom, equality and agency in the face of adversity.

Resilience is a person's ability to engage with ordinary life post trauma in ways that empower them.

Another way in which resilience can be thought of is in terms of the capacity for resistance, the capacity to withstand politically and personally the damage that trauma can inflict. Resistance

> is not just a response to power but a form of power; hence, resistance, like power, is complex. It can be creative and expansive – opening up possibilities and embracing difference, or restrictive and destructive – closing down options and creating more oppression. (Afuape, 2011, p. 36)

For the purposes of this discussion, resistance as resilience is seen as a constructive and creative expression of power. Resistance can be seen in the refusal to be labelled and categorised as a victim, for example, of someone else's actions. Resistance is about the refusal to succumb – a strong political and personal positioning against both the overwhelming causes and the outcomes of trauma (Edkins, 2003).

This is often reflected in a survivor mission as part of the return to ordinary life (Herman, 1992). The new sense of survivor mission is characterised by the need and determination to engage in social action so that structural and cultural change occurs as a result. This exemplifies creative and constructive resistance. We explore this later in the practice implications.

Resilience as power and control

At their core, anti-oppressive approaches attend to the uses and abuses of power inherent in social relationships. While power is often thought of as an inherently negative and destructive force, Foucauldian ideas of power are useful to consider, whereby power

> needs to be considered as a productive network which runs through the whole social body, much more than as a negative instance whose function is repression. (Foucault, 1980, p. 119)

In this way, power is seen as existent in all relationships, with the potential to be positive and productive, negative and repressive (or oppressive) and anywhere in between. Along these lines, it becomes apparent, 'Power is not a possession of particular social groups, but is relational, a strategy which is invested in and transmitted through all social groups' (Lupton, 1997, p. 99).

At the individual level, our ability to exert power in our own lives mediates our access to resources. The extent to which we can access the financial, psychological, political, social and/or physical resources necessary for our well-being, for example, will reflect the extent to which we experience domination and oppression, or liberation and empowerment, within the social hierarchies in which we live. Resilience can be seen as the capacity to exert productive and constructive power within our own relational and structural contexts in order to mobilise our access to resources, be they material or social, for example.

Power is ultimately linked with a sense of control and agency. All the approaches to trauma and resilience that we have considered to date place a sense of control at the core of both trauma and recovery experiences. Anti-oppressive approaches place control centrally also, but it is seen as an aspect of our social and political lives as individuals, families and communities, as much as a psychological construct. Within these approaches, therefore, control, power and rights are understood to be contextually derived and the essential determinants of resilience.

Anti-oppressive approaches to trauma

Given the core emphases outlined above in relation to resilience, it is inevitable that anti-oppressive approaches to trauma focus on both the causal and the consequential aspects of trauma. Anti-oppressive approaches place emphasis on understanding and addressing the inherently unequal and often disempowering circumstances that cause traumatic experiences in the first place, as well as the consequences. This is a significant shift from other approaches, which focus on the consequences primarily, as we now explore.

Conceptualising the causes of trauma

In earlier chapters, the causes of trauma responses were primarily conceptualised as inner world processes – that is, a person's cognitive or emotional experience. In Chapter 4, for example, PTSD was seen as 'a failure of mechanisms involved in recovery and restitution of physiological homeostasis' (Yehuda & LeDoux, 2007, p. 19). Anti-oppressive approaches in many ways also conceptualise the cause of trauma responses as inner world experiences, but a fundamental difference is that these inner world experiences are seen as the internalisation of primarily outer world experiences, not the failure of internal mechanisms. Thus, trauma is both the experience of external oppressions, which in turn manifest as the internal oppressions that trauma imposes. The nature of what is traumatic and why is quite different. This is the case whether we are looking at understanding experiences related to mass trauma – for example, the Holocaust or refugee experiences – or deeply individual experiences of torture or sexual assault.

Critically relevant for our focus on working with individuals who have experienced trauma is the proposal inherent in Thompson's (1993, 2006) PCS model that 'oppression at any level (personal, cultural or structural) is felt eventually by subordinate persons at the individual level' (Mullaly, 2002, p. 56). Research and practice issues at this individual level are the primary focus of this chapter.

Given that there is so much diversity (and conflict) between understandings of oppression, as we look at the causal link with trauma, we will look at only one understanding in this chapter: Young's (1990) 'five faces of oppression'. Alongside Thompson's PCS model, these categories of oppression provide explanations of the abuses of power that underpin many traumatic experiences.

When looking at people's experiences of oppression, Young (1990) identified the need to be more specific rather than talk broadly of oppression. She identified both distributive justice issues – exploitation, marginalisation and powerlessness – and other practices, such as cultural imperialism and violence. Many people face all of the five faces of oppression in their lives, but for some, oppression is experienced in one way primarily.

Exploitation is the first face of oppression. While Young's discussion of oppression as exploitation refers primarily to the social divisions inherent in work structures, exploitation is a profoundly relevant concept in the context of causing trauma. Many traumas occur when people exploit another for their own gain, whether material, psychological, sexual or other. The violations and distress of traumatic experience often relate to the disregard that another person holds in exploiting someone for their own gain. The presence of interpersonal violence and/or violation is consistently identified in research as leading to greater challenges for trauma survivors and to poorer mental health outcomes when compared with trauma experiences that do not have this interpersonal violation aspect inherent in them (see Chapman et al., 2012, for example, and their discussion of the remission of PTSD).

Marginalisation, the second face of oppression, often creates the conditions of vulnerability that lead to trauma. Those experiencing poverty, for example, are often forced to live in vulnerable geographic and social locations, increasing the likelihood of their exposure to traumatic life events such as natural disasters. As Young (1990, p. 53) notes, 'Marginalisation is perhaps the most dangerous form of oppression. A whole category of people is expelled from useful participation in social life.'

Often very much linked with marginalisation is powerlessness, the third face of oppression that perhaps creates the most profound vulnerability to trauma exposures. It consists of inhibitions in the development of one's capacities, a lack of decision-making power in one's working life, and exposure to disrespectful treatment because of the status one occupies. (Mullaly, 2002, p. 44)

Powerlessness establishes the pre-conditions for many traumatic experiences, whether as a characteristic of momentary experience such as in an experience of sexual assault or in the pervasive conditions of fleeing war and political persecution. As Herman (1992, p. 33) notes:

> Psychological trauma is an affliction of the powerless. At the moment of trauma, the victim is rendered helpless by overwhelming force... Traumatic events overwhelm the ordinary systems of care that give people a sense of control, connection and meaning.

These understandings help place far greater attention on the socio-cultural dimensions of people's experiences, that is, how our identities by way of gender, ethnicity or class, for example, and our subsequent experiences in the social hierarchy translate into our vulnerabilities. They bring to the fore the injustices that people experience in everyday life – the realities of people's circumstances and indignities that trauma inflicts on people, the social inequalities that create trauma in the first place – the widespread gender inequalities that lead to violence against women, the economic inequalities that lead to people having to live in unsafe places, which predispose them to other threats and risks. This understanding of powerlessness is not only in relation to the violations of rights that increase people's vulnerability to trauma exposures in the first place. It is in relation to how people are responded to and supported in the aftermath.

Another important aspect of an analysis of power and powerlessness that comes into focus within anti-oppressive approaches is the relative status privileges of professionals. Anti-oppressive thinking reverses the gaze from focusing on clients of services to the professions and seeks to understand disciplinary power. This is extremely appropriate in the field of trauma studies and practice, which has been noted for its internal politics and tensions:

> The central strategies of disciplinary power are observation, examination, measurement and the comparison of individuals against an established norm, bringing them into a field of visibility. It is exercised not primarily through direct coercion or violence... but rather through persuading its subjects that certain ways of behaving and thinking are appropriate for them. (Lupton, 1997, p. 99)

Many have noted the professional power that is vested in psychiatry generally and in the trauma field specifically. This has resulted, and many would argue continues to result, in the capacity to label experiences as illness, for example, as we see later in this chapter with the critique of the PTSD diagnosis and as we considered briefly in Chapter 4.

Power is therefore an inherent force that is noted in the causes of trauma, in the consequences and, as we explore later in this chapter, in the therapeutic relationships arising in the aftermath of trauma.

Mullaly argues that these first three faces of oppression – exploitation, marginalisation and powerlessness – 'all refer to relations of oppression that occur through the social division of work' (Mullaly, 2002, p. 46). While this may be the case in the original conceptualisation of Young's work, they provide useful insights into the conditions of oppression that occur with trauma.

The two other faces of oppression arguably most related to direct experiences of trauma are those of cultural imperialism and violence.

Cultural imperialism refers to the imposition of the dominant group on others:

> This form of oppression comes about when the dominant group universalizes its experience and culture and uses them as the norm. Through a process of ethnocentrism the dominant group, most often without realizing it, projects its experience and culture as representative of all humanity. (Mullaly, 2002, p. 46)

The experiences of indigenous people in colonised countries around the world reflect this process most profoundly. Not only have many experienced the profoundly traumatic experiences of the removal of their children who subsequently experienced both the traumas of separation and often abusive circumstances of their foster homes and care institutions, but they have also experienced intergenerationally the trauma of the loss of culture and identity and the loss of place (Bessarab & Crawford, 2013). Young (1990, p. 59) notes the 'paradoxial oppression' this creates – the culturally dominated group is both 'marked out by stereotypes and at the same time, rendered invisible'. Understanding cultural imperialism as the cause of traumatic responses places all of these understandings at the centre of the cause of trauma. In turn, responses such as anger, mistrust and the internalisation of despair can be heard and acknowledged as responses to pervasive injustices and oppression (Atkinson, 2003).

In this sense, cultural imperialism translates into experiences of violence, the fifth face of oppression, often along with the other experiences of exploitation, marginalisation and powerlessness. As Mullaly (2002, p. 47) notes:

> Almost all oppressed groups suffer systematic violence simply because they are subordinate in the social pecking order. Violence includes not just physical attack,

but harassment, ridicule, and intimidation, all of which serve the purpose of stigmatizing group members.

Placing violence centrally as an experience of oppression highlights the pervasive physical, emotional, social and often ultimately economic damage that trauma reaps. This shift is critical. As Burstow (2005, p. 44) notes with many theoretical approaches: 'Violence is seen as nothing but a preceding event'. Here, it is central as the cause and consequence of trauma. In centralising a focus on violence, due attention is also paid to the violence that is perpetrated through a constant fear of attack, whether it eventuates or not. Thus, the emotional abuse elements of violence are also centralised.

As mentioned in Chapter 1, this is one of the great risks inherent in the new definition of traumatic exposure for a PTSD diagnosis – by only focusing on actual or threatened physical injury or sexual assault, the emotional threats and degradations that are part of a cycle of violence and well established as the cause of traumatic responses may well be overlooked.

Violence is also seen as perpetrated at systems levels, the 'structural violence' mentioned earlier. This concept is critical for understanding that what survivors experience in the processes in the aftermath of traumas can also be violent and traumatic – the legal and social processes, for example (Holman & Silver, 1996), or the sense of violation by the media. This leads to a much broader sense of what is traumatic than, for example, the sense of what is traumatic conveyed in the PTSD diagnosis.

In considering these five faces of oppression, the potential for people to experience multiple oppressions based on their social experiences of gender, age, class or ability, for example, is highlighted. Crenshaw's (1995) introduction of the term 'intersectionality' highlights that people's identities and experiences expose them to multiple risks and traumas in their particular contexts. One of the gaps in many studies is this focus on the intersections of trauma that a person or a community is experiencing. This reduces understandings of trauma as single incidents or issues, for example, rather than seeing them as connected with often much broader, more complex experiences encompassing gender, class and ethnicity.

Conceptualising the consequences of trauma

These experiences of exploitation, marginalisation, powerlessness, cultural imperialism and violence provide a useful framework to understand not only the causes of many traumatic experiences but also trauma responses. Rather than seeing traumatic events as relatively random experiences,

154 Understanding Trauma and Resilience

anti-oppressive approaches see a strong connection between people's contexts and their subsequent vulnerability to traumatic experiences:

> specific traumatic events happen to specific people in specific locations and within specific contexts, and they inevitably involve other human beings. As such, trauma is inherently political. (Burstow, 2003, p. 1306)

The recognition of the inevitable involvement of other people means also that central to the understanding of trauma is that there are in many instances both 'obvious perpetrators and obvious oppressive structures' (Burstow, 2003, p. 1306). This applies to both individual and mass trauma experiences, whereby they are not seen as random environmental events but as predictable events in vulnerable places often affecting the most vulnerable people.

As such, the consequences of trauma are thought about quite differently, in relation to both the labelling of trauma responses and the ways in which they are experienced.

Conceptualising trauma responses

Within anti-oppressive approaches, there are mixed views regarding the diagnostic category of PTSD. Some have been staunch advocates for recognising the impact of trauma at this level of individual experience. For example, feminist activists, along with Vietnam veterans, were instrumental in arguing for the inclusion of PTSD in *DSM III* in 1980, as it was seen to validate the individual effects of trauma, particularly domestic violence (Herman, 1992; Brown, 2004). The diagnosis that seemed to validate the idea that external events could cause inner distress. This was seen as a major shift away from focusing on pathological understandings of women's experiences. This politicising rather than psychologising was a critical step.

Part of the current critique of the PTSD diagnostic category is whether it has achieved this outcome. The unintended consequence of the PTSD diagnosis has been the extent to which recognition has been shifted from specific external events (therefore from social and political understandings of them) to inner world, medicalised and neurobiological responses. Humphreys and Joseph (2004), for example, question whether the social support and active social movements inherent in the original PTSD thinking have been adequately taken up, as per Herman's three stages of recovery.

Other feminist practitioners and researchers have vehemently opposed the diagnosis of PTSD, seeing it as medicalising trauma (Burstow, 2005), or at least critiqued the limiting focus of this approach. Therefore, some call for a total rejection of the PTSD diagnosis, such as feminist author and practitioner, Burstow, who states that the:

Inadvisability of feminist trauma practitioners tying themselves to PTSD or other trauma-related diagnoses is that they cannot facilitate sensitive work, for the diagnoses are not sensitising, nor could they be. (Burstow, 2003, p. 1300)

She then proposes that the category of PTSD 'cannot do justice to the psychological misery of people's lives, never mind the social conditions that give rise to the misery' (Burstow, 2003, p. 1300). The two fundamental assumptions behind the PTSD approach and subsequent cognitive work are that 'the world is essentially benign and safe, and so general trust is appropriate' and that 'People who have been traumatised have a less realistic picture of the world than others' (Burstow, 2003, p. 1298). In the context of many people's lives, where traumatic events are not rare, these assumptions cannot hold, and it is not possible to develop such a 'cloak of invulnerability' (Burstow, 2005, p. 435).

Thus, it is also seen to ignore cultural factors (Tummala-Nara, 2007; Ungar, 2013). As Drozdek and Wilson (2007, p. 9) note:

It also ignores the socio-political-cultural context in which trauma occurs. However, the context is central to how people respond to, comprehend, and recover from trauma.

The cultural criticism of PTSD is that it attends to symptoms that are not considered relevant in so many parts of the world, that it is a Western imposition on ways of thinking about human responses to trauma.

In decentring the PTSD criteria, the individual experience of distress and suffering is not denied and is addressed through the therapeutic interventions we look at later in this chapter; the assumptions about the cause and the consequences of traumatic experience and theorising of these is radically different. As Brown (2004) notes, many of the interventions used in other approaches we have discussed in earlier chapters are still used in feminist therapy, for example. What differs is the political stance of the practitioner, which in turn influences the understanding of trauma experiences and processes of recovery.

As a result of these different understandings of what causes traumatic responses, the manifestation of distress is understood quite differently from the other approaches we have considered. As Afuape (2011, p. 5) notes, the cause of this emotional distress relates to specific types of experiences:

I do not see forms of mental and emotional distress as indications of individual pathology, deficit or disorder, but believe they are manifestations of people's experiences of abuse, oppression and violence.

This provides a much broader definition of distress and its causes. Such understandings underpin a strengths perspective in that it sees these manifestations as efforts to resist the overwhelming impacts of trauma. As Herman (1992, p. 159) notes: 'Trauma robs the victim of a sense of power and control; the guiding principle of recovery is to restore power and control to the survivor.'

It also sees the manifestations of trauma in wider terms, as social suffering and not just individual level suffering:

> Social suffering draws attention to the lived experience of inhabiting social structures of oppression; and the pain that arises from this. (Frost & Hoggett, 2008, p. 441)

Thus, the trauma of dislocation and resettlement for refugees can be understood in terms of PTSD responses (although by virtue of the new definition, many of the traumas that they encounter as part of their dislocation and resettlement may not perceived as capable of causing a PTS response). Within anti-oppressive frameworks, trauma responses can also be seen through the lens of a much wider range of responses that still warrant being perceived as trauma responses.

Broader understandings of the impacts of trauma

Anti-oppressive approaches give attention to a wider range of trauma responses, including changed identities, dehumanisation, silencing and loss. These four key impacts reflect the five faces of oppression described earlier – exploitation, marginalisation, powerlessness, cultural imperialism and violence experiences. While anti-oppressive approaches focus on cultural and structural levels of analysis, it is appreciated that oppression is experienced at individual levels. Given that this is the primary focus of this book, the discussion here relates primarily to this level of individual experience.

The process of the formation of our individual identities is one process that gains significant attention; for this discussion, we focus on trauma identities. As noted in Chapter 6, survivors are confronted post trauma with a trauma identity that is often at odds with pre-trauma identity (although as we're seeing in this chapter, this would not always be the case where people continue to live in traumatic contexts). Identity in this sense 'is the process and product of an individual's interactions with influences in the physical and social worlds' (Mullaly, 2002, p. 59). Through traumatic experiences, new personal and social identities can form.

Anti-oppressive approaches assert that trauma identities are formed through the internalisation of the experiences rather than seeing them as external. An explanation for this process is as follows:

Because the exercise of 'power over others' appears natural and legitimate, the hurt that produces shame and humiliation and the losses that lead to grief become detached from the social relations which generate them. The suffering that then results becomes individualised and internalised – built into subjectivity. (Frost & Hoggett, 2008, p. 442)

This often creates the subsequent sense of alienation and marginalisation from wider social relationships. A sense of self-blame is more tolerable than thinking that a dominant group could be wrong, for example, or that a seemingly trusted caregiver could be violent or exploitative, as we explored in Chapter 3. Thus, beliefs such as 'If only I had done things differently' can inadvertently become the focus of trauma therapy, thinking about this as a faulty cognition rather than addressing the wider social oppression and crime of gendered violence that have generated such a belief, as anti-oppressive approaches emphasise.

Anti-oppressive approaches also highlight that social as well as individual identities form. Many survivors of trauma find themselves labelled for their victim identity only. A status can be imposed by others, which does not accord with the self-identification of the survivor – people are talked about as 'patients', 'clients', 'victims' or 'community members'. The disempowerments can be many.

Along with changed identities, anti-oppressive approaches highlight the dehumanising and depersonalising aspects of trauma and the loss of dignity and respect. In recognising the human capacity to engage in brutal dehumanising behaviour that is beyond just self-interest but is destructive for the sake of it, anti-oppressive approaches highlight the need to restore a sense of dignity and respect, both for self and by others. The dehumanising processes used by perpetrators of trauma create conditions whereby others can become blind and deaf to the suffering experienced; for example, when politicians refer to asylum seekers as 'illegals', this both depersonalises and criminalises them as human beings. This leads to a lack of witnessing and marginalising of their traumatic experiences.

As with the other approaches we have considered, anti-oppressive approaches value the processes of remembering and mourning. There is key recognition of the ways in which both trauma survivors lose their voice, rights and authority and are rendered silent, as well as how societies can silence these voices of trauma:

Silence is profoundly destructive, for it attests to the person's, the family's, the society's, the community's, and the nation's inability to integrate (and constructively respond to) the trauma. (Danieli, 2009, p. 352)

Thus, the tendency to forget and the dangers in doing so are well noted within anti-oppressive approaches. This awareness sits at the core of many interventions, which become social action interventions in particular:

> In the absence of strong political movements for human rights, the active process of bearing witness inevitably gives way to the active process of forgetting. Repression, dissociation and denial are phenomena of social as well as individual consciousness. (Herman, 1992, p. 9)

Part of the continuing history of trauma understandings is this phenomenon of remembering and forgetting at social and collective levels (Rieff, 2011).

By remembering and acknowledging people's experiences of trauma, the losses can also be acknowledged. When people's rights are violated, the losses may include a loss of control, coherence, agency, autonomy, identity, memory and place. These are all issues that anti-oppressive, particularly rights-based, approaches privilege. Trauma is seen as resulting in the loss of voice, control, dignity, autonomy and rights. These losses of experiences are the manifestations of the five faces of oppression.

These losses are not only of a personal nature. They are understood as material losses as well, and the secondary traumas continue to reverberate. Some of these are experienced very profoundly in asylum seeker experiences, for example. The task of proving a 'well-founded fear of persecution', a necessary step for seeking asylum, in the aftermath of fleeing is one many are faced with. Yet:

> Proving that one has suffered and that the suffering was politically motivated are difficult tasks, complicated by cultural differences, bureaucratic demands, and the challenges presented by any representation of trauma. (Shuman & Bohmer, 2004, p. 394)

The secondary traumatisation of going through such processes is self-evident. Many studies of refugee mental health outcomes have highlighted that the violations that continue to be experienced as a part of everyday life have more impact on mental health and well-being than those associated with the original traumas of fleeing (McFarlane & Kaplan, 2012).

There is an unfortunate irony in the fact that research is consistently supporting the finding that it is typically not the original traumatic event that creates the ongoing psychological distress (Brewin et al., 2000) but, rather, it is the nature of the post-trauma environment; yet, many interventions still do not adequately address this aspect of recovery. As we noted in Chapter 7:

> psychological interventions should not be a substitute for interventions that directly relieve threat or that furnish the material resources needed for recovery and restoration of losses incurred. (Hobfoll et al., 2007, pp. 292–293)

Anti-oppressive approaches do draw attention to the need for access to material resources in the aftermath of trauma. The loss of resources is well understood as leading to lost opportunities. These include the basic survival needs of housing, food and water and medical resources.

Attention is also drawn to thinking about the sometimes less tangible needs and rights of autonomy and self-determination, for example. These latter rights are often seen to be the profoundly influential rights in determining how people live with their trauma experiences. Without these acknowledgements and in rendering human suffering a private experience, the result is that 'the political is not fully integrated' (Burstow, 2003, p. 1294).

Anti-oppressive approaches therefore see these areas as important areas to address – to tackle the determinants of oppression and trauma.

Implications for practice

All the approaches to trauma that we have considered to date place a sense of control at the core of both the trauma and resilience/recovery experiences. While many of the strategies of anti-oppressive practice are similar to other approaches, there are some unique features. As with other approaches, anti-oppressive approaches see restoring control over the domains of our lives is core to our well-being, as individuals, families and communities. However, an anti-oppressive approach understands this sense of control much more broadly than the approaches we have looked at so far. Within anti-oppressive approaches, control, power and rights are understood to be contextually derived and enacted, not independent of a person's place in the social hierarchy. In this sense, rights and control are relational, including relational in terms of the physical environment.

Forming an alliance

As with the other approaches we have looked at, within anti-oppressive therapeutic practice contexts, the relationship between the practitioner and the trauma-impacted person is considered a core aspect of the therapeutic process. This relationship is conceptualised in terms of an alliance or partnership, mirroring anti-oppressive conditions of practice:

> Feminist practice aspires to the creation of an egalitarian relationship between therapists and clients. Clients are construed as possessing expertise and authority about themselves, their lives, and their needs. Therapy then becomes a process of empowering clients to identify and own that authority. (Brown, 2004, p. 465)

This requires paying acute and mutual attention to the relationship, whether over a short- or long-term period of engagement. One of the key elements in ensuring a more egalitarian relationship is the recognition of client strengths and expertise.

For the practitioner, critical reflection is a constant process, therefore, of reflecting on their role in the therapeutic process, the ways in which they are influencing it and what they are bringing to their listening, and of addressing any power-related differentials as they arise. This critical reflection also requires an element of 'felt thoughtfulness' (Williams, 1977), which Frost and Hoggett (2008, p. 455) describe as

> a capacity to feel the pain of the other, even in their angry, violent or self-destructive enactments, and to think critically about the injustices that produce it.

This mindfulness and active attention to a person's pain and suffering in the wider context of injustice and oppression is vital. Pain and suffering are understood as both personal and political. It forms the basis of the therapeutic social justice approaches, whereby:

> Therapeutic interventions directly address social and economic equality and attempt to enhance social justice for the most vulnerable in a particular society. (Breckenridge & James, 2012, p. 246)

As we see later in this section, actively addressing these wider forces is part of the therapeutic process also.

Another feature of the therapeutic alliance is that it is not uncommon that survivors themselves become practitioners, as part of their survivor mission. This draws on their expertise as survivors and provides clients with strong mentors in relation to their own resilience and recovery.

Witnessing and politicising the trauma narrative

As Brown (2004) notes, many of the techniques used in undertaking trauma work are used in anti-oppressive practice, such as grounding and trauma-focused cognitive behavioural therapy techniques. The importance of giving voice to trauma experiences, of forming a coherent narrative that is emotionally and cognitively aligned, is emphasised, as with other approaches.

One of the key points of difference, however, is how the symptoms of traumatic stress are interpreted. Hyperarousal, intrusion and avoidance symptoms may be described as follows:

> posttraumatic symptoms are explicitly framed as coping strategies and evidence of clients' attempts to manage intolerable affects and knowledge arising from the

trauma. Symptoms are thus evidence of resistance by the client to being coerced into silence and invisibility. (Brown, 2004, p. 465)

This enables recognition of a person's strengths and efforts to manage the overwhelming fear of their experiences.

In addition, as with narrative approaches, anti-oppressive approaches maintain a strong focus on an individual's experiences in their social and cultural domains as well as on an individual's inner world experience. This is where the sites of intervention expand to include the socio-cultural context as much as in the individual therapeutic and experiential context. This is done in the belief that 'ultimately the witnessing provided by a professional cannot satisfy the larger existential, social and political needs' (Burstow, p. 1312). These larger needs must be addressed through more politically active approaches and is why individual therapy alone is often only part of the healing process. As Davis (1999, p. 763) notes:

> Individualised, curative responses divert attention from: the inequalities of resources and power which underpin the distribution of traumatic distress; the meanings attached to, and moral evaluation of its different manifestations; and the questions of responsibility, accountability and reintegration which follow.

Trauma experiences are typically seen as reflecting broader social inequalities, and consciousness raising to this effect is a key component of anti-oppressive interventions.

For people affected directly by trauma, developing this politicised understanding is part of creating a sense of liberation from the traumatic experiences. As Bishop (2002, p. 99) eloquently states: 'Consciousness and healing melts the seals keeping the blueprint of oppression locked inside the individuals.' The transformation of awareness means that

> one's own suffering arises not from individual deficits but rather from the ways in which one has been systemically invalidated, excluded, and silenced because of one's status as a member of a nondominant group in the culture. (Brown, 2004, p. 464)

Support groups and social action groups that seek to politicise and de-individualise experiences are often engaged with to enable individuals to reframe their experiences in this way. These are critical 'actions that counter alienation' (Burstow, 2003, p. 1313) and serve to give voice to those who may otherwise be rendered powerless and marginalised.

A critical step in consciousness-raising processes has been that of 'reversing the gaze', that is, rather than examining the experience of the survivor, examining the experiences of the dominant, privileged voices to bring about recognition of how oppressive circumstances arise. One of the areas where this has been critical has been in examining whiteness and encouraging dominant white people to consider the ways in which beliefs and actions create oppressive conditions for others. All of these interventions go towards building collective processes of restitution, justice and remembering and witnessing.

Advocating within and beyond the therapeutic relationship

As described throughout this chapter, engaging in a 'survivor mission' in order to protect the rights of others is seen as an important step for many in the recovery processes (Herman, 1992). With the politicised insights, a desire to engage in social action is not uncommon:

> Social action offers the survivor a source of power that draws upon her own initiative, energy and resourcefulness, but that magnifies these qualities far beyond her own capacities. It offers her an alliance with others based on cooperation and shared purpose. (Herman, 1992, p. 207)

Thus, anti-oppressive intervention is not treatment focused but is focused on the need for work focused upon the society to which the survivor returns, advocacy work, educational, media and political work (Davis, 1999, p. 771).

For many people, seeking legal redress for their trauma experience is also a critical step. Anti-oppressive approaches regard this as an essential step in bringing about the necessary cultural and structural changes to prevent traumas from recurring. These justice-based processes are seen as necessary processes and 'opportunities for redress and healing' (Danieli, 2009). While some focus on the legal redress as a process of financial compensation (often a necessary dimension to address), many see its central value in it as a process that has the potential to offer acknowledgement, witnessing, and an affirmation of experiences. It is the externalising and formalising of narratives at a broader social level that is healing.

The literature highlights mixed findings as to the psychological outcomes of pursuing these interventions. While many support the process, for the reasons outlined above, many others highlight the potential for unsuccessful outcomes, which may be experienced as traumatic in and of themselves and for experiences of retraumatisation, given that these processes often lead to a person losing control over their own narrative, or worse, being invalidated in their experiences. Thus, as Herman (1992) notes, legal approaches do not always bring the symbolic and practical together.

For other survivors, engaging in the lobbying of governments for changes in policy and wider access to resources is a core aspect of their survivor mission. The National Apology to Aboriginal and Torres Strait Islander people in 2008 in Australia arose as a result of extensive lobbying by people who had been profoundly affected by their Stolen Generations experiences. It became a means of publicly and explicitly addressing the harm that had been done by the forcible removal of children from Aboriginal parents. Such symbolic actions, alongside material ones, arguably recognised the trauma embedded in the cultural imperialism that had led to such actions being justified in the first place.

A case scenario

How would you go about working with John and/or his mother in anti-oppressive ways?

John worked part-time. While he wanted more work, he couldn't access it, given the high local unemployment situation. He was a reckless driver and had received a few warnings from the police. One night, he ran into the back of another car at the traffic lights. The occupants of that car violently attacked him in an act of road rage, leaving him seriously injured by the side of the road. He sustained a mild brain injury, which now leaves him tired, irritable and lacking insight into his interactions with others. His girlfriend left him after several months, and he has had to return to live with his mother. His mother despairs at his anger and drinking and doesn't know what to do. He feels the world is unjust. He wants to find work, and he wants to take action about the events that led to his injury.

Critically reflecting on anti-oppressive approaches

The criticisms of anti-oppressive approaches are consistent with some of the other approaches we have looked at and also different.

Firstly, a criticism is that these approaches perpetuate the very outcome that they are seeking to address – that is, that they disempower and oppress people. This is a common criticism of human rights approaches generally – that in seeking to protect the rights of people who have experienced trauma, they are imposing Western notions of both what is traumatic in the first place and what is appropriate by way of protection or other interventions (Shell-Duncan, 2008). For example, some have argued that feminist practice and research has been imposing a political perspective to gender and violence that may not be consistent with all victims' experiences or perceptions of sexual violence. Or in the complex territory of relational and cultural rights, female genital mutilation has been seen as a fraught issue. While some argue that the practice is not violating or traumatic and that it is justified on the grounds of being a cultural rights issue, questions arise as to what the criteria are by which these practices are assessed. How can all people's rights be adequately protected in these instances (Shell-Duncan, 2008)? Efforts to provide social protection can very quickly tip into protectionism and paternalism and cultural imperialism. This is what underpins much of the critique of human rights approaches such as those articulated in the UN Declaration of Human Rights.

Secondly, a distinct criticism is that in focusing on the outer world dimensions of causation and consequence, inadequate attention is paid to the individual distress and difficulty experienced after trauma. In one way, there is not a strong emphasis within all anti-oppressive approaches on theorising the cause of the inner world responses. Some argue that appropriate treatment is therefore not sought or people referred to for appropriate psychiatric care. Rather, there is a very active engagement with preventing the consequences of harm, actively articulating what people's needs are and moving towards protecting rights and needs. In this sense, it is the opposite criticism of many of the other approaches, in that not enough attention is paid to individual factors.

Thirdly, what perhaps shifts most here is that it is difficult to propose causal links, given the breadth of factors considered critical and the difficulties in theorising and researching the intersectionality of experience. There are arguably more descriptive accounts of variables and issues that influence mental health experiences and outcomes than causal explanations. One benefit alongside this criticism is that there is an appreciation of a much more complex interactional approach of individual, relational, social and cultural dimensions and an appreciation of the uniqueness of each person's experience.

Conclusion

Anti-oppressive approaches powerfully emphasise what lies at the heart of the trauma experience – the loss of power, control, dignity and loss of rights. They seek to redress these experiences at individual, structural and cultural levels, seeing that traumatic experiences arise as a result of social inequality and oppression. They also seek to understand and address the role of human behaviour explicitly in causing traumas – the intentional and unintentional acts of commission and omission that lead to harm being done. The interventions that arise from these approaches support a very active engagement with preventing the consequences of harm and a commitment to preventing the recurrence of oppressions that lead to and flow from traumatic experiences.

9

Promoting Resilience and Recovery: An Integrative Approach

Introduction

In this chapter, we draw the themes of this book together by revisiting a multidimensional approach that was introduced in Chapter 1. We look at what the particular approaches have contributed to thinking about trauma, resilience and recovery by applying a multidimensional approach; we look at the similarities and differences of their and we also practice and research implications and some of the questions that remain.

Drawing together understandings of trauma and resilience

As we have looked across the various approaches, hopefully a sense of the differences and commonalities of understandings of trauma and resilience has emerged, along with an appreciation of their constantly evolving nature. Over 150 years in Western practice and research contexts, our perspectives have shifted as new traumatic events have occurred and as new awareness has emerged or been privileged in relation to the human experience. In the decades ahead, advances in fields as diverse as technology and sociology will enhance our knowledge further. What this means for us now, as emphasised in Chapter 1, is that we need to be aware of these shifts and their implications, given these theoretical approaches continue to shape our knowledge and practice.

In Chapter 1, Figure 1.1 highlighted some key points of difference across the theoretical approaches, which have been borne out in the chapters that followed. The emphasis in this book has been on several of these areas –

the different theories of causation, the different levels of impact, the ways in which different outcomes and processes occur and, to a lesser extent, the different configurations of people that can be considered. The figure provides a map to use as a basis for teasing out the assumptions behind the ways in which we work in practice and research.

Another way of teasing out these assumptions can be gleaned from Table 9.1. This table summarises the practice implications that have been identified in relation to each of the approaches. While we have looked at them as the implications for interventions, they also highlight what the key areas of change are as identified by the various approaches and areas of focus in future research.

This table shows that there are three themes common to all seven of these approaches: the importance of forming a trauma narrative, of re-establishing a sense of safety and of considering context. Here, we look at these commonalities briefly before considering some of the points of difference when we look at the approaches through a multidimensional lens.

The first theme is the importance of listening to a person's trauma narrative. All of the approaches identify this as a core task, recognising that traumatic stories are characterised by their initially fragmentary nature. The task is to bring thoughts and feelings together into a coherent narrative that fits with our sense of who we are. Supporting a person in being able to tell and hear their own story for their particular purpose and need (Kirmayer et al., 2007), as well as witnessing this as practitioners and researchers, begins the processes of healing and restoration. Establishing a coherent narrative, however it is theorised, is seen as restoring the fracturing harm of trauma.

The second theme identified is that of safety. All of the approaches seek to support people in establishing or re-establishing a sense of safety, as an inner physical and psychological state of being and in the sense of being able to function in daily life. This connects with an understanding that to feel unsafe is to be in a state of suffering. All of the approaches articulate, in some way, an intention to alleviate this suffering and distress that trauma brings to people and to promote new ways of living, be that through relief, restoration and/or recovery.

The third theme is the importance of context. All of the approaches see that the wider social, political, economic and cultural context matters for recovery. Lundy (2004, pp. 56–57) highlights the challenge of this reality when she states the following:

> Many of the issues and problems facing people in need are rooted in broad social, political and economic conditions. At the same time, much of the 'help' that we are prepared to provide is done at an individual level and assumes that problems are personal rather than a reflection of wider social structural problems.

Table 9.1 A comparative analysis of practice implications according to theoretical approach

Theoretical approaches	Implications for interventions
Psychodynamic *Reintegrating the self*	Building a trusting working alliance
	Working with transference and countertransference issues
	Bringing to conscious awareness the trauma that has been experienced
	Integrating experiences into conscious awareness
Attachment *Regulating self and relationships*	Individual therapy contexts:
	• Building a secure attachment within the therapeutic relationship • Revisiting the 'fright' (and finding ways of self-soothing) • Establishing new internal working models
	Optimising family functioning where there has been maltreatment
	Optimising child welfare, hospital and education systems
Symptom *Reducing PTSD*	Reducing immediate distress and restoring a sense of safety
	Longer-term distress reduction and affect regulation
	Modifying the negative appraisals
	Reducing re-experiencing by developing an understanding of memories and triggers
	Developing new coping strategies
Person-centred *Recreating congruence*	Creating an authentic therapeutic relationship
	Understanding the incongruence and symbolisation created by traumatic experience
	Restoring a congruent self-structure
	Promoting actualisation and growth
Narrative *Re-authoring for meaning and coherence*	Articulating a politicised therapeutic stance
	Witnessing survivors' stories in non-psychologised ways
	Using a particular style of questioning
	Forming testimony for advocacy and social change

Table 9.1 (Continued)

Theoretical approaches	Implications for interventions
Social-ecological	Maintaining a systems focus of thinking
Rebuilding and sustaining systems	Rapidly engaging in a resourcing relationship
	Mobilising resources and capacity at individual, family and community levels
	Rebuilding social ecological systems
Anti-oppressive	Forming an alliance
Recognising rights and redressing oppression	Witnessing and politicising the trauma experience
	Advocating within and beyond the therapeutic relationship

While there is recognition that context matters, what we do see across the approaches is considerable variation in the way 'help' is then conceptualised. In our hospital and health care, education, and welfare systems, we need to think critically about our context and how this is influencing how we see our roles.

Thinking dimensionally about trauma and resilience

At the outset in Chapter 1, a multidimensional approach was introduced. Each of the approaches we have looked at vary in the extent to which they conceptualise trauma and resilience according to those dimensions, with a conclusion now justified that some privilege the inner world dimensions and others the outer world ones. In many ways, the movement through the chapters from beginning to end has reflected a shift from a focus on our inner worlds through to our outer worlds.

As a first step, a multidimensional approach provides a map for looking at how the approaches have contributed by way of understandings of definitions of traumatic experiences and of the various inner and outer world dimensions of significance. Table 9.2 provides an overview of the dimensional aspects considered by each of the theoretical approaches. While in one way it is reductionist to do this, it shows some of the key points of difference across the approaches we have considered. It highlights some of

Table 9.2 Reviewing the multidimensional aspects of the approaches

The dimensions	The approaches that focus on this dimension	Key points of commonality and difference across the approaches
Event-related	Psychodynamic Attachment Symptom Person-centred Narrative Social-ecological Anti-oppressive	Variation in the extent to which the traumatic exposure(s) is: • understood as externalised and/or internalised • subjectively and/or objectively positioned • politicised and/or psychologised • actively addressed in therapeutic work
Biological	Attachment Symptom Social-ecological Anti-oppressive	Variation in the extent to which biological dimensions are related to the following: • the brain and to internal regulation • lived experience and the embodiment of trauma and social conditions
Psychological	Psychodynamic Attachment Symptom Person-centred Narrative Social-ecological Anti-oppressive – to the least extent	Variation in the extent to which psychological dimensions are related to the following: • cognitions and/or emotions • brainhood and/or personhood
Spiritual	Narrative Person-centred	Variation in the extent to which spiritual dimensions are: • incorporated into understandings of an individual's trauma and resilience experiences
Relational and social	Psychodynamic Attachment Symptom – to the least extent Person-centred Narrative Social-ecological Anti-oppressive	Variation in the extent to which relational and social dimensions are: • incorporated into understandings of an individual's trauma and resilience experiences • seen as supports and activated as such • interdependence and interaction with individual and structural is yet to be accounted for • reflected in the nature of therapeutic relationships

Table 9.2   (Continued)

The dimensions	The approaches that focus on this dimension	Key points of commonality and difference across the approaches
Structural	Narrative Social-ecological Anti-oppressive	Variation in the extent to which structural dimensions are: • incorporated into understandings of an individual's trauma and resilience experiences • actively addressed in therapeutic work
Cultural	Attachment Narrative Social-ecological Anti-oppressive	Variation in the extent to which cultural dimensions are: • incorporated into understandings of an individual's trauma responses and recovery • actively addressed in therapeutic work
Time and place	Narrative Social-ecological Anti-oppressive	Variation in the extent to which structural dimensions are: • incorporated into understandings of an individual's trauma and resilience experiences

the key tensions in current trauma and resilience understandings. It is the second step, then, where the true complexity and contribution of a multi-dimensional approach lies. This involves holding in mind and in practice all dimensions together simultaneously, in seeing the interactive nature of them. This is when reductionism is avoided.

Event-related dimensions

A multidimensional understanding of trauma takes into consideration the triggering events or circumstances. As our discussion has highlighted, definitions of what constitutes a traumatic exposure are diverse. There is general, although not unanimous, agreement across the approaches that traumatic responses are driven by external events that overwhelm our capacity to function. Psychodynamic and attachment approaches, for example, listen for the precipitating circumstances to understand how they have been internalised, whereas social-ecological and anti-oppressive approaches listen for these processes too but also seek to actively address them.

In our research and practice, central questions therefore are raised about our own understandings as to how traumatic experiences enter into and intersect with people's lives, how they travel with us and influence us and how they become woven into our personal histories. Questions are also raised as to whether trauma damages and/or precipitates growth and change for us as individuals, families and communities and whether we focus in on the deeply subjective aspects of experiences and/or see them in more objective terms. These core beliefs about what is the nature of trauma in turn influence assumptions about where responsibility lies for recovery – whether our recovery is situated at an individual level of inner world processes, at family or relational levels and/or at our broader social and structural influences.

As we have seen with each edition of the *Diagnostic and Statistical Manual of Mental Disorders* (APA, 2013) and in the development of new approaches to trauma understandings such as those proliferating in the neuroscientific literature, trauma definitions will continue to evolve. Some practitioners have argued that a more nuanced view of the type of trauma event that people have experienced is necessary, in order to understand the subsequent trauma response – such as distinguishing between informational and sensory trauma (Gordon, 2007). Such a typology of trauma exposures may highlight why there is such diversity of trauma responses, with sensory trauma potentially more linked to PTSD, for example.

Inner world dimensions of trauma

As introduced in Chapter 1, the inner world dimensions of a multidimensional approach emphasise the biological, psychological and spiritual dimensions of a person. At this point in time in Western contexts, in particular, the biological and psychological dimensions of trauma are the primary domains of interest.

Within practice and research, a very strong biological emphasis is evident, reflected in the symptom approaches to trauma and resilience. The continuing research into the role of the brain in mediating trauma responses is critical. However, alongside that, the other approaches we have considered emphasise that trauma and resilience experiences are far more all-encompassing than our neurobiological processing of trauma exposures. While the symptom approaches and also, more recently, attachment approaches have brought important attention to these processes, the other approaches, particularly social-ecological and anti-oppressive ones, highlight that both the immediate experiences and their aftermath are profoundly influenced by the systems and resources we have available to us.

A dominant emphasis throughout all the approaches has been on the psychological dimensions of trauma. In part, this is because of the theoretical approaches we have looked at, but more so because they reflect the dominant emphasis within Western understandings of trauma's impacts. The suffering and pain of trauma are seen as occupying our psychological dimensions – although these are differently interpreted. Psychodynamic, attachment and symptom approaches have focused our thinking on PTSD and other internal dysregulating processes that occur. Many approaches throughout this book have gone beyond the PTSD lens, to see the psychological dimensions in much more existential terms, and in affective terms (Frost & Hoggett, 2008). Person-centred and narrative approaches have focused thinking more on our need for meaning-making, for understanding broader existential questions and how we seek to restore a sense of coherence. These psychological aspects of our experience in turn influence our identities and self-structure. These psychological dimensions have varied from being highly medicalised through to being seen through the lens of social discourses. All of them address in some way the critically important processes of releasing and relieving trauma's hold on our psychological lives.

One of the key tensions to emerge from these approaches in relation to our psychological dimensions is the extent to which trauma recovery and resilience are currently perceived to be primarily cognitive processes. In this sense, Vidal's (2009) argument that we are seen as 'cerebral subjects' is worthy of attention. He argues that notions of personhood have been replaced with notions of brainhood. This tension between trauma and resilience as connected with our broader personhood, with all of its existential, affective and social connotations, rather than reduced to brainhood, has been evident across the chapters.

This trend towards brainhood links with the finding that very rarely have the approaches we have looked at touched on spiritual dimensions. Relative to the other dimensions that are seen as influential in trauma recovery and resilience, they tend to be neglected aspects in practice in research. Yet, they connect with our existential and meaning-making processes profoundly. Narrative and person-centred approaches contribute extensively in this space, but there is scope to understand the role of the spiritual dimensions much more fully. This is one of the key points of departure from Indigenous perspectives, which see culture and spirituality as so fundamental to well-being, and inseparable from, for example, psychological and physical well-being (Bennett et al., 2013).

Outer world dimensions of trauma

As we turn to the outer world dimensions, some approaches have seen these dimensions as influential but not as a site for intervention, whereas others, such as anti-oppressive approaches, have both placed these dimensions as causal and as critical sites for intervention.

All of the approaches have drawn attention to the role of relational and social factors. Some of them have incorporated the relational dimensions, in particular, into the very heart of understanding trauma reactions – particularly psychodynamic, attachment, person-centred and narrative approaches. Social-ecological and anti-oppressive approaches have incorporated the relational and social dimensions into the causal understandings of trauma, but more so in terms of the relationship with vulnerability. Some of these approaches have tended to see the relational and social dimensions as more related to the recovery environment and as enablers or inhibitors of social and material support provision, for example the symptom approaches.

All of the approaches we have considered provide a way of thinking about the important relational context of therapeutic work. All the approaches see the relationship as providing safety and trust for survivors. Beyond that, however, as Table 9.1 shows, this relationship functions as a change agent in vastly different ways. Broadly speaking, psychodynamic, attachment, symptom and social ecological approaches see this relationship as primarily reparative compared with narrative, person-centred and anti-oppressive approaches, which see the relationship as more of a political alliance.

These differences are reflected then in the different understandings of the structural dimensions. Again, these are identified most prominently in narrative, social-ecological and anti-oppressive approaches. In their own ways, they actively address the experiences of oppression and powerlessness that are both the causes and consequences of trauma. In other approaches, such as psychodynamic, attachment and person-centred approaches, structural dimensions are not addressed, highlighting a key divergence in thinking. Within symptom approaches, though, an interesting tension is emerging. Increasingly, research related to PTSD is identifying economic difficulties as a key predictor of poorer outcomes. However, to date, practice interventions do not focus in this area. The extent to which the structural dimensions of people's lives are addressed in future interventions is an interesting emergent question.

The often seemingly invisible web of our cultural dimension continues to play a critical role in our lives, shaping our beliefs and expectations, and our material realities, both consciously and unconsciously: 'Culture provides all people with existential meaning around the elemental and universal human question of their purpose in being' (Bessarab & Crawford, 2013, p. 94). Many of the approaches acknowledge the role of cultural dimensions but, again, few approaches actively engage with them. Narrative approaches perhaps address these dimensions in the fullest and richest of ways, seeing that collective and social narratives are attended to in ways that the other approaches do not do. Yet, so fundamental is culture to our interpretation and experience of the world that it needs to take a much stronger central role in understandings of trauma and resilience.

The time and place dimensions emphasise the contextual nature of trauma, and ultimately the unique nature of people's experiences. Again, narrative approaches address these dimensions as central to people's experiences, in externalising people's experiences to be understood within these two critical areas. Social-ecological and anti-oppressive approaches also acknowledge the central role these dimensions play in both causing traumatic experiences and contributing to the consequences. Thus, time and place are politicised and appreciated as key influences in people's capacity to function and live well. Psychodynamic and attachment approaches, and to some extent symptom approaches, have an interesting understanding of time. In many ways, there is a focus on time past rather than time present, in order to move towards a new sense of future. The links are to past events and the present experiences of memory, in efforts to unlock the hold of the past. So, time is not politicised in the way of the other approaches but it does play an important part in conceptualising the impact of traumatic experiences.

In relation to place, attachment approaches provide new and untapped opportunities to think about the traumas of dislocation and resettlement, for example. At present, the social-ecological approaches are the ones most concerned with place, as both a source of vulnerability and resilience. Time and place dimensions are vital to hold in mind in our conceptualisations of well-being.

Thinking and working in multidimensional ways

Thinking in multidimensional ways means we are taking into account all of the dimensions discussed in the previous pages, and then bringing them together into a more interactive understanding, so that we look at each person in context. The tendency to partialise and focus in on one of the dimensions is well acknowledged. If we focus on the traumatic events and their impact only, for example, as Gordon (2007, p. 12) notes, 'we are in danger of losing the person'. In the person-centred approach of Rogers (1944), he too cautioned against becoming atomistic in thinking about people. In thinking in multidimensional ways, how we listen to the whole person beyond and including their trauma experiences becomes the key point of focus. In this regard, a multidimensional approach provides a useful map for these critical, interacting dimensions.

A multidimensional approach, therefore, encourages us to think outside of a particular approach and more broadly map out the domains of risk as well as resilience. It helps us to identify the strengths and limitations of each of the approaches, as we have done in the previous section. Then, it encourages thinking about the interaction of the issues that influence experience, not seeing them in isolation or ignoring them altogether. It helps us also hone in on why we use a particular approach over and above another – what appeals to us and what motivates us in our work – so that we can in more targeted ways address our core assumptions.

The challenge of a multidimensional approach to trauma and resilience is to overcome the tendency to maintain a singularity of focus. Rather than see and work with only the psychological dimensions of a person's difficulties, for example, we can see them in all their complexity. There is still quite a considerable step to go in achieving multidimensional understandings of trauma. As has been highlighted throughout the chapters, we have reasonably good understandings of individual resilience or of a community as resilient. What we know far less about is how both are resilient by virtue of the other. Fully embedding these understandings of the interactive and interdependent nature of trauma and resilience are the next challenge for practitioners and researchers alike. This means researching and understanding the mechanisms by which a person's spiritual groundedness brings about a physical and psychological centredness, for example, or the processes by which structural strengths enable physical well-being and social connectedness. Our understanding of these process elements can emerge from a multidimensional conceptualisation of trauma and resilience.

Some of this need for more interactive understandings is found in the critical neurosciences literature. Exemplifying multidimensional thinking, Slaby (2010, p. 397) asks:

> Does neuroscience indeed have such wide-ranging effects or are we collectively overestimating its impacts at the expense of other important drivers of social and cultural change? Via what channels is neuroscience interacting with contemporary conceptions of selfhood, identity and well-being?

This exemplifies multidimensional thinking.

Another example can be found in the conceptualisation of our relational and social dimensions. Within the trauma literature generally, the focus tends to be on either individual relationships or communities. Families and households have been the focus to a far lesser extent. A multidimensional approach emphasises that the interactions of our relationships at individual, family or household and community levels need to be better understood. Understanding these interactions will involve understanding broader structural, cultural, time and place dimensions, but these in turn need to be connected with individual motivations and capacities. In listening and analysing these interactive elements, the picture of a person's life and their unique experiences of trauma and resilience come to be more deeply understood.

Conclusion

Trauma work is complex and uncertain by its very nature. Whether in practice or research, it is tapping into the very heart of people's experiences of suffering, distress and hopelessness. It is also tapping into what people value most, how growth and change are possible and how new meaning can be found. It is tapping into the specific circumstances and particularities of all of our lives.

Traumatic life experiences demand change and adaptive responses. Sometimes this is more possible than others, with so many factors in play. For all of us, whether as survivors, practitioners and researchers, our contexts differ and so we understand these responses and effects through the eyes of that context and our own unfolding experiences. The aim of this book has been to introduce you to ways of thinking about the transformative work that is possible. Each of the approaches we have looked at shares that commitment but provides a different way of achieving this outcome. Whether the language is that of integration, regulation, congruence, absence of symptoms, new meaning, capacity or empowerment, the hope is always that practice and research, in small and large ways, can transform people's suffering, distress and despair into new ways of living well.

References

Acosta, J., Chandra, A., & Feeney, K. (2010). *Navigating the road to recovery: Assessment of the coordination, communication, and financing of the Disaster Case Management Pilot in Louisiana*. Santa Monica: RAND Corporation.

Adger, W. N. (2000). Social and ecological resilience: are they related? *Progress in Human Geography, 24*(3), 347–364.

Adger, W. N., Hughes, T. P., Folke, C., Carpenter, S. R., & Rockström, J. (2005). Social-ecological resilience to coastal disasters. *Science, 309*(5737), 1036–1039.

Affleck, G., & Tennen, H. (1996). Construing benefits from adversity: Adaptational significance and dispositional underpinnings. *Journal of Personality, 64*(4), 899–922.

Affleck, G., Tennen, H., Croog, S., & Levine, S. (1987). Causal attribution, perceived benefits and morbidity after heart attack: An 8 year study. *Journal of Consulting and Clinical Psychology, 55*, 29–35.

Afuape, T. (2011). *Power, resistance and liberation in therapy with survivors of trauma*. New York: Routledge.

Agaibi, C. E., & Wilson, J. P. (2005). Trauma, PTSD, and resilience: A review of the literature. *Trauma, Violence & Abuse, 6*(3), 195–216.

Ainsworth, M. S. (1993). Attachments and other affectional bonds across the life cycle. In C. Parkes, J. Stevenson-Hinde & P. Marris (Eds.), *Attachment across the life cycle* (pp. 33–51). London: Tavistock/Routledge.

Ainsworth, M. S., Blehar, M., Waters, E., & Wall, S. (1978). *Patterns of attachment: A psychological study of the Strange Situation*. Hillsdale, NJ: Lawrence Erlbaum Associates.

Alden, L. E., Regambal, M. J., & Laposa, J. M. (2008). The effects of direct versus witnessed threat on emergency department healthcare workers: Implications for PTSD Criterion A. *Journal of Anxiety Disorders, 22*(8), 1337–1346.

Alexander, J. (2012). *Trauma: A social theory*. Cambridge: Polity Press.

Allen, J. (2012). *Mentalizing in the development and treatment of attachment trauma*. London: Karnac Books.

Allen, J., & Fonagy, P. (Eds.), (2011). *The handbook of mentalization-based treatment*. Chichester: John Wiley & Sons.

Alston, M. (2013). Environmental social work: Accounting for gender in climate disasters. *Australian Social Work, 66*(2), 218–233.

American Psychiatric Association. (1980). *Diagnostic and statistical manual of mental disorders* (3rd ed.). Washington, DC: APA.

American Psychiatric Association. (2000). *Diagnostic and statistical manual of mental disorders* (4th, Text Revision ed.). Washington, DC: American Psychiatric Association.

American Psychiatric Association. (2013). *Diagnostic and statistical manual of mental disorders* (5th ed.). Washington, DC: American Psychiatric Association.

Antonovsky, A. (1998). The sense of coherence: An historical and future perspective. In H. McCubbin, E. A. Thompson, A. I. Thompson & J. E. Fromer (Eds.), *Stress, coping, and health in families: Sense of coherence and resiliency* (pp. 3–20). California: Sage Publications Inc.

Atkinson, J. (2003). *Trauma trails, recreating song lines: The transgenerational effects of trauma in Indigenous Australia.* North Melbourne: Spinifex Press.

Atkinson, P. (2009). Illness narratives revisited: The failure of narrative reductionism. *Sociological Research Online,* 14(5), 1.

Augusta-Scott, T. (2007). Challenging essentialist anti-oppressive discourse: Uniting against racism and sexism. In C. Brown & T. Augusta-Scott (Eds.), *Narrative therapy: Making meaning, making lives* (Chapter 11, pp. 211–228). Thousand Oaks: Sage Publications.

Australian Centre for Posttraumatic Mental Health. (2007). *Australian guidelines for the treatment of adults with acute stress disorder and posttraumatic stress disorder.* Melbourne: ACPMH.

Australian Government (2013). *Royal commission into institutional responses to child sexual abuse.* Available at: http://www.childabuseroyalcommission.gov.au/ (accessed 15/8/2014).

Bankoff, G., Frerks, G., & Hilhorst, D. (Eds.). (2004). *Mapping vulnerability: Disasters, development & people.* London New York: Earthscan.

Barrett-Lennard, G. T., & Neville, B. (2010). The person-centered scene in Australia: Then and now. *Person-Centered & Experiential Psychotherapies,* 9(4), 265–273.

Barth, R. P., Crea, T. M., John, K., Thoburn, J., & Quinton, D. (2005). Beyond attachment theory and therapy: Towards sensitive and evidence-based interventions with foster and adoptive families in distress. *Child & Family Social Work,* 10(4), 257–268.

Bartholomew, K., & Horowitz, L. (1991). Attachment styles among young adults: A test of a four-category model. *Journal of Personality and Social Psychology,* 61(2), 226–244.

Bedard-Gilligan, M., & Zoellner, L. A. (2012). Dissociation and memory fragmentation in post-traumatic stress disorder: An evaluation of the dissociative encoding hypothesis. *Memory,* 20(3), 277–299.

Beels, C. (2009). Some historical conditions of narrative work. *Family Process,* 48, 363–378.

Bennett, B., Green, S., Gilbert, S., & Bessarab, D. (Eds.). (2013). *Our voices: Aboriginal and Torres Strait Islander social work.* South Yarra: Palgrave Macmillan.

Berger, R. (2005). An ecological community-based approach for dealing with traumatic stress: A case of terror attack on a Kibbutz. *Journal of Aggression, Maltreatment & Trauma,* 10(1/2), 513–526.

Berger, W., Coutinho, E., Figueira, I., Marques-Portella, C., Luz, M. P., Neylan, T. C., Marmar, C. R., & Mendlowicz, M. V. (2011). Rescuers at risk: A systematic review and meta-regression analysis of the worldwide current prevalence and correlates of PTSD in rescue workers. *Social Psychiatry and Psychiatric Epidemiology,* 47(6), 1–11.

Berke, P. R., & Campanella, T. (2006). Planning for postdisaster resiliency. *The Annals of the American Academy of Political and Social Science,* 604(1), 192–207.

Bessarab, D. (2000). Working with aboriginal families: A cultural approach. In W. Weeks & M. Quinn (Eds.), *Issues facing Australian families: Human services respond* (3rd ed., Chapter 7, pp. 79–90). Frenchs Forest: Longman.

Bessarab, D. & Crawford, F. (2013). Trauma, grief and loss: The vulnerability of Aboriginal families in the child protection system. In B. Bennett, S. Green, S. Gilbert, & D. Bessarab, D. (Eds). *Our voices: Aboriginal and Torres Strait Islander social work* (pp. 93–113). South Yarra: Palgrave Macmillan.

Bishop, A. (2002). *Becoming an ally: Breaking the cycle of oppression.* Crows Nest: Allen & Unwin.

Black, D. & Trickey, D. (2005). *Children bereaved by murder and manslaughter.* Seventh International Conference on Grief and Bereavement in Contemporary Society, 12 July, London.

Black, D., & Tufnell, G. (2006). When is counselling indicated after a major traumatic life event? *Current Paediatrics,* 16, 464–471.

Blackburn, P. (2005). Speaking the unspeakable: bearing witness to the stories of political violence, war and terror. *International Journal of Narrative Therapy and Community Work,* 2005(3/4), 97–105.

Blackwell, D. (1997). Holding, containing and bearing witness: The problem of helpfulness in encounters with torture survivors. *Journal of Social Work Practice,* 11(2), 81–89.

Blankenship, K. (1998). A race, class and gender analysis of thriving. *Journal of Social Issues,* 54(2), 393–404.

Block, J., & Colvin, C. (1994). Positive illusions and well-being revisited: Separating fiction from fact. *Psychological Bulletin,* 116(1), 28–28.

Blum, H. (2003). Psychoanalytic controversies: Repression, transference and reconstruction. *International Journal of Psychoanalysis,* 84(3), 497–513.

Boals, A., Banks, J. B., Hathaway, L. M., & Schuettler, D. (2011). Coping with stressful events: Use of cognitive words in stressful narratives and the meaning-making process. *Journal of Social and Clinical Psychology,* 30(4), 378–403.

Bohleber, W. (2007). Remembrance, trauma and collective memory: The battle for memory in psychoanalysis. *International Journal of Psychoanalysis,* 88(2), 329–352.

Bombay, A., Matheson, K., & Anisman, H. (2009). Intergenerational trauma: Convergence of multiple processes among first nations peoples in Canada. *Journal of Aboriginal Health,* 5(1–3), 6–47.

Bonanno, G. (2004). Loss, trauma and human resilience: Have we underestimated the human capacity to thrive after extremely aversive events? *American Psychologist,* 59(1), 20–28.

Bonanno, G. A., & Mancini, A. D. (2012). Beyond resilience and PTSD: Mapping the heterogeneity of responses to potential trauma. *Psychological Trauma: Theory, Research, Practice, and Policy,* 4(1), 74–83.

Bonanno, G. A., Westphal, M., & Mancini, A. D. (2011). Resilience to loss and potential trauma. *Annual Review of Clinical Psychology,* 7(5), 511–535.

Boon, H. J., Cottrell, A., King, D., Stevenson, R. B., & Millar, J. (2012). Bronfenbrenner's bioecological theory for modelling community resilience to natural disasters. *Natural Hazards*, 60(2), 381–408.

Boss, P. (2006). *Loss, trauma, and resilience: Therapeutic work with ambiguous loss*. New York: W.W. Norton.

Boulanger, G. (2012). Psychoanalytic witnessing: Professional obligation or moral imperative? *Psychoanalytic Psychology*, 29(3), 318–324.

Bourdieu, P. (1999). *The weight of the world: Social suffering in contemporary society*. Cambridge: Polity Press.

Bowlby, J. (1969). *Attachment* (Vol. 1). London: Penguin Books.

Bowlby, J. (1980). *Loss: Sadness and depression* (Vol. 3). London: Penguin Books.

Bowlby, J. (2005). *A secure base: Clinical applications of attachment theory*. London: Routledge.

Bowman, M. (1997). *Individual differences in posttraumatic response: Problems with the adversity-distress connection*. Mahwah: Lawrence Erlbaum Associates.

Bragin, M. (2010). Can anyone here know who I am? Co-constructing meaningful narratives with combat veterans. *Clinical Social Work Journal*, 38(3), 316–326.

Breckenridge, J., & James, K. (2012). Therapeutic responses to communities affected by disasters: The contribution of family therapy. *Australian and New Zealand Journal of Family Therapy*, 33(3), 242–256.

Breidenstine, A. S., Bailey, L. O., Zeanah, C. H., & Larrieu, J. A. (2011). Attachment and trauma in early childhood: A review. *Journal of Child & Adolescent Trauma*, 4(4), 274–290.

Breslau, J. (2004). Cultures of trauma: Anthropological views of posttraumatic stress disorder in international health. *Culture, Medicine and Psychiatry*, 28(2), 113–126.

Breslau, N. (2001). The epidemiology of posttraumatic stress disorder: What is the extent of the problem? *Journal of Clinical Psychiatry*, 62, 16–22.

Breslau, N. (2009). The epidemiology of trauma, PTSD, and other posttrauma disorders. *Trauma, Violence, & Abuse*, 10(3), 198–210.

Breslau, N., Bohnert, K., & Koenen, K. (2010). The 9/11 terrorist attack and posttraumatic stress disorder revisited. *The Journal of Nervous and Mental Disease*, 198(8), 539–543.

Breuer, J., & Freud, S. (1936 [1895]). *Studies in hysteria*. New York: Nervous and Mental Disease Publishing Co.

Brewin, C. R., Andrews, B., & Valentine, J. D. (2000). Meta-analysis of risk factors for posttraumatic stress disorder in trauma-exposed adults. *Journal of Consulting and Clinical Psychology*, 68(5), 748–766.

Briere, J., & Scott, C. (2006). *Principles of trauma therapy: A guide to symptoms, evaluation and treatment*. Thousand Oaks: SAGE Publications.

Bronfenbrenner, U. (1979). *The ecology of human development: Experiments by nature and design*. Cambridge, MA: Harvard University Press.

Brothers, D. (2008). *Toward a psychology of uncertainty: Trauma-centered psychoanalysis*. New York: Analytic Press.

Brothers, D. (2009). Trauma-centered psychoanalysis. *Annals of the New York Academy of Science*, 1159, 51–62.

Brown, C. (2007). Situating knowledge and power in the therapeutic alliance. In C. Brown & T. Augusta-Scott (Eds.), *Narrative therapy: Making meaning, making lives* (Chapter 1, pp. 3–22). Thousand Oaks: Sage Publications.

Brown, C. & Augusta-Scott, T. (2007). *Narrative therapy: Making meaning, making lives*. Thousand Oaks: Sage Publications.

Brown, L. (Ed.). (1993). *The new shorter Oxford English dictionary*. Oxford: Clarendon Press.

Brown, L. S. (1995). Not outside the normal range. In C. Caruth (Ed.), *Trauma: Explorations in memory* (pp. 100–112). Baltimore: The John Hopkins University Press.

Brown, L. S. (2004). Feminist paradigms of trauma treatment. *Psychotherapy: Theory, Research, Practice, Training,* 41(4), 464–471.

Bruneau, M., Chang, S., Eguchi, R., Lee, G., O'Rourke, T., Reinhorn, A., Shinozuka, M., Tierney, K., Wallace, W., & von Winterfeld, D. (2003). A framework to quantitatively assess and enhance the seismic resilience of communities. *Earthquake Spectra,* 19(4), 733–752.

Bryant, R., Waters, E., Gibbs, L., Gallagher, C., Pattison, P., Lusher, D., MacDougall, C., Harms, L., Block, K., Snowdon, E., Sinnott, V., Ireton, G., Richardson, J., & Forbes, D. (2014). Psychological outcomes following the Victorian Black Saturday bushfires. *Australian and New Zealand Journal of Psychiatry,* 48(7), 634–643.

Bunting, B., Ferry, F., Murphy, S., O'Neill, S., & Bolton, D. (2013). Trauma associated with civil conflict and posttraumatic stress disorder: Evidence from the Northern Ireland study of health and stress. *Journal of Traumatic Stress,* 26, 134–141.

Burstow, B. (2003). Toward a radical understanding of trauma and trauma work. *Violence Against Women,* 9(11), 1293–1317.

Burstow, B. (2005). A critique of posttraumatic stress disorder and the DSM. *Journal of Humanistic Psychology,* 45(4), 429–445.

Butler, J. (2003). *The Judith Butler reader*. Malden, MA: Blackwell Publishers.

Calhoun, L. & Tedeschi, L. (1998). Beyond recovery from trauma: Implications for clinical practice and research. *Journal of Social Issues,* 54(2), 357–371.

Carey, M., Walther, S., & Russell, S. (2009). The absent but implicit: A map to support therapeutic enquiry. *Family Process,* 48(3), 319–331.

Carolan, M., Burns-Jager, K., Bozek, K., & Chew, R. (2010). Women who have their parental rights removed by the State: The interplay of trauma and oppression. *Journal of Feminist Family Therapy,* 22, 171–186.

Carr, R. B. (2011). Combat and human existence: Toward an intersubjective approach to combat-related PTSD. *Psychoanalytic Psychology,* 28(4), 471–496.

Caruth, C. (1995). *Trauma: Explorations in memory*. Baltimore: The John Hopkins University Press.

Carver, C. S. (1998). Resilience and thriving: Issues, models, and linkages. *Journal of Social Issues,* 54(2), 245–266.

Castells, M. (2011). A network theory of power. *International Journal of Communication,* 5, 773–787.

Chamlee-Wright, E., & Storr, V. H. (2011). Social capital as collective narratives and post-disaster community recovery. *Sociological Review,* 59(2), 266–282.

Chandler, D. (2002). Introduction: Rethinking human rights. In D. Chandler (Ed.), *Rethinking human rights: Critical approaches to international politics* (pp. 1–15). Basingstoke: Palgrave Macmillan.

Chang, C.-M., Lee, L.-C., Connor, K. M., Davidson, J. R. T., Jeffries, K., & Lai, T.-J. (2003). Posttraumatic distress and coping strategies among rescue workers after an earthquake. *The Journal of Nervous and Mental Disease, 191*(6), 391–398.

Chapman, C., Mills, K., Slade, T., McFarlane, A. C., Bryant, R. A., Creamer, M., Silove, D., & Teesson, M. (2012). Remission from post-traumatic stress disorder in the general population. *Psychological Medicine, 42*(8), 1695–1703.

Cicchetti, D., Rogosch, F., & Toth, S. (2006). Fostering secure attachments in infants in maltreating families through preventive interventions. *Development and Psychopathology, 18*(3), 623–649.

Clarke, S., Hoggett, P., & Thompson, S. (Eds.). (2006). *Emotion, politics and society.* Basingstoke: Palgrave Macmillan.

Cohen, D. (2011). Does experimental research support psychoanalysis? *Journal of Physiology Paris, 105*(4–6), 211–219.

Connolly, M., & Harms, L. (2012). *Social work from theory to practice.* Port Melbourne: Cambridge University Press.

Cooper, M., & McLeod, J. (2011). Person-centered therapy: A pluralistic perspective. *Person-Centered & Experiential Psychotherapies, 10*(3), 210–223.

Cork, S. (2010). Resilience of social-ecological systems. In S. Cork (Ed.), *Resilience and transformation: Preparing Australia for uncertain futures* (pp. 131–142). Victoria: CSIRO Publishing.

Council of Australian Governments. (2009). National Strategy for Disaster Resilience. Canberra: Commonwealth of Australia.

Cox, R. S., & Perry, K. M. E. (2011). Like a fish out of water: Reconsidering disaster recovery and the role of place and social capital in community disaster resilience. *American Journal of Community Psychology, 48*(3–4), 395–411.

Crawford, E., Wright, M., & Masten, A. (2006). Resilience and spirituality in youth. In E. Roehlkepartain, P. King, L. Wagener & P. Benson (Eds.), *The handbook of spiritual development in childhood and adolescence* (pp. 355–370). Thousand Oaks: SAGE Publications.

Creamer, M., Burgess, P., & McFarlane, A. C. (2001). Post-traumatic stress disorder: Findings from the Australian national survey of mental health and well-being. *Psychological Medicine, 31*(7), 1237–1247.

Crenshaw, K. (1995). Mapping the margins: intersectionality, identity politics and violence against women of colour. In K. Crenshaw, N. Gotanda & G. Peller (Eds.), *Critical race theory: The key writings that informed the movement* (pp. 357–383). New York: New York Press.

Crossley, M. L. (2003). Formulating narrative psychology: The limitations of contemporary social constructionism. *Narrative Inquiry, 13*(2), 287–300.

Crumpton-Cook, R. (1996). But we have the expertise. *Psychotherapy in Australia, 3*(1), 16–17.

Danieli, Y. (2009). Massive trauma and the healing role of reparative justice. *Journal of Trauma Stress, 22*(5), 351–357.

Darves-Bornoz, J.-M., Alonso, J., de Girolamo, G., de Graaf, R., Haro, J.-M., Kovess-Masfety, V., Lepine, J.-P., Nachbaur, G., Negre-Pages, L., Vilagut, G., & Gasquet,

I. (2008). Main traumatic events in Europe: PTSD in the European study of the epidemiology of mental disorders survey. *Journal of Traumatic Stress,* 21(5), 455–462.

Davis, H. (1999). The psychiatrization of post-traumatic distress: Issues for social workers. *British Journal of Social Work,* 29(5), 755–777.

Davis, R., Cook, D., & Cohen, L. (2005). A community resilience approach to reducing ethnic and racial disparities in health. *American Journal of Public Health,* 95(12), 2168–2173.

De Fazio, V. (1978). Dynamic perspectives on the nature and effects of combat stress. In C. Figley (Ed.), *Stress disorders among Vietnam Veterans: Theory, research, treatment* (pp. 23–42). New York: Brunner/Mazel Inc.

Denborough, D. (2005). A framework for receiving and documenting testimonies of trauma. *International Journal of Narrative Therapy and Community Work,* 2005(3/4), 34–42.

Denborough, D. (Ed.). (2006). *Trauma: Narrative responses to traumatic experience.* Adelaide: Dulwich Centre Publications.

Denborough, D. (2012). A storyline of collective narrative practice: A history of ideas, social projects and partnerships. *International Journal of Narrative Therapy and Community Work,* 1, 40–65.

Doidge, N. (2010). *The brain that changes itself: Stories of personal triumph from the frontiers of brain science.* Carlton North: Scribe Publications.

Doka, K. (1989). *Disenfranchised grief: Recognizing hidden sorrow.* New York: Lexington Books.

Dorahy, M., Corry, M., Shannon, M., Webb, K., McDermott, B., Ryan, M., & Dyer, K. (2013). Complex trauma and intimate relationships: The impact of shame, guilt and dissociation. *Journal of Affective Disorders,* 147, 72–79.

Dozier, M., Manni, M., Gordon, M., Peloso, E., Gunnar, M., Stovall-McClough, K,. Edlreth, D. & Levine, S. (2006). Foster children's diurnal production of cortisol: An exploratory study. *Child Maltreatment,* 11(2), 189–197.

Drozdek, B. (2007). The rebirth of contextual thinking in psychotraumatology. In B. Drozdek & J. Wilson (Eds.), *Voices of trauma: Treating psychological trauma across cultures* (pp. 1–26). New York: Springer.

Du Plooy, L., Harms, L., Muir, K., Martin, B., & Ingliss, S. (2014). ' "Black Saturday' " and its aftermath: Reflecting on postdisaster social work interventions in an Australian trauma hospital. *Australian Social Work,* 67(2), 274–84.

Edkins, J. (2003). *Trauma and the memory of politics.* Cambridge; New York: Cambridge University Press.

Egan, G. (2014). *The skilled helper: A problem-managemetn and opportunity-development approach to helping* (10th ed.). Belmont: Brooks/Cole.

Ehlers, A., & Clark, D. M. (2000). A cognitive model of posttraumatic stress disorder. *Behaviour Research and Therapy,* 38(4), 319–345.

Ehlers, A., & Clark, D. M. (2008). Post-traumatic stress disorder: The development of effective psychological treatments. *Nordic Journal of Psychiatry,* 62 (Suppl 47), 11–18.

Ehlers, A., Clark, D. M., Hackmann, A., Grey, N., Liness, S., Wild, J., Manley, J., Waddington, L., & McManus, F. (2010). Intensive cognitive therapy for PTSD: A feasibility study. *Behavioural and Cognitive Psychotherapy,* 38(4), 383–398.

Ehlers, A., Clark, D. M., Hackmann, A., McManus, F., & Fennell, M. (2005). Cognitive therapy for post-traumatic stress disorder: Development and evaluation. *Behaviour Research and Therapy,* 43(4), 413–431.

Ellard, J. (1997). The epidemic of post-traumatic stress disorder: A passing phase? *Medical Journal of Australia,* 166(20), 84–87.

Ellenberger, H. (1970). *The discovery of the unconscious: The history and evolution of dynamic psychiatry.* New York: Basic Books.

Erikson, K. (1976). *Everything in its path: Destruction of community in the Buffalo Creek flood.* New York: Simon and Schuster Paperbacks.

Farmer, E., Selwyn, J. & Meakings, S. (2013). 'Other children say you're not normal because you don't live with your parents'. Children's views of living with informal kinship carers: social networks, stigma and attachment to carers. *Child and Family Social Work,* 18(1), 25–34.

Figley, C. (Ed.). (1978). *Stress disorders among Vietnam Veterans.* New York: Brunner/Mazel Publishers.

Figley, C. (Ed.). (1995). *Compassion fatigue: Coping with secondary traumatic stress disorder in those who treat the traumatized.* New York: Brunner/Mazel.

Figley, C. (2002). Compassion fatigue: Psychotherapists' chronic lack of self care. *Journal of Clinical Psychology,* 58(11), 1433–1441.

Flory, K., Hankin, B., Kloos, B., Cheely, C., & Gurecki, G. (2009). Alcohol and cigarette use and misuse among Hurricane Katrina survivors: Psychosocial risk and protective factors. *Substance Use and Misuse,* 44(12), 1711–1724.

Foa, E., Gillihan, S., & Bryant, R. (2013). Challenges and successes in dissemination of evidence-based treatments for posttraumatic stress: Lessons learned from prolonged exposure therapy for PTSD. *Psychological Science in the Public Interest,* 14(2), 65–111.

Foa, E., Keane, T., Friedman, M., & Cohen, J. (2009). *Effective treatments for PTSD: practice guidelines from the international society for traumatic stress studies* (2nd ed.). New York: Guilford Press.

Folke, C. (2006). Resilience: The emergence of a perspective for social–ecological systems analyses. *Global Environmental Change,* 16(3), 253–267.

Folke, C., Carpenter, S. R., Walker, B., Scheffer, M., Chapin, T., & Rockström, J. (2010). Resilience thinking: Integrating resilience, adaptability and transformability. *Ecology & Society,* 15(4), 1–9.

Fonagy, P. (2001). *Attachment theory and psychoanalysis.* New York: Other Press.

Fook, J. (2002). *Social work: Critical theory and practice.* London: SAGE.

Forbes, D., Lewis, V., Varker, T., Phelps, A., O'Donnell, M., Wade, D., Ruzek, J., Watson, P., Bryant, R., & Creamer, M. (2011). Psychological first aid following trauma: Implementation and evaluation framework for high-risk organizations. *Psychiatry,* 74(3), 224–239.

Foucault, M. (1980). Truth and power. In C. Gordon (Ed.), *Power/Knowledge: Selected interviews and other writings 1972–1977* (pp. 109–133). London: Harvester Wheatsheaf.

Frank, A. (1995). *The wounded storyteller.* Chicago/London: The University of Chicago Press.

Frank, A. W. (2010). In defence of narrative exceptionalism. *Sociology of Health & Illness*, 32(4), 665–667.

Frankl, V. (1984). *Man's search for meaning* (Revised and Updated ed.). New York: Washington Square Press.

Frattaroli, J. (2006). Experimental disclosure and its moderators: A meta-analysis. *Psychological Bulletin*, 132(6), 823–865.

Frazier, P., Tennen, H., Gavian, M., Park, C., Tomich, P., & Tashiro, T. (2009). Does self-reported posttraumatic growth reflect genuine positive change? *Psychological Science*, 20(7), 912–919.

Freud, A. (1968). *The ego and the mechanisms of defence* (Revised ed.). London: The Hogarth Press.

Freud, S. (1962 [1896]). The aetiology of hysteria. *The Standard Edition of the Complete Psychological Works of Sigmund Freud, Volume III (1893–1899): Early Psycho-Analytic Publications.* (pp.189–223). London: Random House.

Freud, S. (1966 [1917]). *The introductory lectures on psychoanalysis.* New York: Norton.

Freud, S. (1969). *An outline of psycho-analysis.* New York: W. W. Norton & Company.

Freud, S. (1984 [1928]). Beyond the pleasure principle. In J. Strachey & A. Richards (Eds.), *The Pelican Freud library: On metapsychology: The theory of psychoanalysis* (Vol. 11, pp. 269–338). Ringwood: Penguin Books.

Freyd, J. J., DePrince, A. P., & Gleaves, D. N. (2007). The state of betrayal trauma theory: Reply to McNally – Conceptual issues and future directions. *Memory*, 15(3), 295–311.

Friedman, M., Resick, P., Bryant, R., & Brewin, C. (2011a). Considering PTSD for DSM-5. *Depression & Anxiety*, 28, 750–769.

Friedman, M., Resick, P., Bryant, R., Strain, J., Horowitz, M., & Spiegel, D. (2011b). Classification of trauma and stressor-related disorders in DSM-5. *Depression & Anxiety*, 28, 737–749.

Frisina, P. G., Borod, J. C., & Lepore, S. J. (2004). A meta-analysis of the effects of written emotional disclosure on the health outcomes of clinical populations. *Journal of Nervous and Mental Disease*, 192, 629–634.

Frost, L., & Hoggett, P. (2008). Human agency and social suffering. *Critical Social Policy*, 28(4), 438–460.

Gay, P. (1988). *Freud: A life for our time.* Basingstoke: Macmillan.

Germain, C., & Bloom, M. (1999). *Human behavior in the social environment: An ecological view.* New York: Columbia University Press.

Gilligan, R. (2004). Promoting resilience in child and family social work: Issues for social work practice, education and policy. *Social Work Education*, 23(1), 93–104.

Gilman, S., King, H., Porter, R., Rousseau, G., & Showalter, E. (Eds.). (1993). *Hysteria beyond Freud.* Berkeley: University of California Press.

Gist, R., & Lubin, B. (Eds.). (1999). *Response to disaster: Psychosocial, community and ecological approaches.* Philadelphia: Brunner/Mazel.

Gleiser, K. A. (2003). Psychoanalytic perspectives on traumatic repetition. *Journal of Trauma & Dissociation*, 4(2), 27–47.

Goddard, C., & Hunt, S. (2011). The complexities of caring for child protection workers: The contexts of practice and supervision. *Journal of Social Work Practice*, 25(4), 413–432.

Goldsmith, D., Oppenheim, D., & Wanlass, J. (2004). Separation and reunification: Using attachment theory and research to inform decisions affecting the placements of children in foster care. *Juvenile and Family Court Journal*, 55(2), 1–14.

Gordon, C. (Ed.). (1980). *Power/knowledge: Selected interviews and other writings, 1972–1977 Michel Foucault*. Brighton: Harvester Press.

Gordon, R. (2007). Thirty years of trauma work: Clarifying and broadening the consequences of trauma. *Psychotherapy in Australia*, 13(3), 12–19.

Green, D., & McDermott, F. (2010). Social work from inside and between complex systems: Perspectives on person-in-environment for today's social work. *British Journal of Social Work*, 40(8), 2414–2430.

Greene, R., & Greene, D. (2009). Resilience in the face of disasters: Bridging micro- and macro-perspectives. *Journal of Human Behavior in the Social Environment*, 19(8), 1010–1024.

Guha-Sapir, D., Vos, F., Below, R., & Ponserre, S. (2011). *Annual disaster statistical review 2010: The numbers and trends*. Brussels: CRED.

Gunderson, L. (2010). Ecological and human community resilience in response to natural disasters. *Ecology & Society*, 15(2), 1–11.

Habibis, D., & Walter, M. (2009). *Social inequality in Australia: Discourses, realities and futures*. South Melbourne: Oxford University Press.

Haebich, A. (2000). *Broken circles: Fragmenting indigenous families 1800–2000*. Fremantle: Fremantle Press.

Hafkenscheid, A. (2005). Event countertransference and vicarious traumatization: Theoretically valid and clinically useful concepts? *European Journal of Psychotherapy & Counselling*, 7(3), 159–168.

Hamilton, C. (2000). Continuity and discontinuity of attachment from infancy through adolescence. *Child Development*, 71(3), 690–694.

Harms, L. (2001). *An analysis of experiences of psychosocial recovery from road trauma*. Unpublished PhD, The University of Melbourne, Melbourne.

Harms, L. (2010). *Understanding human development: A multidimensional approach* (2nd ed.). South Melbourne: Oxford University Press.

Harvey, M. (1996). An ecological view of psychological trauma and trauma recovery. *Journal of Traumatic Stress*, 9(1), 3–23.

Hawkins, R. L., & Maurer, K. (2011). You fix my community, you have fixed my life: The disruption and rebuilding of ontological security in New Orleans. *Disasters*, 35(1), 143–159.

Hepworth, D., Rooney, R., & Larsen, J. A. (2002). *Direct social work practice: Theory and skills*. Pacific Grove: Brooks/Cole.

Herman, J. (1992). *Trauma and recovery*. New York: Basic Books.

Hesse, E. (2008). The adult attachment interview: Protocol, method of analysis, and empirical studies. In J. Cassidy & P. Shaver (Eds.), *Handbook of attachment: Theory, research, and clinical applications* (pp. 552–598). New York: Guilford Press.

Hildreth, W. (2009). The financial logistics of disaster: The case of Hurricane Katrina. *Public Performance and Management Review*, 32(3), 400–436.

Hilhorst, D. (2004). Complexity and diversity: Unlocking social domains of disaster response. In G. Bankoff, G. Frerks & D. Hilhorst (Eds.), *Mapping vulnerability: Disasters, development & people* (pp. 52–66). London New York: Earthscan.

Hilhorst, D. & Bankoff, G. (2004). Introduction: Mapping vulnerability. Chapter 1. In G. Bankoff, G. Frerks & D. Hilhorst (Eds.) *Mapping vulnerability: Disasters, development & people* (pp. 1–9). London New York: Earthscan.

Hobfoll, S. (2001). The influence of culture, community, and the nested-self in the stress process: Advancing conservation of resources theory. *Applied Psychology: An International Review*, 50(3), 337–421.

Hobfoll, S., Ennis, N., & Kay, J. (2000). Loss, resources and resiliency in close interpersonal relationships. In J. Harvey & E. Miller (Eds.), *Loss and trauma: General and close relationship perspectives* (pp. 267–285). Philadelphia: Brunner-Routledge.

Hobfoll, S. E., Watson, P., Bell, C. C., Bryant, R. A., Brymer, M. J., Friedman, M. J., Friedman, M., Gersons, B. P. R., de Jong, J. T. M. V., Layne, C. M., Maguen, S., Neria, Y., Norwood, A. E., Pynoos, R. S., Reissman, D., Ruzek, J. I., Shalev, A. Y., Solomon, Z., Steinberg, A. M., & Ursano, R. J. (2007). Five essential elements of immediate and mid–term mass trauma intervention: Empirical evidence. *Psychiatry: Interpersonal and Biological Processes*, 70(4), 283–315.

Hoffman, K., Marvin, R., Cooper, G., & Powell, B. (2006). Changing toddlers' and preschoolers' attachment classifications: the Circle of Security intervention. *Journal of Consulting and Clinical Psychology*, 74(6), 1017–1027.

Holling, C. S. (1973). Resilience and stability of ecological systems. *Annual Review of Ecology & Systematics*, 4, 1–23.

Holling, C. S. (2001). Understanding the complexity of economic, ecological, and social systems. *Ecosystems*, 4(5), 390–405.

Holman, E., & Silver, R. (1996). Is it the abuse or the aftermath? A stress and coping approach to understanding responses to incest. *Journal of Social and Clinical Psychology*, 15(3), 318–339.

Holmstrom, L., & Burgess, A. (1975). Assessing trauma in the rape victim. *American Journal of Nursing*, 75(8), 1288–1291.

Hopper, E., Bassuk, E., & Olivet, J. (2010). Shelter from the storm: Trauma-informed care in homelessness services settings. *The Open Health Services and Policy Journal*, 3, 80–100.

Horowitz, M. (1992). *Stress response syndromes* (2nd ed.). Northvale: Jason Aronson Inc.

Howe, M. L., Goodman, G. S., & Cicchetti, D. (Eds.), (2008). *Stress, trauma, and children's memory development: Neurobiological, cognitive, clinical, and legal perspectives*. New York: Oxford University Press.

Humphreys, C., & Joseph, S. (2004). Domestic violence and the politics of trauma. *Women's Studies International Forum*, 27(5–6), 559–570.

Ife, J. (2012). *Human rights and social work: Towards rights-based practice*. Cambridge: Cambridge University Press.

International Federation of Red Cross and Red Crescent Societies. (n.d). Gender policy. from http://www.ifrc.org/Global/Governance/Policies/gender-policy-en.pdf

Jack, G. (2010). Place matters: The significance of place attachments for children's wellbeing. *British Journal of Social Work,* 40(3), 755–771.

Jackson, A., Frederico, M., Tanti, C., & Black, C. (2009). Exploring outcomes in a therapeutic service response to the emotional and mental health needs of children who have experienced abuse and neglect in Victoria, Australia. *Child and Family Social Work,* 14, 198–212.

Janoff-Bulman, R. (1992). *Shattered assumptions: Towards a new psychology of trauma.* New York: The Free Press.

Janoff-Bulman, R. (1995). Victims of violence. In G. Everly & J. Lating (Eds.), *Psychotraumatology: Key papers and core concepts in post-traumatic stress* (pp. 73–85). New York: Plenum Press.

Janoff-Bulman, R., & Berger, A. (2000). The other side of trauma: Towards a psychology of appreciation. In J. Harvey & E. Miller (Eds.), *Loss and trauma: General and close relationship perspectives* (pp. 29–41). Philadelphia: Brunner-Routledge.

Jaycox, L., Stein, B., & Amaya-Jackson, L. (2009). School-based treatment for children and adolescents. In E. B. Foa, T. Keane, M. J. Friedman & J. Cohen (Eds.), *Effective treatments for PTSD: Practical guidelines from the international society for traumatic stress studies* (2nd ed., pp. 327–345). New York: The Guilford Press.

Johnson, H., Thompson, A., & Downs, M. (2009). Non-Western interpreters' experiences of trauma: the protective role of culture following exposure to oppression. *Ethnicity and Health,* 14(4), 407–418.

Johnson, J., Maxwell, A., & Galea, S. (2009). The epidemiology of posttraumatic stress disorder. *Psychiatric Annals,* 39(6), 326–334.

Joseph, S., Yule, W., Williams, R. and Hodgkinson, P. (1993). Increased substance use in survivors of the Herald of Free Enterprise disaster, *British Journal of Medical Psychology,* 66(2), 185–91.

Joseph, S. (2005). Understanding posttraumatic stress from the person-centred perspective. In S. Joseph & R. Worsley (Eds.), *Person-centred psychopathology: A positive psychology of mental health* (pp. 190–201). Ross-on-Wye, England: PCCS Books.

Joseph, S. (2011). *What doesn't kill us: The new psychology of posttraumatic growth.* New York: Basic Books.

Joseph, S., & Murphy, D. (2012). Person-centered approach, positive psychology, and relational helping: Building bridges. *Journal of Humanistic Psychology,* 53, 26–51.

Joseph, S., & Murphy, D. (2014). Trauma: A unifying concept for social work. *British Journal of Social Work,* 44(5), 1094–1109.

Jung, C. (1977). *Memories, dreams, reflections.* London: Collins.

Kagan, J. (1984). *The nature of the child.* New York: Basic Books.

Kaplan, T., Black, D., Hyman, P., & Knox, J. (2001). Outcome of children seen after one parent killed the other. *Clinical Child Psychology and Psychiatry,* 6, 9–22.

Kardiner, A. (1941). *The traumatic neuroses of war.* Washington, DC: National Research Council.

Kemp, S. (2011). Recentring environment in social work practice: Necessity, opportunity, challenge. *British Journal of Social Work,* 41(6), 1198–1210.

Kendall-Tackett, K. (Ed.). (2005). *Handbook of women, stress and trauma.* New York: Brunner-Routledge.

Kendall-Tackett, K. (2009). Psychological trauma and physical health: A psychoneu-roimmunology approach to etiology of negative health effects and possible interventions. *Psychological Trauma: Theory, Research, Practice, and Policy,* 1(1), 35–38.

Kessler, R. C., Berglund, P., Demler, O., Jin, R., Merikangas, K. R., & Walters, E. E. (2005). Lifetime prevalence and age-of-onset distributions of DSM-IV disorders in the national comorbidity survey replication. *Archives of General Psychiatry,* 62(6), 593–602.

Kessler, R. C., Sonnega, A., Bromet, E., Hughes, M., & Nelson, C. B. (1995). Posttraumatic stress disorder in the national comorbidity survey. *Archives of General Psychiatry,* 52(12), 1048–1060.

Keyes, K., McLaughlin, K., Demmer, R., Cerdá, M., Koenen, K., Uddin, M., & Galea, S. (2013). Potentially traumatic events and the risk of six physical health conditions in a population-based sample *Depression and Anxiety,* 30(5), 451–460.

Kirmayer, L. J., Dandeneau, S., Marshall, E., Phillips, M. K., & Williamson, K. J. (2011). Rethinking resilience from Indigenous perspectives. *The Canadian Journal of Psychiatry,* 56(2), 84–91.

Kirmayer, L. J., Lemelson, R., & Barad, M. (Eds.). (2007). *Understanding trauma: Integrating biological, clinical, and cultural perspectives.* New York: Cambridge University Press.

Klein, S., & Alexander, D. A. (2009). Epidemiology and presentation of post-traumatic disorders. *Psychiatry,* 8(8), 282–287.

Klein, M., Heimann, P., & Money-Kyrle, R. (Eds.), (1955). *New directions in psycho-analysis: The significance of infant conflict in the pattern of adult behaviour.* London: Tavistock Publications.

Kleinman, A., Das, V. & Lock, M. (Eds) (1997). *Social suffering.* Berkeley: University of California Press.

Knudson-Martin, C. (2012). Attachment in adult relationships: A feminist perspec-tive. *Journal of Family Theory and Review,* 4(4), 299–305.

Kobak, R., & Madsen, S. (2008). Disruptions in attachment bonds: Implications for theory, research and clinical intervention. In J. Cassidy (Ed.), *Handbook of attachment: Theory, research and clinical applications* (pp. 23–47). New York: Guilford Press.

Kudler, H., Krupnick, J. L., Blank, A., Herman, J., & Horowitz, M. (2009). Psychodynamic therapy for adults. In E. B. Foa, T. Keane, M. Friedman & J. A. Cohen (Eds.), *Effective treatments for PTSD: Practice guidelines from the international society for traumatic stress studies* (pp. 346–369). New York: The Guilford Press.

Lambert, M. J. (2005). Early response in psychotherapy: Further evidence for the importance of common factors rather than 'placebo effects'. *Journal of Clinical Psychology,* 61(7), 855–869.

Lambert, M. & Ogles, B. (2004). The efficacy and effectiveness of psychotherapy. In M. Lambert (Ed.), *Bergin and Garfield's handbook of psychotherapy and behavior change* (5th ed., pp. 139–193). New York: Wiley.

Laub, D. (1995). Truth and testimony: The process and the struggle. In C. Caruth (Ed.), *Trauma: Explorations in memory* (pp. 61–75). Baltimore: The Johns Hopkins University Press.

Laub, D. & Auerhahn, N. (1993). Knowing and not knowing massive psychic trauma: Forms of traumatic memory. *International Journal of Psycho-Analysis*, 74, 287–302.

Lazarus, R. (1998). *Fifty years of the research and theory of R. S. Lazarus: An analysis of historical and perennial issues.* Mahwah, NJ: Lawrence Erlbaum Associates.

Lazarus, R. (2001). Conservation of Resources theory (COR): Little more than words masquerading as a new theory. *Applied Psychology: An International Review*, 50(3), 381–391.

Lehman, D., Davis, C., Delongis, A., Wortman, C., Bluck, S., Mandel, D., & Ellard, J. (1993). Positive and negative life changes following bereavement and their relations to adjustment. *Journal of Social and Clinical Psychology*, 12, 90–112.

Lerner, G. (1993). *The creation of feminist consciousness.* New York: Oxford University Press.

Lester, D. (2005). Suicide in Vietnam veterans: The suicide wall. *Archives of Suicide Research*, 9, 385–387.

Levine, S. Z., Laufer, A., Stein, E., Hamama-Raz, Y., & Solomon, Z. (2009). Examining the relationship between resilience and posttraumatic growth. *Journal of Trauma Stress*, 22(4), 282–286.

Levy, M. (2000). A conceptualization of the repetition compulsion. *Psychiatry: Interpersonal and Biological Processes*, 63(1), 45–53.

Lieberman, A. F., Ippen, C., & Marans, S. (2009). Psychodynamic therapy for children. In E. B. Foa, H. Keane, M. Friedman & J. A. Cohen (Eds.), *Effective treatments for PTSD: Practice guidelines from the international society for traumatic stress studies* (pp. 370–387). New York: The Guilford Press.

Lilly, M. M., & Valdez, C. E. (2012). Interpersonal trauma and PTSD: The roles of gender and a lifespan perspective in predicting risk. *Psychological Trauma: Theory, Research, Practice, and Policy*, 4(1), 140–144.

Little, G. (1999). *The public emotions: From mourning to hope.* Sydney: ABC Books.

Lundy, C. (2004). *Social work and social justice: A structural approach to practice.* Sydney: Broadview Press Ltd.

Lupton, D. (1997). Foucault and the medicalisation critique. In A. Petersen & R. Bunton (Eds.), *Foucault, health and medicine* (pp. 94–111). New York: Routledge.

Luthar, S. S., Cicchetti, D., & Becker, B. (2000). The construct of resilience: A critical evaluation and guidelines for future work. *Child Development*, 71(3), 543–562.

Lyons-Ruth, K., Dutra, L., Schuder, M., & Bianchi, I. (2006). From infant attachment disorganization to adult dissociation: Relational adaptations or traumatic experiences? *Psychiatric Clinics of North America*, 29, 63–86.

Magnavita, J. (2002). *Comprehensive handbook of psychotherapy: Volume 1 psychodynamic/object relations.* New York: John Wiley & Sons.

Main, M., & Hesse, E. (1990). Parents' unresolved traumatic experiences are related to infant disorganized attachment status: Is frightened or frightening parental behavior the linking mechanism? In M. Greenberg, D. Cicchetti & E. Cummings (Eds.), *Attachment in the preschool years: Theory, research and intervention* (pp. 161–184). Chicago: The University of Chicago Press.

Main, M., & Solomon, J. (1990). Procedures for identifying infants as disorganized/disoriented during the Ainsworth strange situation. In M. Greenberg, D. Cicchetti & E. Cummings (Eds.), *Attachment in the preschool years: Theory, research and intervention* (pp. 121–160). Chicago: The University of Chicago Press.

Martin, C. G., Cromer, L. D., DePrince, A. P., & Freyd, J. J. (2013). The role of cumulative trauma, betrayal, and appraisals in understanding trauma symptomatology. *Psychological Trauma: Theory, Research, Practice, and Policy,* 52(2), 110–118.

Maru, D., & Farmer, P. (2012). Human rights and health systems development: Confronting the politics of exclusion and the economics of inequality. *Health and Human Rights,* 14(2), 1–9.

Marx, K. (1959). Manifesto of the Communist Party. In K. Marx & F. Engels (Eds.), *Basic writings on politics and philosophy* (pp. 1–41). Garden City, NY: Anchor Publishing Co.

Maslach, C. (1982). *Burnout: The cost of caring.* Englewood Cliffs, NJ: Prentice Hall.

Maslow, A. (1968). *Toward a psychology of being* (2nd ed.). New York: D. Van Nostrand Co.

Masson, J. (2012). *Against therapy.* Untreed Reads. Available at: www.untreedreads.com.

Mayseless, O. (2005). Ontogeny of attachment in middle childhood: Conceptualization of normative changes. In K. Kerns & R. Richardson (Eds.), *Attachment in middle childhood* (pp. 1–23). New York: The Guilford Press.

McCann, L., & Pearlman, L. A. (1990). Vicarious traumatization: A framework for understanding the psychological effects of working with victims. *Journal of Traumatic Stress,* 3(1), 131–149.

McColl, M., Bickenbach, J., Johnston, J., Nishihama, S., Schumaker, M., Smith, K., Smith, M., & Yealland, B. (2000). Spiritual issues associated with traumatic-onset disability. *Disability and Rehabilitation,* 22(12), 555–564.

McCrory, E., De Brito, S. A., & Viding, E. (2010). Research review: The neurobiology and genetics of maltreatment and adversity. *Journal of Child Psychology & Psychiatry,* 51(10), 1079–1095.

McCrory, E., De Brito, S. A., & Viding, E. (2011). The impact of childhood maltreatment: a review of neurobiological and genetic factors. *Frontiers in Psychiatry,* 2, 48–48.

McFarlane, A. C., & Williams, R. (2012). Mental health services required after disasters: Learning from the lasting effects of disasters. *Depression Research and Treatment,* 2012, 1–13.

McFarlane, C., & Kaplan, I. (2012). Evidence-based psychological interventions for adult survivors of torture and trauma: A 30-year review. *Transcultural Psychiatry,* 49(3–4), 539–567.

McIntosh, D., Poulin, M., Silver, R., & Holman, E. (2011). The distinct roles of spirituality and religiosity in physical and mental health after collective trauma: a national longitudinal study of responses to the 9/11 attacks. *Journal of Behavioral Medicine,* 34, 497–507.

McKinney, K. (2007). 'Breaking the conspiracy of silence': Testimony, traumatic memory, and psychotherapy with survivors of political violence. *Ethos,* 35(3), 265–299.

McMillen, J. C. (1999). Better for it: How people benefit from adversity. *Social Work,* 44(5), 455–468.

McMillen, J. C., Smith, E., & Fisher, R. (1997). Perceived benefit and mental health after three types of disaster. *Journal of Consulting and Clinical Psychology,* 65(5), 733–739.

McNally, R. (2003). Progression and controversy in the study of posttraumatic stress disorder. *Annual Review of Psychology,* 54, 229–252.

McNally, R. (2005). Debunking myths about trauma and memory. *Canadian Journal of Psychiatry,* 50(13), 817–822.

McPhie, L. & Chaffey, C. (1999). The journey of a lifetime: Group work with young women who have experienced sexual assault. In Dulwich Centre Publications (Eds.), *Extending narrative therapy: A collection of practice-based papers* (pp. 31–61). Adelaide: Dulwich Centre Publications.

Mendez, M. F., & Fras, I. A. (2011). The false memory syndrome: Experimental studies and comparison to confabulations. *Medical Hypotheses,* 76(4), 492–496.

Mercer, J. (2012). Reply to Sudbery, Shardlow and Huntington: Holding therapy. *British Journal of Social Work,* 42, 556–559.

Middleton, W., Stavropoulos, P., Dorahy, M. J., Krüger, C., Lewis-Fernández, R., Martínez-Taboas, A., Sar, V., & Brand, B. (2014). Institutional abuse and societal silence: An emerging global problem. *Australian and New Zealand Journal of Psychiatry,* 48(1), 22–25.

Mikulincer, M., Shaver, P., & Pereg, D. (2003). Attachment theory and affect regulation: The dynamics, development, and cognitive consequences of attachment-related strategies. *Motivation and Emotion,* 27, 77–102.

Miller, K., & Rasmussen, A. (2010). War exposure, daily stressors, and mental health in conflict and post-conflict settings: Bridging the divide between trauma-focused and psychosocial frameworks. *Social Science & Medicine,* 70, 7–16.

Mitchell, J. (1983). When disaster strikes: The critical incident stress debriefing process. *Journal of Emergency Medical Service,* 8(1), 36–39.

Moser, J. S., Hajcak, G., Simons, R. F., & Foa, E. B. (2007). Posttraumatic stress disorder symptoms in trauma-exposed college students: The role of trauma-related cognitions, gender, and negative affect. *Journal of Anxiety Disorders,* 21(8), 1039–1049.

Mullaly, B. (2002). *Challenging oppression: A critical social work approach.* Ontario: Oxford University Press.

Muller, D. (2011). *Media ethics and disasters: Lessons from the Black Saturday's bushfires.* Carlton: Melbourne University Press.

Murphy, D., Archard, P. J., Regel, S., & Joseph, S. (2013). A survey of specialized traumatic stress services in the United Kingdom. *Journal of Psychiatric and Mental Health Nursing,* 20(5), 433–441.

National Child Traumatic Stress Network and National Center for PTSD. (2016). *Appendix A: Overview of psychological first aid.* Washington, DC: US Department of Veteran Affairs.

National Collaborating Centre for Mental Health. (2005). *Post-traumatic stress disorder: The management of PTSD in adults and children in primary and secondary care.* Trowbridge: Gaskell and the British Psychological Society.

National Inquiry into the Separation of Aboriginal and Torres Strait Islander Children from their Families (Australia). (1997). *Bringing them home: Report of the national inquiry into the separation of aboriginal and Torres strait islander children from their families.* Sydney: Human Rights and Equal Opportunity Commission.

National Research Council. (2008). *Treatment of posttraumatic stress disorder: An assessment of the evidence.* Washington, DC: The National Academies Press.

National Research Council and Institute of Medicine. (2000). *From neurons to neighborhoods: The science of early childhood development.* Washington, DC: National Academy Press.

Neimeyer, R., & Stewart, A. (1996). Trauma, healing and the narrative emplotment of loss. *Families in Society: The Journal of Contemporary Human Services, 77*(6), 360–375.

Neville, B. (2009). Book Review: Gillian Proctor, Mick Cooper, Pete Sanders & Beryl Malcolm (Eds.): Politicizing the person-centred approach: An agenda for social change. *Person-centered and Experiential Psychotherapies, 8*(1), 65–67.

Newman, L., & Dale, A. (2005). Network structure, diversity and proactive resilience building: A response to Tompkins and Adger. *Ecology and Society, 10*(1), 1–4.

Norcross, J., & Barnett, J. (2008). Self-care as ethical imperative. *The National Register* 2008. Retrieved on 3/3/2013 from http://www.nationalregister.org/trr_spring08_norcross.html

Norman, S. (2006). New Zealand's holistic framework for disaster recovery. *Australian Journal of Emergency Management, 21*(4), 16–20.

Norris, F. (1992). Epidemiology of trauma: Frequency and impact of different potentially traumatic events on different demographic groups. *Journal of Consulting and Clinical Psychology, 60*(3), 409–418.

Norris, F., Perilla, J., Ibanez, G., & Murphy, A. (2001). Sex differences in symptoms of posttraumatic stress: Does culture play a role? *Journal of Traumatic Stress, 14*(1), 7–28.

Norris, F. H., & Stevens, S. P. (2007). Community resilience and the principles of mass trauma intervention. *Psychiatry: Interpersonal and Biological Processes, 70*(4), 320–328.

Norris, F., Stevens, S., Pfefferbaum, B., Wyche, K., & Pfefferbaum, R. (2008). Community resilience as a metaphor, theory, set of capacities, and strategy for disaster readiness. *American Journal of Community Psychology, 41*, 127–150.

Norton, J. (2007). Putting the brakes on the influence of neuroscience on psychotherapy. *Psychotherapy in Australia, 13*(3), 60–65.

O'Connor, P. (1985). *Understanding Jung, understanding yourself.* North Ryde: Methuen Haynes.

O'Leary, V. E. (1998). Strength in the face of adversity: Individual and social thriving. *Journal of Social Issues, 54*(4), 425–446.

O'Leary, V., & Ickovics, J. (1995). Resilience and thriving in response to challenge: An opportunity for a paradigm shift in women's health. *Women's Health: Research on Gender, Behavior and Policy, 1*, 121–142.

Ost, J., Wright, D., Easton, S., Hope, L., & French, C. (2013). Recovered memories, satanic abuse, dissociative identity disorder and false memories in the UK: A survey of clinical psychologists and hypnotherapists. *Psychology, Crime & Law, 19*(1), 1–19.

Padykula, N., & Conklin, P. (2010). The self regulation model of attachment trauma and addiction. *Clinical Social Work Journal,* 38(4), 351–360.

Parkes, C. (2008). Bereavement following disasters. In M. Stroebe, R. Hansson, H. Schut & W. Stroebe (Eds.), *Handbook of bereavement research and practice: Advances in theory and intervention* (Chapter 22, pp. 463–484). Washington, DC: American Psychological Association, chapter 22, pp. 463–484.

Payne, M. (2011). Risk, security and resilience work in social work practice. *Social Work Review,* 1, 7–14.

Pearlman, L. A., & Saakvitne, K. W. (1995). *Trauma and the therapist: Countertransference and vicarious traumatization in psychotherapy with incest survivors.* New York: Norton.

Pennebaker, J. (Ed.) (1995). *Emotion, disclosure and health.* Washington: American Psychological Society.

Pennebaker, J. W., & Seagal, J. D. (1999). Forming a story: The health benefits of narrative. *Journal of Clinical Psychology,* 55(10), 1243–1254.

Perry, B. (2009). Examining child maltreatment through a neurodevelopmental lens: Clinical applications of the neurosequential model of therapeutics. *Journal of Loss & Trauma,* 14(4), 240–255.

Perry, B., & Hambrick, E. (2008). The neurosequential model of therapeutics. *Reclaiming Children and Youth,* 17(3), 38–43.

Perry, B., Pollard, R., Blakley, T., Baker, W., & Vigilante, D. (1995). Childhood trauma, the neurobiology of adaptation, and 'use-dependent' development of the brain: how 'states' become 'traites'. *Infant Mental Health Journal,* 16(4), 271–291.

Petchkovsky, L., & San Roque, C. (2002). Tjunguwiyanytja, attacks on linking: Forced separation and its psychiatric sequelae in Australia's 'Stolen Generations'. *Transcultural Psychiatry,* 39(3), 345–366.

Pinquart, M., Feussner, C., & Ahnert, L. (2013). Meta-analytic evidence for stability in attachments from infancy to early adulthood. *Attachment & Human Development,* 15(2), 189–218.

Poole, D. A., Lindsay, D. S., Memon, A., & Bull, R. (1995). Psychotherapy and the recovery of memories of childhood sexual abuse: U.S. and British Practitioners' opinions, practices, and experiences. *Journal of Consulting and Clinical Psychology,* 63, 426–437.

Powers, M. B., Halpern, J. M., Ferenschak, M. P., Gillihan, S. J., & Foa, E. B. (2010). A meta-analytic review of prolonged exposure for posttraumatic stress disorder. *Clinical Psychology Review,* 30(6), 635–641.

Price, J. P. (2007). Cognitive schemas, defence mechanisms and post-traumatic stress symptomatology. *Psychology and Psychotherapy,* 80(3), 343–353.

Price-Robertson, R., & Knight, K. (2012). Natural disasters and community resilience: A framework for support. CFCA Paper no. 3. Australian Institute of Family Studies.

Raphael, B., & Meldrum, L. (1994). Helping people cope with trauma. In R. Watts & D. Horne (Eds.), *Coping with trauma: The victim and the helper* (pp. 1–19). Brisbane: Australian Academic Press.

Read, P. (1996). *Returning to nothing: The meaning of lost places.* Oakleigh: Cambridge University Press.

Reis, B. (2009). Performative and enactive features of psychoanalytic witnessing: the transference as the scene of address. *International Journal of Psychoanalysis*, 90(6), 1359–1372.

Reiter, A. (2000). *Narrating the Holocaust*. London: Continuum.

Remen, R. N. (1996). *Kitchen table wisdom: Stories that heal*. Camberwell: Penguin Group.

Rieff, D. (2011). *Against remembrance*. Carlton: Melbourne University Press.

Riley, P. (2010). *Attachment theory and the teacher-student relationship: A practical guide for teachers, teacher educators and school leaders*. London: Taylor & Francis.

Robertson, J., & Robertson, J. (1971). Young children in brief separation–a fresh look. *Psychoanalytic Study of the Child*, 26, 264–315.

Robinson, R., & Mitchell, J. (1995). Getting some balance back into the debriefing debate. *The Bulletin of The Australian Psychological Society*, 17(5), 5–10.

Robson, M. (2010). Therapeutic work with children: A contextual overview. *British Journal of Guidance and Counselling*, 38(3), 247–261.

Rodriguez-Llanes, J., Vos, F., & Guha-Sapir, D. (2013). Measuring psychological resilience to disasters: are evidence-based indicators an achievable goal?. *Environmental Health: A Global Access Science Source*, 12(1), 2–20.

Rogers, C. (1944). Psychological adjustments of discharged service personnel. *Psychological Bulletin*, 41(10), 689–696.

Rogers, C. (1965). *Client-centered therapy: Its current practice, implications, and theory*. New York: Houghton Mifflin Company.

Rogers, C. (1967). *On becoming a person: A therapist's view of psychotherapy*. London: Constable & Company Ltd.

Rogers, C. (1986). A client-centered/person-centered approach to therapy. In L. Kutash & A. Wolf (Eds.), *Psychotherapist's casebook* (pp. 197–208). San Francisco: Jossey Bass.

Rogers, C. (2007 [1957]). The necessary and sufficient conditions of therapeutic personality change. *Psychotherapy: Theory, Research, Practice, Training*, 44(2), 240–248.

Rose, S. C., Bisson, J., Churchill, R., & Wessely, S. (2002). Psychological debriefing for preventing post traumatic stress disorder (PTSD). *The Cochrane Database of Systematic Reviews* (Publication no. 10.1002/14651858.CD000560).

Roth, A., & Fonagy, P. (2005). *What works for whom?: A critical review of psychotherapy research*, (2nd Ed.). New York: The Guilford Press.

Rothschild, B. (2000). *The body remembers: The psychophysiology of trauma and trauma treatment*. New York: W. W. Norton and Co.

Rowlands, A. (2013). Disaster recovery management in Australia and the contribution of social work. *Journal of Social Work in Disability & Rehabilitation*, 12(1–2), 19–38.

Rutter, M. (2008a). Implications of attachment theory and research for child care policies. In J. Cassidy (Ed.), *Handbook of attachment: Theory, research and clinical applications* (pp. 958–974). New York: Guilford Press.

Rutter, M. (2008b). Today's neuroscience, tomorrow's history. Retrieved from http://www.ucl.ac.uk/histmed/downloads/hist_neuroscience_transcripts/rutter.pdf

Rutter, M., Beckett, C., Castle, J., Colvert, E., Kreppner, J., Mehta, M., Stevens, S., & Sonuga-Barke, E. (2007). Effects of profound early institutional deprivation: An overview of findings from a UK longitudinal study of Romanian adoptees. *European Journal of Developmental Psychology,* 4(3), 332–350.

Rutter, M., Kreppner, J., & Sonuga-Barke, E. (2009). Emanuel Miller lecture: Attachment insecurity, disinhibited attachment, and attachment disorders: Where do research findings leave the concepts? *The Journal of Child Psychology and Psychiatry,* 50(5), 529–543.

Ryan, F. (2011). Kanyininpa (Holding): A way of nurturing children in Aboriginal Australia. *Australian Social Work,* 64(2), 183–197.

Sabin-Farrell, R., & Turpin, G. (2003). Vicarious traumatization: Implications for the mental health of health workers. *Clinical Psychology Review,* 23(3), 449–480.

Salazar, A., Keller, T., Gowen, L., & Courtney, M. (2013). Trauma exposure and PTSD among older adolescents in foster care. *Social Psychiatry and Psychiatric Epidemiology,* 48(4), 545–551.

Saleebey, D. (1997). *The strengths perspective in social work practice* (2nd ed.). New York: Longman.

Sanders, P. (2005). Principled and strategic opposition to the medicalisation of distress and all of its apparatus. In S. Joseph & R. Worsley (Eds.), *Person-centred psychopathology: A positive psychology of mental health* (pp. 21–42). Ross-on-Wye, England: PCCS Books.

Sandler, J., & Freud, A. (1985). *The analysis of defense: The ego and the mechanisms of defense revisited.* New York: International Universities Press.

Schaefer, J., & Moos, R. (1992). Life crises and personal growth. In B. Carpenter (Ed.), *Personal coping: Theory, research and application* (pp. 149–170). Westport: Praeger.

Schafer, M., & Ferraro, K. (2013). Childhood misfortune and adult health: Enduring and cascadic effects on somatic and psychological symptoms? *Journal of Aging and Health,* 25(1), 3–28.

Schauer, M., Neuner, F., & Elbert, T. (2011). *Narrative exposure therapy: A short-term treatment for traumatic stress disorders* (2nd revised and expanded ed.). Cambridge, MA: Hogrefe Publishing.

Schlenger, W., Caddell, J., Ebert, L., Jordan, B. K., Rourke, K., Wilson, D., Thalji, L., Dennis, J. M., Fairbank, J., & Kulka, R. (2002). Psychological reactions to terrorist attacks: Findings from the national study of Americans' reactions to September 11. *The Journal of the American Medical Association,* 288(5), 581–588.

Schore, A. N. (2001). The effects of early relational trauma on right brain development, affect regulation, and infant mental health. *Infant Mental Health Journal,* 22(1–2), 201–269.

Schore, A. (2002a). Dysregulation of the right brain: a fundamental mechanism of traumatic attachment and the psychopathogenesis of posttraumatic stress disorder. *Australian and New Zealand Journal of Psychiatry,* 36, 9–30.

Schore, A. N. (2002b). Advances in neuropsychoanalysis, attachment theory and trauma research. *Psychoanalytic Inquiry,* 22(3), 433–484.

Schore, A. (2009). Relational trauma and the developing right brain: An interface of psychoanalytic self psychology and neuroscience. *Self and Systems: Annals of the New York Academy of Science,* 1159, 189–203.

Schore, J., & Schore, A. N. (2008). Modern attachment theory: The central role of affect regulation in development and treatment. *Clinical Social Work Journal,* 36(1), 9–20.

Schottenbauer, M. A., Glass, C. R., Arnkoff, D. B., & Gray, S. H. (2008). Contributions of psychodynamic approaches to treatment of PTSD and trauma: A review of the empirical treatment and psychopathology literature. *Psychiatry: Interpersonal and Biological Processes,* 71(1), 13–34.

Schwartz-Barcott, T. (2008). *After the disaster: Re-creating community and well-being at Buffalo Creek since the notorious coal-mining disaster in 1972.* Amherst: Cambria Press.

Scott, C. (2009). Trauma's presentation. In K. Golden & B. Bengo (Eds.), *The trauma controversy: Philosophical and interdisciplinary dialogues* (pp. 115–126). Albany, NY: SUNY press.

Seng, J., Lopez, W., Sperlich, M., Hamama, L., & Meldrum, C. (2012). Marginalised identities, discrimination burden, and mental health: Empirical exploration of an interpersonal-level approach to modeling intersectionality. *Social Science and Medicine,* 75, 2437–2445.

Shapiro, F. (2001). *Eye movement desensitization and reprocessing (EMDR): Basic principles, protocols and procedures.* New York: Guilford Press.

Shapiro, F. (2002). EMDR 12 years after its introduction: Past and future research. *Journal of Clinical Psychology,* 58, 1–22.

Shardlow, S., & Sudbery, J. (2014). Holding techniques in the care of children: Response to Mercer. *British Journal of Social Work,* 44(1), 181–184.

Shaver, P., & Mikulincer, M. (2010). Mind-behavior relations in attachment theory and research. In C. Agnew, D. Carlston, W. Graziano & J. Kelly (Eds.), *Then a miracle occurs: Focusing on behavior in social psychological theory and research* (pp. 342–367). New York: Oxford University Press.

Shear, K., Monk, T., Houck, P., Melhem, N., Frank, E., Reynolds, C., & Sillowash, R. (2007). An attachment-based model of complicated grief including the role of avoidance. *European Archives of Psychiatry and Clinical Neuroscience* 257, 453–461.

Shell-Duncan, B. (2008). From health to human rights: Female genital cutting and the politics of intervention. *American Anthropologist,* 110(2), 225–237.

Sherrieb, K., Norris, F. H., & Galea, S. (2010). Measuring capacities for community resilience. *Social Indicators Research,* 99(2), 227–247.

Shonkoff, J. P. (2003). From neurons to neighborhoods: Old and new challenges for developmental and behavioural pediatrics. *Developmental and Behavioral Pediatrics,* 24(1), 70–76.

Showalter, E. (1997). *Hystories: Hysterical epidemics and modern media.* New York: Columbia University Press.

Shuman, A., & Bohmer, C. (2004). Representing trauma: Political asylum narrative. *Journal of American Folklore,* 117(466), 394–414.

Silver, R., Boon, C., & Stones, M. (1983). Searching for meaning in misfortune: Making sense of incest. *Journal of Social Issues,* 39(2), 81–102.

Slaby, J. (2010). Steps towards a critical neuroscience. *Phenomenology and the Cognitive Sciences,* 9, 397–416.

Smyke, A., Zeanah, C., Gleason, M., Drury, S., Fox, N., Nelson, C., & Guthrie, D. (2012). A randomized controlled trial comparing foster care and institutional care for children with signs of Reactive Attachment Disorder. *American Journal of Psychiatry*, 169(5), 508–514.

Smyth, J. M. (1998). Written emotional expression: Effect sizes, outcome types, and moderating variables. *Journal of Consulting & Clinical Psychology*, 66, 174–184.

Solomon, E. P., & Heide, K. M. (2005). The biology of trauma: Implications for treatment. *Journal of Interpersonal Violence*, 20(1), 51–60.

Solomon, J. & George, C. (2011). The disorganized attachment-caregiving system: Dysregulation of adaptive processes at multiple levels. In J. Solomon & C. George (Eds.), *Disorganized attachment and caregiving* (Chapter 1, pp. 3–24). New York: Guilford Press.

Solomon, R., & Shapiro, F. (2008). EMDR and the adaptive information processing model: Potential mechanisms of change. *Journal of EMDR Practice and Research*, 2(4), 315–325.

Somers, M. (1994). The narrative constitution of identity: A relational and network approach. *Theory and Society*, 23, 605–649.

Spila, B., Makara, M., Kozak, G., & Urbanska, A. (2008). Abuse in childhood and mental disorder in adult life. *Child Abuse Review*, 17, 133–138.

Steel, Z., Steel, C. R., & Silove, D. (2009). Human rights and the trauma model: Genuine partners or uneasy allies? *Journal of Traumatic Stress*, 22(5), 358–365.

Steele, W. & Malchiodi, C. (2012). *Trauma-informed practices with children and adolescents*. New York: Routledge.

Stolorow, R. (2008). The contextuality and existentiality of emotional trauma. *Psychoanalytic Dialogues*, 18(1), 113–123.

Stroebe, M., & Schut, H. (2008). The Dual Process Model of coping with bereavement: Overview and update. *Grief Matters: The Australian Journal of Grief and Bereavement*, Autumn, 4–11.

Stroebe, M., Schut, H., & Finkenauer, C. (2001). The traumatization of grief? A conceptual framework for understanding the trauma-bereavement interface. *Israel Journal of Psychiatry and Related Sciences*, 38(3–4), 185–201.

Sudbery, J., Shardlow, S., & Huntington, A. (2010). To have and to hold: Questions about a therapeutic service for children. *British Journal of Social Work*, 40, 1534–1552.

Tang, S., & Freyd, J. (2012). Betrayal trauma and gender differences in posttraumatic stress. *Psychological Trauma: Theory, Research, Practice, and Policy*, 4(5), 469–478.

Taylor, S., & Armor, D. (1996). Positive illusions and coping with adversity. *Journal of Personality*, 64(4), 873–898.

Taylor, S., & Brown, J. (1988). Illusion and well-being: A social psychological perspective on mental health. *Psychological Bulletin*, 103(2), 193–210.

Teague, B., McLeod, R. & Pascoe, S. (2010). *2009 Victorian bushfires royal commission: Final report*. Melbourne: Government Printer for the State of Victoria.

Tedeschi, R., & Calhoun, C. (1995). *Trauma and transformation: Growing in the aftermath of suffering*. London: SAGE Publications.

Tedeschi, R. G., & Calhoun, L. G. (2004). Posttraumatic growth: Conceptual foundations and empirical evidence. *Psychological Inquiry*, 15(1), 1–18.

Tedeschi, R., Park, C., & Calhoun, L. (1998). *Posttraumatic growth: Positive changes in the aftermath of crisis*. London: Lawrence Erlbaum Associates.

Thomas, C. (2010). Negotiating the contested terrain of narrative methods in illness contexts. *Sociology of Health & Illness*, 32(4), 647–660.

Thompson, N. (1993). *Anti-discriminatory practice*. Basingstoke: Macmillan.

Thompson, N. (2003). *Promoting equality: Challenging discrimination and oppression* (2nd ed.). Houndmills, Basingstoke: Palgrave Macmillan.

Thompson, N. (2006). *Anti-discriminatory practice* (4th ed.). Houndmills, Basingstoke: Palgrave Macmillan.

Tolin, D. F., & Foa, E. B. (2006). Sex differences in trauma and posttraumatic stress disorder: A quantitative review of 25 years of research. *Psychological Bulletin*, 132(6), 959–992.

Trevithick, P. (2012). *Social work skills and knowledge: A practice handbook* (3rd ed.). Milton Keyes: Open University Press.

Tumarkin, M. (2005). *Traumascapes: The power and fate of places transformed by tragedy*. Carlton: Melbourne University Press.

Tummala-Narra, P. (2007). Conceptualizing trauma and resilience across diverse contexts: A multicultural perspective. *Journal of Aggression, Maltreatment, and Trauma*, 14(1/2), 33–53.

Turner, A. (2012). Person-centred approaches to trauma, critical incidents and post-traumatic stress disorder. In J. Tolen & P. Wilkins (Eds.), *Client issues in counselling and psychotherapy: person-centred practice* (pp. 30–46). London: SAGE.

Ulman, R., & Brothers, D. (1988). *The shattered self: A psychoanalytic study of trauma*. Hilldale: The Analytic Press.

Ungar, M. (2009). Resilience practice in action: Five principles for intervention. *Social Work Now*, 43, August, 32–38.

Ungar, M. (2010). Families as navigators and negotiators: Facilitating culturally and contextually specific expressions of resilience. *Family Process*, 49(3), 421–435.

Ungar, M. (2013). Resilience, trauma, context, and culture. *Trauma, Violence, & Abuse*, 14(3), 255–266.

United Nations General Assembly (1948). *Universal Declaration of Human Rights*. Retrieved 15/1/2015 from http://www.un.org/en/documents/udhr

Urbis Social Planning and Social Research. (n.d.). *Evaluation of the Victorian bushfire case management service*. Melbourne: Department of Human Services.

Vachon, M. (1998). Caring for the caregiver in oncology and palliative care. *Seminars in Oncology Nursing*, 14(2), 152–157.

Vaillant, G. (2002). *Ageing well: Surprising guideposts to a happier life from the landmark Harvard study of adult development*. Melbourne: Scribe Publications

Van der Kolk, B. (1994). Foreword. In J. Wilson & J. Lindy (Eds.), *Countertransference in the treatment of PTSD* (pp. vii–xii). New York: Guilford Press.

Van der Kolk, B. (2005). Developmental trauma disorder: Toward a rational diagnosis for children with complex trauma histories. *Psychiatric Annals*, 35, 401–408.

Van Der Kolk, B. A., & Fisler, R. (1995). Dissociation and the fragmentary nature of traumatic memories: Overview and exploratory study. *Journal of Traumatic Stress*, 8(4), 505–525.

Van der Kolk, B., van der Hart, O., & Burbridge, J. (2004). Approaches to the treatment of PTSD. *David Baldwin's Trauma Information Pages* Retrieved 02/01/2014, from http://www.trauma-pages.com/a/vanderk.php

Vandell, D., Belsky, J., Burchinal, M., Steinberg, L., Vandergrift, N., & NICHD Early Child Care Research Network. (2010). Do effects of early child care extend to age 15 years? Results from the NICHD study of early child care and youth development. *Child Development,* 81(3), 737–756.

van IJzendoorn, M., Juffer, F., & Duyvesteyn, M. (1995). Breaking the intergenerational cycle of insecure attachment: A review of the effects of attachment-based interventions on maternal sensitivity and infant security. *Journal of Child Psychology and Psychiatry,* 36, 225–248.

Vidal, F. (2009). Brainhood, anthropological figure of modernity. *History of the Human Sciences,* 22(1), 5–36.

Walsh, F. (2002). Bouncing forward: Resilience in the aftermath of September 11. *Family Process,* 41(34–36).

Walsh, F. (2006). *Strengthening family resilience* (2nd ed.). New York: The Guilford Press.

Ward, T. (2012). Narrative identity and forensic psychology: A commentary on Youngs and Canter. *Legal and Criminal Psychology,* 17, 250–261.

Waters, E., Hamilton, C. E., & Weinfield, N. S. (2000). The stability of attachment security from infancy to adolescence and early adulthood: General introduction. *Child Development,* 71(3), 678–683.

Waters, E., Merrick, S., Treboux, D., Crowell, J., & Albersheim, L. (2000). Attachment security in infancy and early adulthood: A twenty-year longitudinal study. *Child Development,* 71(3), 684–689.

Waters, H. S., & Waters, E. (2006). The attachment working models concept: Among other things, we build script-like representations of secure base experiences. *Attachment & Human Development,* 8(3), 185–197.

Weathers, F., & Keane, T. M. (2007). The criterion a problem revisited: Controversies and challenges in defining and measuring psychological trauma. *Journal of Traumatic Stress,* 20, 107–121.

Weinberg, M., & Tronick, E. (1996). Infant affective reactions to the resumption of maternal interaction after the still-face. *Child Development,* 96, 905–914.

Weiss, T. (2002). Posttraumatic growth in women with breast cancer and their husbands: An intersubjective validation study. *Journal of Psychosocial Oncology,* 20(2), 65–80.

Weiss, T., & Berger, R. (Eds.), (2010). *Posttraumatic growth and culturally competent practice: Lessons learned from around the globe.* Hoboken, NJ: John Wiley & Sons, Inc.

Werner, E., & Smith, R. (1992). *Overcoming the odds: High risk children from birth to adulthood.* Ithaca: Cornell University Press.

Westphal, M., & Bonanno, G. A. (2007). Posttraumatic growth and resilience to trauma: Different sides of the same coin or different coins? *Applied Psychology,* 56(3), 417–427.

Wethington, H. R., Hahn, R. A., Fuqua-Whitley, D. S., Sipe, T. A., Crosby, A. E., Johnson, R. L., Liberman, A. M., Moscicki, E., Price, L. N., Tuma, F. K., Kalra, G., &

Chattopadhyay, S. K. (2008). The effectiveness of interventions to reduce psychological harm from traumatic events among children and adolescents: A systematic review. *American Journal of Preventitive Medicine,* 35(3), 287–313.

White, M. (1987). Family therapy and schizophrenia: Addressing the 'in-the-corner' lifestyle. *Dulwich Centre Newsletter,* Spring, 14–21. Reprinted in M. White (1989), *Selected Papers* (pp. 47–57). Adelaide: Dulwich Centre Publications.

White, M. (2004). Working with people who are suffering the consequences of multiple trauma: A narrative perspective. *The International Journal of Narrative Therapy and Community Work,* 1, 45–76.

White, M. (2011). *Narrative practice: Continuing the conversations.* New York: W. W. Norton & Company.

Wilkins, D. (2012). Disorganised attachment indicates child maltreatment: How is this link useful for child protection social workers? *Journal of Social Work Practice,* 26(1), 15–30.

Williams, M. B., & Sommer, J. (Eds.), (1994). *Handbook of post-traumatic therapy.* Westport, CT: Greenwood Press.

Williams, R. (1977). *Marxism & Literature.* Cambridge: Cambridge University Press.

Wilson, J. (1995). The historical evolution of PTSD diagnostic criteria: From Freud to DSMIV. In G. Everly & J. Lating (Eds.), *Psychotraumatology* (pp. 9–26). New York: Plenum Press.

Wilson, J., & Lindy, J. (Eds.), (1994). *Countertransference in the treatment of PTSD.* New York: Guilford Press.

Wingard, B. & Lester, J. (2001). *Telling our stories in ways that make us stronger.* Adelaide: Dulwich Centre Publications.

Winkworth, G., Healy, C., Woodward, M., & Camilleri, P. (2009). Community capacity building: Learning from the 2003 Canberra bushfires. *Australian Journal of Emergency Management,* 24(2), 5–12.

Woon, F. L., Sood, S., & Hedges, D. W. (2010). Hippocampal volume deficits associated with exposure to psychological trauma and posttraumatic stress disorder in adults: A meta-analysis. *Progress in Neuro-Psychopharmacology and Biological Psychiatry,* 34(7), 1181–1188.

World Health Organization. (2003). *Constitution of the World Health Organization.* Geneva: United Nations.

World Health Organization. (2010). Mental and behavioural disorders: *ICD-10* Retrieved 22/07/2013, from http://apps.who.int/classifications/icd10/browse/2010/en#/F40-F48

Yehuda, R., & LeDoux, J. (2007). Response variation following trauma: A translational neuroscience approach to understanding PTSD. *Neuron,* 56(1), 19–32.

Yehuda, R., Koenen, K. C., Galea, S., & Flory, J. D. (2011). The role of genes in defining a molecular biology of PTSD. *Disease Markers,* 30(2–3), 67–76.

Young, I. (1990). *Justice and the politics of difference.* Princeton: Princeton University Press.

Ypinazar, V. A., Margolis, S. A., Haswell-Elkins, M., & Tsey, K. (2007). Indigenous Australians' understandings regarding mental health and disorders. *Australian and New Zealand Journal of Psychiatry,* 41(6), 467–478.

Yuen, A. (2007). Discovering children's responses to trauma: A response-based narrative practice. *International Journal of Narrative Therapy and Community Work*, 2007(4), 3–18.

Zepf, S., & Zepf, F. D. (2008). Trauma and traumatic neurosis: Freud's concepts revisited. *International Journal of Psychoanalysis*, 89(2), 331–353.

Index

accurate symbolisation, 90–1
Acosta, J., 140
actualisation, 90, 96, 102–4
  post-traumatic, 95
adaptation, 1–2, 10–12, 72, 89, 105,
  123–6, 130
adaptive capacity, 75, 126
Adger, W. N., 124
adult trauma, 21, 35, 77
Affleck, G., 97, 105
Afuape, T., 25, 148, 155
Agaibi, C. E., 10
Ahnert, L., 53
Ainsworth, M. S., 47, 50–2, 54, 64
Alden, L. E., 68
Alexander, J., 147
Allen, J., 19, 49, 54–6, 61, 86
Alston, M., 130
American Psychiatric Association (APA),
  6, 16, 38, 53, 56–8, 66–72, 171
amygdala, 66, 75, 77, 88
anti-oppressive approaches, 144–64
  alliance, 159–60
  criticisms of, 163–4
  PCS model, 145–6
  power and powerlessness, 151
  practical implications, 159–63
  resilience and, 144–5
  therapist, 159
  trauma, 149–59; consequences of,
    conceptualising, 153–4; responses,
    conceptualising, 154–6
  violence, 153
Antonovsky, A., 147
anxiety, 7, 12, 29, 31–2, 38, 50, 52, 55,
  61, 75, 77, 85–6, 90
approaches (trauma and resilience), 1

attachment, *see* attachment
  approaches
  ecological, 13
  feminist, 20
  multidimensional, 13
  neurobiological, 16
  psychiatric, 7
  psychodynamic, 7
  rights-based, 7
  salutogenic, 8
  stage, 9
Armor, D., 104
Atkinson, J., 18, 20, 152
Atkinson, P., 122
attachment approaches, 46–65
  Bowlby's approach, 46–9
  children and, 62–3
  criticism of, 63–5
  internal working models, 49–50
  maltreatment and, 62
  place and culture, 53–4
  practical implications, 59–63
  relationship, 47
  of resilience, 46–54
  security, 49
  styles, 51–3
  therapies, 60–3
  of trauma, 54–9
attachment behaviour, 47
attachment relationship, 47
  children and, 63–4
  devastating impacts, 46
  distinctive qualities, 50–1
  infants and adults, 48
  maltreatment, 54–6
  trauma and, 54–6, 58
  violation, recognition of, 38, 56
Auerhahn, N., 32, 36, 39–40

Augusta-Scott, T., 120
Australian Centre for Posttraumatic
    Mental Health, 22, 82
Australian Government, 112
Australian National Survey of Mental
    Health and Well-being, 73
avoidance symptoms, 69, 72, 105, 160

Bankoff, G., 5, 19
Barrett-Lennard, G. T., 93
Bartholomew, K., 51
Barth, R. P., 63
Becker, B., 11
behavioural repetition, 34
Bennett, B., 172
Berger, R., 13
Berger, W., 68
Berke, P. R., 126, 141
Bessarab, D., 152, 173
Betrayal Trauma Theory, 19, 114
biological dimensions, 16–17, 171
Bishop, A., 161
Blackburn, P., 114, 116, 118–19
Blankenship, K., 13
Block, J., 104
Bloom, M., 126
Blum, H., 36, 41
Boals, A., 119
Bohleber, W., 32, 35–6
Bohmer, C., 158
Bombay, A., 7
Bonanno, G., 9–11, 13
Boon, H. J., 127
Boulanger, G., 36, 40, 44
Bourdieu, P., 144
Bowlby, J., 46–51, 58, 60–1
    attachment theory, 46–9
Bragin, M., 38
Breckenridge, J., 140, 160
Breslau, J., 20
Breslau, N., 68, 74–5
Breuer, J., 30, 33, 42
Brewin, C. R., 136, 158
Briere, J., 83–4
Bronfenbrenner, U., 13, 20, 124
Brothers, D., 30–1, 33, 108

Brown, C., 109, 120
Brown, J., 104
Brown, L. S., 12, 67–8, 154–5,
    159–61
Bruneau, M., 127, 129, 138
Bryant, R., 43, 135
Bunting, B., 73
Burstow, B., 4, 66, 70, 134, 153–5, 159,
    161
Butler, J., 144

Calhoun, C., 8, 13, 96, 98, 99, 105
Calhoun, L. G., 96
Campanella, T., 126, 141
Canadian First Nation people, 110
Carey, M., 118
Carolan, M., 5
Carr, R. B., 45
Caruth, C., 112
Carver, C. S., 9
Castells, M., 144
CBT, see cognitive behavioural therapy
    (CBT)
Chaffey, C., 117
Chamlee-Wright, E., 114
Chandler, D., 147
Chang, C.-M., 68
Chapman, C., 150
childhood trauma, 7, 35, 55, 75–6
chronological age, 17, 21
Cicchetti, D., 62
civilian life, areas of adjustments to,
    93–4
Clark, D. M., 16, 82–3
client-centred approaches, see
    person-centred approaches
cognitive behavioural therapy
    (CBT), 81
Cohen, D., 45
Cohen, J., 22
collective narrative therapy, 119–21
    see also narrative approaches
Colvin, C., 104
community competence, 128–30, 137
community resilience, 126–9, 142
compassion fatigue, 26

complex trauma, 18–19, 55
Conklin, P., 47
Connolly, M., 1
conscious awareness, 37, 42–4
conservation of resources (COR) theory,
    128–32
Cooper, M., 91, 99, 103
COR theory, *see* conservation of
    resources (COR) theory
cortisol, 75
counsellors, 5, 79–80
countertransference, 41–2
Courtney, M., 196
Coutinho, E., 68
Cox, R. S., 131
Crawford, E., 10, 152, 173
Creamer, M., 73–4
Crenshaw, K., 153
critical reflections
  anti-oppressive approaches,
      163–4
  attachment approaches, 62
  narrative approaches, 121–2
  person-centred approaches, 103–5
  practitioners and researchers (in
      trauma), 24–7
  psychodynamic approaches, 45
  social-ecological approaches,
      141–2
  symptom approaches (reducing
      PTSD), 85–8
Crossley, M. L., 108, 122
Crumpton-Cook, R., 137, 142
cultural imperialism, 150, 152–3, 156,
    163–4

Dale, A., 125
Danieli, Y., 157, 162
Darves-Bornoz, J.-M., 73
Davis, H., 85–7, 161–2
debriefing, 37, 78–9
De Fazio, V., 34
defence mechanisms, 12, 31–2, 37–9, 43,
    45, 70, 90, 141
Denborough, D., 118, 119
developmental stage, 17, 39, 88

*Diagnostic and Statistical Manual of
    Mental Disorders,* 66, 171
dimensions (of trauma and resilience)
  cultural, 20–1
  inner world, 15
  psychological, 15–16
  relational and social, 18–19
  social capital, 130
  spiritual, 17–18
  structural, 19–20
  time and place, 21–2
disaster
  defined, 133
  impacts of, 135–7
  mobilise resources, 140
  rebuilding processes, 141
  social and ecological systems,
      disruption of, 134
  trauma, exposure of, 133
disenfranchised trauma, 5
disrupted narratives, 110–11
dissociation, traumatic, 37–8, 54, 56, 71,
    77
distress, 155
  acute, 63
  defence mechanisms and, 37
  emotional, 155
  infant's, 92
  inner world, 28
  intense, 52
  psychological, 158
  reducing, 78–85
  separation from parents, 47
documentation, 118–19
Doidge, N., 77
Doka, K., 5
Dorahy, M., 55
Downs, M., 8
Dozier, M., 75
Drozdek, B., 86, 155
DSM III, 67
DSM IV, 73
DSM V, 6, 67
  intrusion symptoms, 69
  PTSD, definition of, 72
Du Plooy, L., 137, 139

ecological approaches, 13
  resources and attributes, 128–33
Edkins, J., 148
Egan, G., 102
Ehlers, A., 82–3
Ellard, J., 70, 86
Ellenberger, H., 30
EMDR, *see* Eye Movement
    Desensitisation and Reprocessing
    (EMDR)
emotional abuse, 7, 18, 153
enhanced relationships, 13, 97
Erikson, K., 136
event-related dimensions, 170–1
exploitation, 150, 152, 153, 156
exposure therapy, 84, 111
exposure, traumatic, 4–7, 67
  defined, 67, 153
  ICD-10, 68
  PTSD and, 67; symptoms of, 68–72
Eye Movement Desensitisation and
    Reprocessing (EMDR), 81, 83

false memory syndrome, 35
Farmer, E., 56
Farmer, P., 145
Farrell, R., 26
felt security, *see* safety regulation system
feminist approaches, 20
Ferraro, K., 55
Feussner, C., 53
Figley, C., 26, 115
Finkenauer, C., 7
Fisler, R., 37–8
Flory, K., 16
Foa, E. B., 22–3, 43, 74, 82, 85–6
Folke, C., 134
Fonagy, P., 45, 47, 49, 64
Fook, J., 25
Foucault, M., 144, 148
Frank, A. W., 109, 122
Frankl, V., 112
Fras, I. A., 33, 35–6
Frattaroli, J., 119
Frazier, P., 13
free association, 40, 42

Freud, A., 30
Freud, S., 29–31, 33–5
Freyd, J. J., 19, 114
Friedman, M., 4, 22, 67, 72
Frisina, P. G., 119
From Neurons to Neighborhoods, 76
Frost, L., 16, 156–7, 160, 172

Gay, P., 35
George, C., 48, 50, 54–5
Germain, C., 126
Gilligan, R., 128
Gillihan, S., 43
Gist, R., 79
Gleiser, K. A., 34, 37
Goldsmith, D., 63
gold standards, 45, 82
Gordon, C., 144
Gordon, R., 111–12, 171, 174
Greene, D., 13
Greene, R., 13
grief, 5, 7–8, 22
Guha-Sapir, D., 133
Gunderson, L., 124, 134–5

Habibis, D., 145
Haebich, A., 20
Hafkenscheid, A., 42
Hambrick, E., 76
Hamilton, C., 53
Harms, L., 1, 8, 13, 15, 23
Harvey, M., 13
Hawkins, R. L., 136
health (WHO definition), 9
Heide, K. M., 75
Herman, J., 9–10, 34, 120, 148, 151, 154,
    156, 158, 162
Hesse, E., 55
Hildreth, W., 135
Hilhorst, D., 19
Hobfoll, S., 24, 106, 128–9, 139–40, 158
  resource 'caravans,' 129
Hoffman, K., 52
Hoggett, P., 16, 156–7, 160, 172
Holling, C. S., 134
Holman, E., 5, 153
Hopper, E., 27

Horowitz, L., 51
Horowitz, M., 72
Howe, M. L., 33
HPA, *see* hypothalamic pituitary adrenal (HPA) axis
human rights, 21, 114, 120, 146–7, 163–4
  resilience and, 146–7
Humphreys, C., 154
hypothalamic pituitary adrenal (HPA) axis, 75

ICD-10, 68
  PTSD, definition of, 74
Ickovics, J., 9
Ife, J., 147
incongruence, 89, 91, 94–5, 98, 101–2, 111
infants
  attachment approaches of, 17, 48, 50–3
  maltreating parents and, 62
  physiological regulation, 49
  responsive relationships, 50
informational trauma, 22, 26, 171
inner world dimensions, 15, 171–2
intrusion symptoms, 69, 72
Ippen, C., 31

Jack, G., 54
Jackson, A., 138
James, K., 140, 160
Janoff-Bulman, R., 86, 95, 111
Jaycox, L., 18, 55
Johnson, H., 8
Johnson, J., 8
Joseph, S., 13, 81, 86, 90, 95–6, 102, 154
Jung, C., 29

Kagan, J., 87
Kaplan, I., 158
Kaplan, T., 39
Kardiner, A., 43
Keane, T., 4, 6, 22, 67
Kemp, S., 53
Kendall-Tackett, K., 16, 74

Kessler, R. C., 73–5
Keyes, K., 5
Kirmayer, L. J., 110, 166
Knudson-Martin, C., 64
Kobak, R., 48, 50

Lambert, M., 23
Laub, D., 32, 36, 39–40, 42, 113, 116
Lazarus, R., 131
LeDoux, J., 69, 74–5, 85, 149
Lehman, D., 105
Lester, D., 20, 115
Lester, J., 18, 110
Levine, S., 105
Levy, M., 34
Lilly, M. M., 74
Lindy, J., 41
Little, G., 16
lower stress-response networks, 76
Lubin, B., 79
Lundy, C., 166
Lupton, D., 148, 151
Luthar, S. S., 11
Lyons-Ruth, K., 38

Madsen, S., 48, 50
Magnavita, J., 45
Main, M., 47, 50–2, 54–5
Mancini, A. D., 9–10, 13
Marans, S., 31
marginalisation, 21, 115, 145, 150, 152–3, 156–7
Maru, D., 145
Marx, K., 144–5
Maslach, C., 25
Maslow, A., 97
Masson, J., 45
Masten, A., 10
Maurer, K., 136
Mayseless, O., 48
McCann, L., 26, 41
McColl, M., 97
McCrory, E., 78
McDermott, F., 13
McFarlane, A. C., 136, 158
McIntosh, D., 17

McKinney, K., 118
McLeod, J., 91, 100, 103
McMillen, J. C., 13, 96
McNally, R., 35
McPhie, L., 117
Meldrum, L., 7
memory, 33–6
  cathartic release of, 77
  childhood, 35
  conscious acknowledgement of, 77
  trauma, role in, 16, 43
  traumatic, 16, 33, 35–6, 41, 43, 77–8, 83, 88, 113
  verbal, 39
  visual, 39
Mendez, M. F., 33, 35–6
Mercer, J., 61
Middleton, W., 112
Mikulincer, M., 46, 51
Millar, J., 127
Miller, K., 135
Mitchell, J., 79
moment of threat, 112
Moos, R., 96–7
Moser, J. S., 74
Mullaly, B., 145–6, 150–2, 156
Muller, D., 137
multidimensional approaches, 23, 168
  inner world dimensions, 171
  outer world dimensions, 18
  relationships and, 176
  resilience and, 13, 168–70
  think and work in, 174–6
  trauma and, 13–15, 168–70
Murphy, A., 74
Murphy, D., 81, 86, 90, 96, 103

narrative approaches, 107–22
  beyond, 111–12
  collective therapy, 119–21
  conversation and, 118
  criticisms of, 121–2
  disrupted, 110–11
  documentation, 118–19
  political aspects, 109
  practical implications, 115–21

  of resilience, 108–10
  restorative work, 117–18
  social silencing, 112–13
  socio-cultural and political contexts, 109, 113–15
  testimony method, 119
  therapeutic relationship, 115
  of trauma, 110–15
  truth and, 121
  witnessing survivors, 116–17
Narrative Exposure Therapy, 111
narrative identity, 107–8, 110, 121
National Centre for Posttraumatic Mental Health, 81–2
National Child Traumatic Stress Network and National Center for PTSD, 80
National Collaborating Centre for Mental Health, 22
National Co-morbidity Survey Replication (NCS-R), 73
National Research Council, 85
National Research Council and Institute of Medicine, 76
NCS-R, see National Co-morbidity Survey Replication (NCS-R)
negative appraisals, 82–3
negative life events, 59
Neimeyer, R., 109–11
neural pathways, 49, 75–7
neurobiological approaches, 2, 16–17, 75, 87, 88
  PTSD and, 75
Neville, B., 93, 104
Newman, L., 125
Neylan, T. C., 68
Norris, F., 12, 74, 86, 126–30, 141
Northern Ireland Centre for Trauma and Transformation, 81, 82
Norton, J., 87

Ogles, B., 23
O'Leary, J., 9
O'Leary, V., 9
oppression, 3, 18–19, 122, 144–6, 148–50, 152–61, 168, 173
Ost, J., 35

outer world dimensions
  resilience, 18
  trauma, 18, 173–4

Padykula, N., 47
paradoxial oppression, 152
Parkes, C., 7
Payne, M., 11, 25
PCL-C, 73
PCS model, 145–6
Pearlman, L. A., 26, 41–2
Pennebaker, J., 83, 108, 119
Perilla, J., 74
Perry, B., 75–6, 82, 84–5
  Neurosequential Model of
    Therapeutics, 84
Perry, K. M. E., 131
personal, cultural or structural model,
    see PCS model
person-centred approaches, 89–106
  actualisation, 102–3
  criticism of, 103–5
  incongruence, 101–2
  practical implications, 99–103
  self-structure, 102
  six core conditions, 91
  symbolisation, 101–2
  therapeutic practices, 92
  therapeutic relationship, 100–1
Petchkovsky, L., 7
PFA, see Psychological First Aid (PFA)
Phillips, M. K., 76
physical age, 17
Pinquart, M., 53
Poole, D. A., 35
post disaster, 114, 134, 136,
    138, 141
post-traumatic growth, 8, 13, 93, 95–9,
    103, 105–6
  principles of, 98–9
  therapeutic relationship, 139
post-traumatic stress disorder (PTSD),
    6–8, 15–16, 19, 22, 39, 79
  amygdala attack, 77
  anti-oppressive approaches, 154–6
  assumptions, 155

avoidance criteria, 69–70
causes of, 74–8
checklist (PCL-C), 73
criteria D, 71
criticism of, 85–8
cultural criticism, 155
defined, 86
diagnosis of, 72, 88
EMDR and, 82–3
exposure therapy, 84
gold standards, 82
hyperarousal criteria, 70
intrusion criteria, 69
longer-term interventions, 81–5
medications, 85
model of, 82
negative appraisals, 82–3
neurobiological approaches, 75
Perry's Neurosequential Model of
    Therapeutics, 84
prevalence of, 8, 73–4
psychiatric diagnoses, 75
recovery and, 78
resilience and, 78
risk rate, 73–4
short-term interventions, 78–81
symptoms of, 66–88
therapeutic techniques, 84–5
post-traumatic stress response, 72
potentially traumatic events, 5, 74
powerlessness, 3, 32, 150–3, 156, 173
Powers, M. B., 84
Price, J. P., 37
psychiatric disorder, trauma related, 15,
    43, 66
psychiatrization, 85–6
Psychoanalytic Society, 35
psychodynamic approaches, 7, 28–45
  challenges, 36
  countertransference, 41–2
  criticism of, 45
  defence mechanisms, 37
  dissociation, 37–8
  memory, 33–6
  practical implications, 39–45
  repression, 38–9

psychodynamic approaches (*cont.*):
    for self and resilience, 29–30
    transference, 41–2
    trauma, 30–3
psychological dimensions, 15–16,
        171–2, 175
Psychological First Aid (PFA), 79–81
psychopathology, 8–9, 98, 113
psychosis, 5
psychotherapy, 35, 41, 78
PTEs, *see* potentially traumatic events
PTG, *see* post-traumatic growth
PTSD, *see* post-traumatic stress disorder
        (PTSD)

RAD, *see* reactive attachment disorder
Raphael, B., 7
Rasmussen, A., 135
reactive attachment disorder, 53, 56–7
Read, P., 22
reclaim, 83
recovery
    Bonanno's definition, 9
    conceptualization of, 9
    defined, 8–9
    disaster events, 134, 141
    marker of, 10
    person-centred approaches to, 89–92
    PTSD and, 78, 8
    rebuilding processes, 141
    stage approach, 9
    trajectories and, 9
Reis, B., 41
Reiter, A., 32, 36
relationship
    alliance, 159
    attachment, 38, 50–1, 63–4
    parental, 41
    self and, 44
    therapeutic, 24, 38, 41, 61–2, 89,
        100–2, 115–16, 139–40, 162–3
    trauma and, 54–6, 58, 96
relationship-based practice, 59
religion, trauma and, 18
Remen, R. N., 24
repression, 30, 38–9, 158

resilience
    anti-oppressive approaches, 144–5
    attachment approaches of, 46–54
    attributes/properties of, 127–32
    capacities of, 12
    children identification, 11
    community systems of, 127–8, 131–3
    defined, 10
    dimensions of, *see* dimensions (of
        trauma and resilience)
    family, 128
    human rights, 146
    motivational aspect, 131
    multidimensional approach,
        theorising using, 13–15, 23, 168–70,
        174–6
    narrative approaches, 108–10
    networked resources, 125, 128–32
    person-centred approaches to, 89–92
    power and control, 148–9
    practice and research, implications for,
        22–4
    presence of, 11
    psychodynamic approaches, 29–30
    PTSD and, 78–88
    as resistance, 147–8
    resources, 132–3
    sense of security, 11
    social capital, 129–30
    social-ecological approaches, 123–33
    study of, 10
    systems, 127–32, 138–9
    theoretical approaches, comparative
        analysis of, 167–8
    vs. trauma, 165–8
    trauma and, 13, 14
    see also trauma
resistance, 12, 117, 127
    resilience as, 147–8
resources (in resilience)
    disaster and, 131
    Hobfoll's 'caravans,' 129
    identification of, 129–30
    networked, 128
    social and environmental system, 131
resource systems, 132–3, 135–6, 140

rights-based approaches, 7, 146–7
Riley, P., 63
Robertson, J., 47
Robinson, R., 79
Rodriguez-Llanes, J., 136
Rogers, C., 89–94, 100–3, 174
Rose, S. C., 37, 79
Roth, A., 45
Rothschild, B., 16
Rowlands, A., 136, 138–9
Rutter, M., 53–4, 57, 59, 65, 87–8
Ryan, M., 64

Saakvitne, K. W., 26, 42
safety regulation system, 48
Salazar, A., 7
Saleebey, D., 98
salutogenic approaches, 8
Sanders, P., 86, 90, 93, 100, 104
San Roque, C., 7
Schaefer, J., 96–7
Schafer, M., 55
Schauer, M., 111
Schlenger, W., 68
Schore, A., 49, 75
Schore, J., 49
Schottenbauer, M. A., 41
Schut, H., 7
Scott, C., 77, 83–4
Seagal, J. D., 83, 108, 119
secondary trauma, 133, 137, 140, 158
secure attachment, 19, 46, 50–2, 54, 56,
    59–60, 62–4, 92
  in traumatic life events, 59
secure base, 50–2, 60–3
self and the world, 94–5
self-care, 25, 27
  psychodynamic approaches, 29–30
self-perception, 96
self-structure, 2, 89–97, 96, 102, 172
sense of community closeness, 97, 136
sense of congruence, 90, 94
sense of depersonalisation, 71
sense of safety, restoring, 78–85
sense of security, 11
sense of self-blame, 157

sense of self-reliance, 96
sensory trauma, 26, 43, 171
sexual abuse, 35, 112, 117, 119
Shapiro, F., 83
Shardlow, S., 61
Shaver, P., 46
Shear, K., 58
Shell-Duncan, B., 163–4
Sherrieb, K., 129
Shonkoff, J. P., 76
Showalter, E., 30
Shuman, A., 158
silence, 157
Silver, R., 5, 97, 153
Slaby, J., 175
Smith, R., 11–12
Smyke, A., 57–8
Smyth, J. M., 119
social capital, 129–30
social-ecological approaches
  adaptation, process of, 125–6
  core aspects, 124
  disaster events, 133–4
  networked resources, 128
  practice, implications for, 138–41
  relational aspects, 124
  strengths and limitations, criticisms
    of, 142
  systemic focus, 138–9
  systems theory, 124–5, 138–9
  therapeutic relationship, 139
  trauma exposures, 133–7
social silencing, 112–13
socio-cultural and political contexts,
    113–15
  importance of, 114
Solomon, E. P., 75
Solomon, J., 47–8, 50–2, 54–5
Solomon, R., 83
Somers, M., 114
Spila, B., 55
spiritual dimensions, 17–18, 171–2
  and trauma, 18
stage approaches, 9
  Herman's proposal, 9–10
Steel, C. R., 147

Stewart, A., 109–11
still face experiment, 48
Stolorow, R., 29, 32
Storr, V. H., 114
stress, traumatic
    dissociation, 71
    in infants, 75
Stroebe, M., 7
Sudbery, J., 61
supportive collective narratives, 115
symptom approaches, 66–88

Tang, S., 114
Taylor, S., 104
Tedeschi, R., 8, 13, 96–9, 105
Tennen, H., 105
testimony method, 119
TF-CBT, see trauma-focused cognitive
    behavioural therapy (TF-CBT)
theoretical approaches, 1–2, 7, 15, 17,
    19, 21, 24, 28
    trauma, 7, 15, 19–21, 24
therapists, 26, 35–6, 40–2, 60, 91–2,
    101–2, 108, 124, 131, 159
Thomas, C., 109
Thompson, A., 8
Thompson, N., 145–6, 150
Tolin, D. F., 74
transference, 41–2
transilience, 12–13
trauma
    anti-oppressive approaches, 149–59
    anxiety and, 31
    approaches to, see approaches (trauma
        and resilience)
    attachment approaches of, 54–9
    in attachment relationships, 54–6
    beyond narrative, 111
    civilian life, areas of adjustments
        to, 94
    conscious awareness, 42–4
    core, 31–2, 34
    criticism of, 24–7
    defence mechanisms, 37–9
    defined, 4, 31

dimensions of, see dimensions (of
    trauma and resilience)
disaster events, see disaster
dissociation, 37
exploitation, 150
exposure, 4–7, 67; chronological age,
    17; classification, 5; concept of,
    133–4; developmental stage, 17;
    DSM V, 6; physical age, 17;
    psychosis, 5; vulnerability, 5–6
identities, 156–9
impacts, 7–8, 32, 156–9; theoretical
    approaches, 7
inner world dimensions, 171–2
maltreatment, 54–6
memory, 16, 33, 35–6, 41, 43, 77–8,
    83, 88, 113
multidimensional approach,
    theorising using, 13–15, 23, 168–70,
    174–5
narrative approaches, 110–15
negative symptoms approach, 96
neurobiological approaches, 17
oppression, 150
outer world dimensions, 173–4
person-centred approaches to, 93–9
positive emotions, 16
positive symptoms approach, 96
post traumatic growth, 95–9
practice and research, implications for,
    5, 22–5, 138–41
practitioners and researchers, 24–7
psychiatric disorder, 16
psychoanalytic theories, 17
psychodynamic approaches, 30–3
psycho-economic views, 31
PTSD and, 66–78
re-experiencing of, reducing, 83–4
relationships and, 19
and religion, 18
vs. resilience, 13–14, 165–8
resources, 129
responses, causes of, 149–53
secure attachment, 59
between self and the world, disruptive
    incongruence, 94–5

self structure, impact on, 93–5
silence in, 157
social-ecological approaches, 133–7
social silencing, 112–13
systemic focus, 138–9
theoretical approaches, comparative
    analysis of, 167–8
trust and, 40–1
see also resilience
trauma-focused cognitive behavioural
    therapy (TF-CBT), 81
Trevithick, P., 139
Tronick, E., 48
trust, 2, 40–1
Tumarkin, M., 22
Turner, A., 94
Turpin, G., 26

Ulman, R., 30
Ungar, M., 12, 126, 128, 130–1,
    138, 155
Urbis Social Planning and Social
    Research, 140

Vachon, M., 25
Valdez, C. E., 74
Vandell, D., 64
Van der Kolk, B., 32, 37–8, 54, 80
vicarious traumatization, 25, 42
Vidal, F., 172
violence
    anti-oppressive approaches, 153
    in relationship, 18

structural, 146, 153
    against women, 20, 151
vulnerability, 5–6, 17, 19, 21

Walsh, F., 10, 124, 126, 128, 141
Walter, M., 145
Ward, T., 108
Waters, E., 50, 53, 59
Waters, H. S., 50
Weathers, F., 4, 6, 67
Weinberg, M., 48
Weinfield, N. S., 53
Weiss, T., 13, 105
Werner, E., 11–12
Wethington, H. R., 79
White, M., 108–9, 111, 115–17
WHO, *see* World Health Organisation
    (WHO)
Williams, R., 136, 160
Wilson, J. P., 10, 31, 39, 41, 155
Wingard, B., 18, 110
Winkworth, G., 136–7
Woon, F. L., 77
World Health Organisation (WHO), 9,
    67–8, 74, 75
Wright, M., 10

Yehuda, R., 69, 74–5, 78, 85, 88, 149
Young, I., 144, 150, 152
Ypinazar, V. A., 20
Yuen, A., 108

Zepf, F. D., 34
Zepf, S., 34